"*Phoenix Lights* is a compelling and thoroughly documented account of the most bizarre and widely observed UFO event in modern times. Observed by thousands of citizens, but ignored, denied, or dismissed by government at all levels and by the media, Dr. Lynne Kitei (key-tie), a medical professional, has courageously taken up the challenge of publicly chronicling her personal observations. The Phoenix Lights were a sequence of events, intentionally staged by entities unknown; to what end, other than to be observed, also unknown. Some day the veil of secrecy will surely be lifted, thanks to the efforts of Dr. Lynne and many others. But in the meantime, in the words of Alice: 'Things are curiouser and curiouser!'"

—Edgar Mitchell, Sc.D.
Capt USN (ret), Apollo astronaut

"As a practicing trial attorney with more than thirty years experience, I have developed a healthy skepticism for theories advanced without real, hard evidence. Dr. Lynne Kitei has succeeded, with a plethora of evidence, in overcoming my skepticism and convincing me that we have not as yet discovered the whole truth regarding the Phoenix Lights. Her extensive research has revealed an astonishing story that deserves serious consideration and continued explanation. She deserves praise for her courage in not shying away from a controversial subject. Reading her book opened my eyes. I recommend it to anyone who wishes to explore the unexplainable."

—Barnett Lotstein, Esq.
Special Assistant to the Maricopa County Attorney

"In her excellent book entitled *The Phoenix Lights*, Dr. Lynne submits a steady stream of actual occurrences, with photographic backup, to support her theory of UFOs. Dr. Lynne takes the reader from what would be considered by skeptics as impossible and makes it seem quite plausible. Dr. Lynne, with her very credible credentials, discusses UFOs and takes the reader from the 'what if' to the 'how' and 'what' they are.

"The other really intriguing part of this book reminds me of my experience of twenty-two years in government as an elected official. Often, during my tenure, I have heard that it is better if the public did not know something. I have never agreed with this premise. If involved or knowledgeable, our federal government must fully disclose its information and participation in the age-old question. Every time government officials and bureaucrats try to protect the public, we lose!"

—Robert B. Usdane
Retired Past President, Arizona State Senate

"This book is very important in that most people can identify their own attitudes towards Unexplained Phenomena (UPs) with _____ r. Unlike most people though, Dr. X, when confr_____ s, persisted in trying to understand their meanin_____ e book, she came to the realization that there re_____ ? that is denied or ridiculed by the authorities in _____ y most of our citizens. Using her considerable investigative skills, she has in the last six or seven years transformed her previous naivete into a wide base of knowledge concerning these UPs. She was even able to make the connection of recent events with an extraordinary near-death experience that she lived through in her early childhood.

"After a long period of anonymity, she has bravely decided that if she is ever to find out what the true meaning of these experiences is she must uninhibitedly relate her experiences to all who will listen. By so doing, perhaps enough people will follow her lead and transform the presently ridiculed experiences of thousands of people into an understanding of the most important phenomenon of our era.

"Without denigrating the importance of the 'scientific method' we must admit that there are some happenstances that are not amenable to traditional scientific experimentation and verification. If you look up into the night sky and see a falling star and then describe your visual experience to a companion, chances are good that your companion will believe that you really did see it, even though he or she has never had a similar experience. However there is no way that anyone can 'scientifically' verify that you really did see it because it was a personal experience.

"Similarly, if you look up into the sky and see an unidentified flying object of a type never before seen by you, why should people doubt that you really did see it? Instead of demanding 'scientific proof' for an event that is not scientifically provable, we should at least keep an open mind and accept the possibility that something totally foreign to our previous experience really could happen. Otherwise we will continue to travel through life with restrictive blinders filtering out what could have been the most important experiences of our lives."　　**—A. Swimmer, Ph.D.**
Associate Professor of Mathematics, Arizona State University

"The research Dr. Kitei has done to create this astonishing book is monumental. How anyone could read it and not be deeply moved and convinced that we are not alone on this planet is hard for me to comprehend. The message is clear, concise, and impelling. We have known it as true, now we have the evidence."
—Gladys Taylor McGarey, M.D., M.D.(H)
Scottsdale Holistic Medical Group

"This is a thought-provoking, deeply personal investigation of the Phoenix Lights phenomenon of March 1997 by one of the actual witnesses. Told in a gripping, engaging style, Dr. Kitei's story takes the reader on an incredible journey of discovery and revelation. We're lucky to have such an articulate and perceptive woman tell the story of an event witnessed by several thousand men, women, and children around the state of Arizona that fateful night that the government, to this day, denies ever happened."
—Dr. Paul Cook, Senior Lecturer
Department of English, Arizona State University
author of *The Engines of Dawn* and *The Alejandra Variations*

THE PHOENIX
Lights

LYNNE D. KITEI, M.D.

HAMPTON ROADS
PUBLISHING COMPANY, INC.

Cover design by Marjoram Productions
Interior crop circle drawing © 2004 by Anne L. Louque

Hampton Roads Publishing Company, Inc.
1125 Stoney Ridge Road
Charlottesville, VA 22902

434-296-2772
fax: 434-296-5096
e-mail: hrpc@hrpub.com
www.hrpub.com

If you are unable to order this book from your local
bookseller, you may order directly from the publisher.
Call 1-800-766-8009, toll-free.

Library of Congress Cataloging-in-Publication Data

Kitei, Lynne D., 1948-
The Phoenix lights / Lynne D. Kitei.
    p. cm.
Includes bibliographical references.
ISBN 1-57174-377-4 (alk. paper)
1. Unidentified flying objects--Sightings and encounters--Arizona--Phoenix.
I. Title.
TL789.5.A6K578 2004
001.942'0971'73--dc22

                                    2003027021

ISBN 1-57174-377-4
10 9 8 7 6 5 4 3 2 1
Printed on acid-free paper in Canada

In memory of my parents,
the guiding lights throughout my life,
Ruth and Lou Dumin

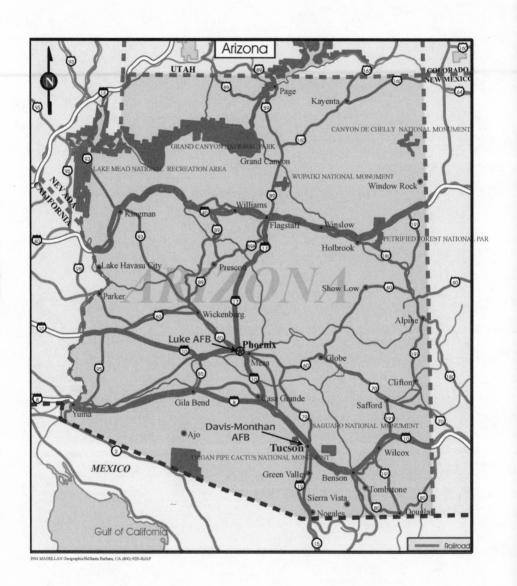

Table of Contents

Introduction

By Gary E. Schwartz, Ph.D.

How would you feel if you knew, *definitively*, that the Earth is being observed and shepherded by an advanced civilization and that it has been going on for a very long time? That the strange and unexplained lights reported for thousands of years by ancient cultures around the globe, witnessed many thousands of times by hundreds of thousands of people worldwide and documented by still, movie, video, and digital cameras with increasing frequency in the latter part of the twentieth century, are not all weather balloons, flares, satellites, secret defense activities, meteors, or hoaxes? That some of these "unexplained phenomena"—what Lynne D. Kitei, M.D., the courageous author of this transformative book, calls "UPs" rather than "UFOs"—require that we embrace the reality of a profound hypothesis entertained by curious and intelligent people throughout recorded history? Just as the late Carl Sagan suggested, "We are not alone in the Universe."

As a serious scientist, I never expected that I would have any interest in writing an introduction for or associating my name with a book that explores the possibility that UFO phenomena are real and that there is genuine evidence for the existence of advanced civilizations and intelligences that are interacting with our planet. Nonetheless, after meeting with the remarkable author of this book and reviewing her data, as a dedicated scientist I cannot avoid endorsing her work.

Dr. Kitei is a wonderful human being whom I feel privileged to have met. She is an accomplished physician, educator, mother of two grown children, creator and producer of the internationally award winning *You Make It!* prevention/education series, director of the nonprofit Health Education Youth-at-Risk Fund at the Arizona Community Foundation, and the wife for over 30 years of a distinguished physician. She also happens to have witnessed a multitude of incidents of unexplained phenomena (UPs), capturing many of them on film and video.

In the beginning, Dr. Lynne, as she became known through her health-reporting work for NBC, USA Cable, and other media, kept her experiences secret. She has a solid reputation to uphold, not only for herself, but for her husband and family. When she made some of her remarkable footage available to the media, she did so anonymously. When she finally agreed to speak with the press, she first did so as Dr. "X," and only recently as Dr. Lynne. Now, after seven years of intensive research, she is giving up her anonymity so that people will listen to the data.

Dr. Lynne is not a "kook," and she is not interested in fame or fortune. She did not ask to have these unexplained experiences, and she definitely did not request the responsibility she was "handed," so to speak, which requires that she go public in order to share with the world what she has documented to be real.

What you are about to read is a true story where "true" does not mean "hyped" by Hollywood or "fabricated" by the sensational side of the press. This really happened to a credible person with substantial credentials. She found herself in the position of receiving information that has direct bearing on how every human being should reenvision reality: that we live in an intelligent universe, a living energy universe.

I am a scientist and clinician, working in various areas of integrative science and medicine, the bridge between conventional and "alternative" science. My research bridges body, mind, and spirit from the biophysics of heart-brain interactions within and between people to bioradiation effects of healing techniques that span the physical, psychological, and spiritual. The motto of our laboratory is simple: "Let the data speak." As far as I can determine, there are no mistakes in the data Dr. Lynne reveals here for the first time.

I received my doctorate from Harvard University in 1971, and taught at both Harvard and Yale before moving to the University of Arizona in 1988, where I am presently professor of psychology, surgery, medicine, neurology, and psychiatry.

I briefly mention my personal academic history because I want you to know that, like Dr. Lynne, I have had the good fortune to be well educated and that I deeply understand the requirement for discerning what is factual and credible. I am aware as I write these words that I am placing my own reputation at risk in endorsing a book on a topic that is obviously controversial.

Before meeting Lynne D. Kitei, M.D., it was easy for me to dismiss the sensational claims I saw on television and read in the newspapers. However, after meeting with Dr. Lynne, hearing her story firsthand, and seeing her videos and photographs, many of which are reproduced in this book, I can no longer deny the totality of the facts.

Dr. Lynne's findings are so strong and her message so important that I have decided I must take this opportunity to contribute to the process of fostering our species' ability to end its history of denial of data. It is time we wake up and bravely face the vast implications capstoned in this book. Its publication will help let the data speak, which as a scientist is my fundamental motto and creed.

After reading this book, I have agreed to help Dr. Lynne continue her work. I have formally established the Ruth and Louis Dumin Project in the Human Energy Systems Laboratory, in honor of her deceased parents, to foster research and education that can help people transform their consciousness to a new reality.

Once you have read and examined the evidence presented here, I am certain that you will feel, as I do, that this book is a tremendous wake-up call for us here on Earth. It is not too late for us to grow up as a species. Through her dedicated investigation and observations, Dr. Lynne has discovered that help is available for us to mature and evolve before we destroy the precious gifts we have been given. We need only look up from our lives and see with new eyes.

The choice is ours. May this book help you break through your denial as much as it has me.

Foreword

By Paul Perry, coauthor of the *New York Times* best-sellers *Saved by the Light* and *Closer to the Light*

On March 13, 1997, thousands of eyewitnesses across the state of Arizona reported seeing a mile-long, V-shaped formation of lights flying close to the ground. This silent formation made its presence known from the top. of the Grand Canyon almost to the Mexican border.

UFO buffs call it the "most public" UFO flyover ever to be recorded.

One of the people who saw it was Dr. Lynne Kitei. She was standing on the porch of her mountainside home in Paradise Valley when the formation passed. Just like everyone else who was looking up that night, Dr. Lynne, as she likes to be called, saw the strange lights. Unlike others, however, Dr. Lynne had seen these lights before.

No one had to take her word for it, either. Since the first time Dr. Lynne had seen three orbs of light hovering near her house, she kept a camera close by to record other extraordinary phenomena should they occur.

And occur they did. Over the course of two years, Dr. Lynne amassed an impressive amount of video and 35-mm photographs, recording multiple sightings of paranormal light experiences that took place in a variety of forms. It was a good thing that she was able to capture them on film and video. Without such a visual record no one would have believed that both she and her husband (also a physician) were witnessing what seemed to be an extraterrestrial light show. They may even have begun to doubt their own eyes.

The March 13 sighting was different for Dr. Lynne. Unlike the other sightings, an entire state had seen what she had been seeing all along. In many ways that made it safe for Dr. Lynne to begin openly researching the lights.

And research them she did. Dr. Lynne joined with a number of others—from photo analysis experts, scientists, and engineers to air traffic controllers and university professors—to expose the web of mystery and intrigue that surrounds the Phoenix Lights and the other sightings like them that take place around the world on an almost daily basis.

This book is a chronicle of Dr. Lynne's persistent desire to uncover the truth and the meaning behind the Phoenix Lights.

Dr. Lynne is a woman of great energy and power, a kind of human dynamo who wants to find the answers to her questions right now, before another minute passes. Yet, despite her impatience, she is thorough, a seeker of truth at supersonic speed.

I don't want to go into her conclusions here, since part of the joy of reading a book like this is the process of discovery. I will say, however, that the work behind this book reveals a great deal of courage. To investigate the paranormal can possibly expose one to a great amount of ridicule. To do it with the attention to care that she has demonstrated here reduces the possibility that any of that ridicule will stick.

What you will conclude when you read this book is anyone's guess. Are we being visited by alien cultures from another dimension? Are they trying to communicate with us through the use of lights? Are there people among us who are more sensitized to these alien communications than others?

These are just some of the many questions that are sure to enter your mind as you read this book.

I remain truly baffled by these lights and their meanings. And I continue to be incredibly impressed with Dr. Lynne Kitei and her search for truth. She has found something in these mysterious lights, something that truly deserves our attention.

Preface

Through the ages, even though humankind has advanced technologically, we have also taken steps backward. Some of us have become distanced, even separated, from our own spiritual potential. The indigenous peoples of the world, including Native Americans, know how significant these connections are, connections that are integral to the welfare of humanity and to our planet Earth. They speak of balance, giving back what we have taken. Some say this inherent balance is a vital force throughout the universe. But somehow in the process of our evolution as a species we have lost this fundamental ingredient that is essential to our survival.

Is it crucial that we regain this balance once again? Is it imperative that we reconnect to the source of spiritual energy and through that connection learn how to heal ourselves and the world around us?

At this momentous turning point in our human and spiritual history there seems to be an increasing number of unexplained happenings alerting us to our destructive ways and the immediate need to nurture our positive human strengths. Poignant messages relayed through out-of-body and near-death experiences, crop circles, unearthly visions, and worldwide UFO phenomena, similar to the Phoenix Lights, are helping us awaken to the compelling truth—before it is too late.

The Phoenix Lights

After experiencing and filming these extraordinary events firsthand, I felt compelled to explore the source and meaning of these mysterious phenomena. Why? Because I too was given a message, an anonymous gift that I soon realized wasn't meant for me alone.

Acknowledgements

There are so many beautiful and loving souls who have helped in the process of making *The Phoenix Lights* possible.

My family tops the list: Frank, Brett and Eliza, Dan and Nicole, Bob and Janice, Murray and Shelley, Jeannette, Mindy, Uncle Milton, Rhoda, Valerie, Tammy, Shirley, Godiva, Jet, and Neeko.

I could not have continued on my quest without the support and encouragement of my treasured friends: Shelley Anderson, Elizabeth Faulkner, Adam Finberg, Barbara Finberg, Flynn Flexer, Denise Gaines, Marcia Gelman, Phyllis Gross, Julie Houck, Sue Jaffe, Jan Jacobson, Susan Krakow, Sandy Levitt, Mark Lewis, Barnett Lotstein, Donna Normandin, Debbie Paris, Judy Pelle, Paul Perry, Danielle Rakow, Keith Ritchie, Sunny Seibel, Sharon Shulman, Jeannie Winograd.

And new friends I met along the way: Carol Adler, Dr. John Alexander, Frances Emma Barwood, Sandra Baum, Captain Eileen Beinz, Charles Byers, John Carpenter, David Hatcher Childress, Roberta Colasanti, Dr. Paul Cook, Peter Davenport, Jim Dilettoso, Tim Edwards, Brit and Lee Elders, Dr. Brad Evans, Steve Filmer, Mike Fortson, Peter Gersten, Susan Goldwater, Bill Grava, Dr. Steven Greer, Dr. Bruce Greyson, Rod Haber, Dr. Richard Haines, Bill Hamilton, Dr. Ruth Hover, Linda Moulton Howe, Cindy Hubeck, Dr. Bruce

Hull, Beth Jacobs, Shelley Jeffrey, Trig Johnson, Colm Kelleher, Tom King, Sue and Mike Krzyston, Vern Latham, Armondo Lauro, Dr. Roger Leir, Tim Ley, Stephanie Lipson, Bruce Maccabee, Jaime Mauson, Dr. Glady McGarey, Pat McMahon, Astronaut Dr. Edgar Mitchell, Dr. Rand Molnar, Robert O'Connor, Scott and Ted Podleski, Dr. Richard Powell, Thomas Ropp, Dr. Linda Russek, Dr. Alvin Swimmer, Dr. Kenneth Ring, Chuck Rairden, Shala and Max Saracen, Jim Schnebelt, Dr. Gary Schwartz, Steve Snow, Whitley Strieber, Michael Tanner, Noel Tyl, Preston Westmoreland, Steve Wilson, Senator Bob Usdane.

Much appreciation goes to all the witnesses of the Phoenix Lights and other unexplained phenomena who have shared and will continue to share their own stories, as well as to the scientists, military, pilots, air traffic controllers, and investigators who generously gave their time and expertise to help in my journey of discovery.

A special thank you to my wonderful and talented literary family: My exceptional agent, William Gladstone, and Kim Valentini of Waterside Productions; Robert Friedman, Jane Hagaman, Sarah Hilfer, Tracey Hill, Lisette Larkins, my editor Richard Leviton, Tiffany McCord, Tania Seymour, and all the others at Hampton Roads Publishing Company who contributed to the completion and dissemination of this heartfelt effort.

1. Showtime . . . The Phoenix Lights

On the evening of March 13, 1997, a collection of unidentified flying objects crossed the state of Arizona from north to south and back again. It was an incident that has become known worldwide as the Phoenix Lights.

It began when a former police officer called the highway patrol from his home in the northern mountains to report a group of "bright red-orange lights formed in the shape of a boomerang" that was headed south. No engines could be heard, he said, which was surprising since the lights were "large and in formation."

Next to witness the mysterious lights were travelers on Interstate 17, the freeway connecting Northern Arizona with the capital city of Phoenix. Some drivers nearly left the road watching the massive array of lights. No sound accompanied the lights and they moved in unison, "as though they were connected," said one witness.

When the display came over the mountains of North Phoenix and moved over the city, thousands of people saw it. The route the mysterious lights took that night can be followed by tracking the 911 calls that came into the Phoenix police department. In the north valley, people talked frantically to emergency operators about a "strange soundless craft" moving over their heads. One man directly under the lights said that looking at the shimmering area between them was like "looking through water at the sky." An 11-year-old boy, Tim MacDonald, came out of his Cub Scout meeting and watched the triangle shape of lights for nearly three minutes. "I thought it was a UFO," he told a newspaper reporter. Golfers at driving ranges froze as they caught sight of the glimmering collection. Commercial airline pilots radioed the tower to find out what those strange lights were. A cement driver, Bill Greiner, watched the lights from a spot near Luke Air Force Base, where he reported seeing fighter planes take off and head for the strange objects, their afterburners roaring at liftoff.

For several minutes the city stood still as these lights swept overhead on their way toward Tucson, where truck drivers called one another on their CB radios, and families on the dark freeway stopped and stared in awe at the passing giant formation.

But unlike others who had been taken by surprise that night and didn't have time to grab a camera, I was ready. For the past two years my husband and I had been taking both still photographs and video footage of the heavenly lights. At times they had been so close that we could have thrown a rock from our bedroom balcony and hit them. At other times they were so distant and high that I knew others must have seen them too. I tracked down a few people who had seen them, including some air traffic controllers at the airport. We were all grateful to know that we were not alone in witnessing these bizarre orbs of light, yet we were surprised that so few of us had seen them.

But this time it would be different. There is no way the entire city couldn't be seeing this, I told myself. About an hour and a half after the triangle shape of lights passed over Arizona, I videotaped the strange orbs that appeared to hover over the city of Phoenix. I filmed the lights from the porch of my home in the mountains overlooking the city.

As my husband, Frank, and I watched the lights, I could only imagine their effect on people. All the while I thought about the first time I saw these lights, and what seeing them had done to me. . . .

2. Seeing the Light

The mystery of the Phoenix Lights began for me at 8 P.M. on my birthday eve, February 6, 1995. I had just settled into a bath. The hot water and vanilla-scented bubbles filled my senses with a delicious calm.

Suddenly the mellow moment was shattered by my husband's frantic call, "Come in here quick and look at this. What *is* it?" He sounded alarmed, so I didn't waste any time. Alarm is out of character for Frank, a family physician who has seen it all. I grabbed a towel and, dripping wet, rushed to his side. He was standing transfixed by the bedroom window, looking at something close to the house. From this window I usually scan the twinkling city skyline in the distance, but this time something else caught my attention. Less than a hundred yards away from our property, three objects hung in midair, about 50 to 75 feet above the ground. I immediately looked underneath and around them to see if something or someone was creating the spectacle, but I saw nothing. No laser beam, no hologram. Except for the soft light within each object, there was only darkness. I stood there intently taking it all in. It seemed important not to move.

I took a mental note of every nuance—size, shape, color, distance. Each sphere was an oval, between three and six feet across. They seemed to be hovering motionlessly in perfect symmetry, one on top and the other two aligned underneath, like a pyramid. The soothing amber light contained within each orb looked different from any light I had ever seen. It didn't glare at all and was uniform throughout, reminding me of a holiday luminary that shines from within, without the light extending beyond its edge. Frank and I were in awe, mesmerized by the extraordinary scene.

I knew no one else would believe this unless we had photographic proof, so I turned to grab our 35-mm camera from the bedroom closet. "Get back here. Look what's happening now. One of them is disappearing," said Frank. I clutched the camera and hurried to the window. The top oval orb was slowly fading. It was meticulously and uniformly disappearing in place, as though it were being controlled by a dimmer switch.

I wanted to get a shot of this impressive phenomenon, whatever it was. I quickly opened the sliding glass door, stepped out onto the balcony and snapped a picture of the two remaining orbs.

How is this astonishing sight even possible? I wondered, noticing the eerie silence, as if time had stopped. The next thing I remember, the left bottom oval started to dissipate, just like the first, slowly and silently fading from view without moving. I took another photo.

In the days that followed, Frank didn't really want to discuss it. To me, the whole experience was exciting and wondrous. Even so, it didn't make sense, especially when I stared at the place where the three mysterious objects had appeared and then dissolved. For weeks afterward, it felt as though they were still there—watching.

It took me more than two weeks to build up the courage to seek out a film shop. When I finally arrived at the photo lab on February 24, 1995, I timidly admitted to the developer that my husband and I had seen something quite unusual outside our window a couple of weeks before. I asked her to please take special care in trying to find some lights among the photos on the two rolls I handed her.

One of the other developers overheard our conversation. He didn't live far from us, he said, and had seen air force jets scouting our area the day after this sighting. Why would the military be zooming at low altitudes around a private residential area? I added this to a growing list of questions about the mysterious lights.

When the photos came back I discovered that only one picture of the lights had turned out, but what a picture it was. I had caught the lower left oval as it was disappearing while the right oval was still in place. One of the unique features of this book is that I have photographs of the Phoenix Lights that I can share with you. Some of these amazing 35-mm shots, including this one, are presented on pages 102–109.

This single print proved to me that what we had seen was not an optical illusion. But what to do with it? Neither my husband nor I was ever into the topic of Unidentified Flying Objects. We didn't know anyone else who was, either, so I ended up mounting the unique photo on our fireplace mantel, just for fun. It seemed so out of place next to our family pictures that I eventually tucked it neatly behind a favorite portrait for safekeeping. Even though the picture was out of sight, the event wasn't out of my mind.

Over the next 23 months there wasn't a glimmer of anything unusual in the Phoenix skies. From time to time I wondered what we had seen. If we had been anywhere else in the house, we would probably have missed it. I was relieved that I had captured a photo of the strange incident; otherwise no one, including ourselves, would have believed it had occurred. After something inexplicable happens to you, with no outside confirmation, you begin to doubt the experience and your perception of it, especially over time. As much as I tried to deny it, the feeling that we were supposed to witness and film the mysterious sight lingered. Maybe one day I would find out why.

Then it happened again, but on a grander scale.

It was about 8 P.M. on the evening of January 22, 1997. I had just slipped into bed and was staring out of our picture window at the beautiful skyline. The view was full of lights: stoplights blinking their green, yellow, and red arrays; car lights whizzing down the main thoroughfares; commercial airplanes crisscrossing the skies as they arrived at and departed from Sky Harbor International Airport.

Then something on the western horizon caught my attention. Three huge amber orbs hung there in a stationary row, strangely similar to the three orbs outside our window in 1995.

"Frank. Come here! There are three amber lights in formation out there behind the buildings down Central Avenue. Hurry!"

After several seconds of silence he replied, "I don't want to hear about it. You enjoy."

"But you don't understand. They look like the three lights we saw two years ago, except this time they're at a distance and in a line!"

"Do I still have to go to work tomorrow?" he jokingly replied.

I watched them alone. After hovering rock-solid for about three or four minutes they each took a turn in fading out. It looked as if each orb was dissipating from the outside in, from right to left, until all three were gone from view.

The next evening, while Frank was at the medical board's monthly meeting, something huge and golden-orange glaring motionlessly in the sky once again caught my attention. Realizing that this sight had to be documented, I grabbed my video camera, scurried out to the pool area, and pressed the record button.

After filming 17 seconds of footage, the camera clicked off. The battery had gone dead. A few minutes later, the lights faded to black.

"Honey, you won't believe this," I said to Frank when he came home. "Remember I told you about the three lights in a row last night? Well, about a half an hour ago the same lights appeared in front of South Mountain."

As I pointed to the spot where they had appeared, they suddenly reappeared. "That's them! That's them!" I shouted, running into the house and up the long stairway to grab my camera from the closet. Just as I aimed my camera at this puzzling display, six amber spheres blinked on, in an equidistant line, directly above the three that were already there. The distance across was probably more than a mile. There was nothing I could relate it to, except maybe *Star Trek*.

"Oh, my, Frank, what is that? It looks like a Mothership or a *fleet* of ships."

I got several shots off as the bottom three started to disappear, one by one from right to left. I kept clicking away.

During my frenzy to get the photos, I could hear Frank mutter, "It's probably a blimp. Isn't the Phoenix Open in town?"

I tried in earnest to visualize it being a blimp, but to no avail. The lights were shaped like large orange orbs, and they didn't move at all. The notion that these lights were part of a colossal blimp was implausible.

I called the newspaper to see if anyone else had reported what I was seeing.

"City desk," said the voice in the newsroom of the *Arizona Republic*.

"Could you tell me what the strange lights are that are hovering right now in front of South Mountain? You should get someone out there to capture the sight on film." As my sentence came to an end, so did the light show. They were gone. There was nowhere else to go with the conversation. Reluctantly, I hung up.

The next morning I felt I had to have an explanation. I wanted to believe that there was a rational explication for the incident. First I phoned the *Arizona Republic* asking if anyone had called the night before to report strange lights. Not a one, said the receptionist.

"Can you tell me who I could contact to find out what they might have been?" I asked.

"Maybe it was an experimental military maneuver," she replied quickly. "Sometimes Luke Air Force Base sends out test flights and they don't report them to the public."

The female lieutenant I spoke to next listened patiently and then responded curtly. "I can tell you that they did not come from Luke and they did not come into Luke. We had nothing to do with them."

Pressing further, I asked, "Could you tell me who I should contact to find out what they were?"

"I have no idea."

Frustrated, I asked, "Would you have a number for a UFO organization?"

She stated emphatically, "No. I certainly would not have that information."

"But there must be someone who knows what they were. My husband and I saw the same thing. We even captured some on videotape. I'm sure there must be a logical explanation. I'm only trying to find out what that might be."

"Well, since it was in front of South Mountain, maybe someone at the airport saw something."

"Good idea," I said. I hung up and looked for the Sky Harbor International Airport telephone number.

The strange phenomena had to have come from somewhere. I would just search until I found an answer. Finally, I got the Federal Aviation Administration on the line. I reiterated my account. The operator asked me to hold while she checked to see if the air traffic controllers had seen anything unusual the night before. It was at least five minutes before she returned.

"You're in luck. One of the controllers who is here this morning was working last night. He did see some strange lights. He's not sure what they were."

"Could I speak with him personally?" I requested. She asked me to wait.

Finally, there was a click on the line. A deep male voice asked, "Did you see those six orange lights hovering equidistant from each other in a formation last night about 8:30 P.M.?"

When I told him we had, he seemed almost relieved that someone else had seen them.

"When we saw the array of six lights appear at 8:30 P.M., out of nowhere, we immediately looked on radar, but nothing showed up," he said. "We then thought maybe they were lights carried by skydivers. But that would be unlikely because it was too late and they were in a perfect formation. They couldn't have been flares either. Flares drift downwards. These stayed right in place. Besides, they were a different color from anything I've ever seen. So we grabbed our binoculars to take a closer look. What startled us was that they were six distinct amber objects, hovering motionless for a time, in perfect synchrony."

I was more curious than ever. "So," I inquired again, "what were they?"

There was silence for several seconds, then a deep breath. "Beats me," he answered.

"Wait a minute. You're an air traffic controller. That's what you do, identify things flying around in air space. And you don't know what they were?"

He hesitated for a moment and then replied, "I'll ask around."

Since I had no clue as to what we were dealing with, I wanted to remain as anonymous as possible and gave him my son's telephone number. "Please call back if you hear of anything," I asked, "I'm just trying to find a logical explanation for what we saw."

I wasn't going to be caught off guard again. I brought the video equipment upstairs, plugged it into the electric socket and placed it next to the bedroom door leading out to our balcony—just in case.

That evening, shortly after dark, two giant amber orbs appeared on the horizon and hovered for several minutes in a side-by-side formation. Grabbing my camera, I rushed outside to capture the sight on tape, documenting the sighting verbally as well. "January 24th, 1997. Huge amber balls of light over Phoenix. Just hovering, not moving, not going anywhere." I tried to keep the hand-held camera steady. Frank joined me on the veranda. After the balls disappeared, we stood there in silence staring at the vacant sky for several seconds, then stepped back inside. I noticed the time was 8:27 P.M.

Not ten minutes later, the lights reappeared. They seemed to be in the same spot, but in a different formation. I picked up a pair of binoculars to get a closer look. Two large golden spheres were now positioned at an angle. "We have to get this on film," I exclaimed, as I grabbed my video camera again.

"Enough already," said Frank. "You have some on tape. You don't even know what they are. Why are you filming any more?"

Determined to capture the fascinating vision hovering in the Phoenix skies, I pointed my camera at the display, describing it as I filmed. "8:40," I said. "It's come back again. Same spot. See the difference of the approaching airplane and them? The jet is so much smaller."

Every night that week was filled with curiosity and amazement, viewing these strange amber creations appearing motionless in formations across the horizon. Whatever these lights were, you could see distinctly that the commercial airlines coming in and out of Sky Harbor Airport, about 20 miles from us, were dwarfed by the gigantic orange luminaries.

On January 30, I stepped onto the veranda to capture another silent sighting on video. As the camera rolled, I began my verbal documentation. "This one has been out there for some time."

I put the camera on the balcony ledge so it would be stable and started chatting with Frank, who had joined me. "There were just two there. This one is really high." It was definitely higher than the red lights of the radio tower on South Mountain, which ruled out the possibility that it was someone on the mountain holding a light.

I had taken the 35-mm film of the January 23 sighting to the developer, but to my dismay, none of these photos turned out. I was told that the negatives were blank, and they looked it. Maybe the orbs had been too far away. After all, the ones in the pictures I had taken two years before had been just beyond our house. Now the lights were appearing at a distance. Disappointed, I put the negatives in a drawer.

But the recent events were too compelling to dismiss. I started sharing them with my close friends. When they saw the videos, they were dumbfounded. No one could explain the formations. Even though the tapes didn't do them justice, because the orbs appeared much smaller, whiter, and flickered in the videos, the sight of these stationary balls hovering over the mountains was still remarkable.

Aside from the verification from the air traffic controller on January 24, there was no other mention of the strange lights, including in the media. I began thinking that, like in 1995, these sightings would remain a mystery.

Whatever they were, I still felt compelled to film them when they reappeared. A little after 9 P.M. on March 4, Frank and I were on the bedroom balcony. He was facing me, leaning against the upstairs railing with the spectrum of white city lights as a backdrop. I forget what we were talking about, but suddenly something amber appeared in the sky right behind Frank's head. "Hold that thought," I blurted, as I rushed into the bedroom to grab the camera.

Frank said he saw something come out of the first one. By the time I got outside, there were two lights very closely aligned, one directly on top of the other. "What day is it?" I asked, after turning on my Sony 8mm.

As a smaller aircraft with blinking lights came into the frame, Frank enthusiastically answered, "March 4th, 1997. You can see the plane moving, but the golden Martian/Venusian/Plutonian lights are just sitting there. Add it to the portfolio of 'Lynne's World of the Unknown.' It's going to air on Thursday at eight o'clock." Frank bantered like this until the lights blinked out.

It seemed as though I had just put my camera back in our bedroom when I found myself outside with it again. Now that I was taking note of the landscape, it looked as though these lights were hovering about 20 miles to the south, above the basin area between the Estrella and South Mountain ranges, which would have placed them over the Gila Bend Indian Reservation.

Frank had given me a telescope for my birthday, which I now focused on the lights. Looking through the eyepiece, I could see that the lights were round, amber-colored balls of swirling energy. No parachutes, no sparks, no smoke trails, no wings in sight. What's more, the spinning orbs didn't move out of frame for the duration of the sighting, about seven minutes.

The next night Frank and I had just entered the bedroom when we noticed through our big window two glowing orbs in the west. They seemed to be hovering directly over the Dial Building downtown. Frank took over the narration, "Wednesday, March 5th, 1997, and this time the light is much farther to the west. It's way over to the west. I would guess about 19th Avenue, perhaps 35th. We just noticed it . . . yep . . . it's gone."

Within seconds, another light appeared in the same spot. When the orbs blinked on, Frank couldn't resist their fascination either. He spoke excitedly. "It's on again. Appears to be only one yellow light now."

"What time is it?" I interrupted, then answered myself. "About 8:30, Wednesday evening. And it's orange."

Frank interjected, "Nah . . . it's yellow."

I compromised. "Orangey-yellow."

"Yellowy-orange," countered Frank, and chanted, "You like tomato . . . I like *tomaato.*" The unknown object started fading from view as Frank jokingly whispered, "It's cloaking."

Mid-morning on Thursday, March 6, my son's phone started ringing. I usually don't answer it, but something told me I should.

"Hello," said a strong male voice. "Is Lynne there, please?"

"Speaking," I said.

"Hi, this is Vern at the airport. I was just wondering if you heard anything more about the lights we saw back in January."

"You were going to find out what they were. Did you?"

"I asked around, but nobody here knew what they were. Did you hear anything?"

"I haven't heard a thing, but I've been filming them. Haven't you been seeing them?"

He said "no" and then conjectured that perhaps the lights were behind the ridgeline of South Mountain, obstructing them from the view of anyone lower than we were, which included the airport. That would mean that each light was enormous, much bigger than a commercial aircraft.

Still no answers, only more questions. The newspaper and Luke Air Force Base had snubbed me, so where else could I turn?

After searching out someone associated with a credible UFO organization, I was finally referred to Richard, a field investigator for MUFON, the Mutual UFO Network. After I briefly described the picture I had taken of the February 1995 sighting and the appearance of the recent lights, we set up an appointment to meet at his home office on March 12. He asked if the current state director of MUFON, Tom Taylor, could attend. It was curious that neither of the men had heard about the strange lights, but they were eager to analyze my photos. At the least, I hoped they could tell me what I had been filming.

The huge amber orbs continued their nightly visits, usually three sightings in succession with several minutes in between, reappearing in just about the same place. On March 10, things got more cryptic. While I was downstairs cleaning up after dinner, I heard Frank call out, urging me to come upstairs. When I got there, he said that I had just missed an astounding formation of three orbs intersecting four orbs. It was amusing to see him so excited about the lights, particularly since he usually teased me during the mysterious nightly visitations. He drew a sketch of the formation, so I could visualize it. Sadly, we didn't capture it on film.

Meanwhile, I was bursting with curiosity, counting the hours until my meeting with the UFO investigator. But that meeting was not to take place, at least not on the day we had planned. The following afternoon Richard called to tell me that Taylor's mother had passed away and we would have to reschedule the meeting. We both checked our schedules and agreed on a new date—March 14.

3. The Buzz Begins

I woke with a start. I had slept so soundly that I hadn't heard Frank get ready and leave for work. As I was dressing, it occurred to me that I needed to make a copy of the footage from the night before, but I was running late. I had already edited a few sightings from the previous weeks in preparation for my meeting that morning. Looking at the time, I figured I'd just let the field investigator dub the rest directly onto his equipment from my camera. He should get the idea.

As I drove to Richard's home, I breathed a sigh of relief that someone from a credible UFO organization might finally be able to tell me what was going on in the Arizona skies. I approached the porch and saw an older man with thinning white hair, glasses, and a friendly smile.

"Hello," he said, as the screen door swung wide and we both extended our hands for a shake.

"I'm glad to meet you at last," I replied.

He led me through his modest home into a small back room. As I glanced around the makeshift lab filled with dismantled computers, stacks of videotapes, books, and papers, I wondered if this UFO authority could, after all, provide a valid explanation for what was happening.

He, on the other hand, seemed filled with excitement. "Did you get the big sighting on video last night?" he asked.

"What big sighting? About 10 P.M., I captured part of a formation that seemed identical to what we saw on January 23. It happened so quickly that by the time I got my camera focused I was only able to record three of the lights."

He said, "Oh, last night there was a *major* sighting of UFOs throughout Arizona. There were reports of strange lights and flying objects from all over the state. My phone has been ringing off the wall."

I was speechless as I handed Richard the photo from 1995 to scan onto his computer for analysis. Even though he seemed pleased to have something so unusual in his possession, he continued ruminating about the preceding night's events. "Something really strange happened last night. Dozens of people from all over Arizona reported the sighting to Peter Davenport, the head of the Seattle UFO hotline. Hundreds of others have been calling the police stations, newspapers, and TV newsrooms all night to find out what they saw in the sky. NBC will be here in about half an hour to interview me to get a take on what occurred."

A possible mass sighting was intriguing, but not knowing for sure what we were dealing with—a hoax, the military, whatever—I didn't want to get involved with the media. But I did want to help. Besides, it was the evidence that was important, not me.

"You know what? Why don't you take a copy and share the footage I took last night with the news people? I'll leave it up to you to handle. I'm happy to chat over the phone, but I would prefer to remain anonymous."

He understood.

The doorbell interrupted us. The NBC crew came in with their gear. I stood silently off to one side of the tiny back room. I tried to remain inconspicuous, just watching as they set up their equipment for the evening news interview. They never even asked who I was.

The field investigator showed them my video from the night before, as he dubbed the original footage onto his own tape. He started briefing them about what he had heard thus far, remaining cautiously evasive throughout the reporter's inquiry.

I was itching to tell my side of the story, and finally piped in. "I don't want to be on camera and I can't tell you my name, but I can give you some firsthand background about the strange activities in our skies for the past couple of months. In fact, that's why I'm here—to have what I've been videotaping analyzed."

Richard interjected enthusiastically, "Yes, it is really something that we were supposed to meet on Wednesday, but I had to cancel. Now she walks in the morning after a statewide sighting with fantastic footage, just in time for the news media. How coincidental."

His statement made me realize something ironic. Had there not been a massive sighting the night before, my photos might never have been taken seriously. But now dozens, if not hundreds, of reports of strange objects witnessed in the Arizona skies could not be dismissed. I was thankful for this turn of events and that I had documented evidence for it.

With the reporter standing just a few feet away, I wanted to answer some of his questions. I was a witness, ready to give him the inside scoop with proof in hand. But because I wouldn't be interviewed on film, nothing I said impressed him.

As the cameraman took a break to change angles, I whispered to Richard, "I'm on my way. It was a pleasure meeting you. I look forward to your expert evaluation of the situation." And I left with the original evidence clutched to my chest.

When I arrived home, there was a phone message from the air traffic controller: "I wanted you to know that the sighting last night was almost identical to the one on January 23. Again, nothing showed up on radar. By the way, a commercial pilot called into the tower asking, 'What the hell are these lights over me?'"

I called the field investigator to report the new data. Before I could finish my sentence, he interrupted. "Jim Schnebelt from the local FOX TV affiliate is here filming. Would you mind talking with him over the phone?"

"Of course not, I'd be happy to share what I know," I replied. After being ignored by the first reporter, I was delighted that someone in the media wanted to listen to my anonymous account.

Moments after I hung up from the reporter, the telephone started ringing. It was a reporter from another station asking if I would be interviewed that afternoon for the evening news.

"No, I don't think I'm ready for that," I responded, "but you're welcome to retrieve a copy of last night's footage from the MUFON field investigator who gave you this number. I'll answer any questions you might have over the phone." I was inundated with calls from all the Phoenix news stations, asking for a description of what I had witnessed the night before. It was thrilling to be able to help.

By late afternoon, I had the TV on and the VCR cued up. Beginning at 4:30 P.M., every network affiliate and local channel ran the story, most as their lead. And with the strange twist of fate, they were all showing my video. Here are a few excerpts to illustrate how the TV news media introduced the unusual statewide event to the Arizona public.

Reporter Jim Schnebelt from KSAZ-FOX 10 News at 5 P.M. explained that the home video they were showing of three strange objects hovering directly over downtown hadn't been explained yet, but that something strange did happen in the sky over Arizona last night. At least two local people caught the strange lights on videotape, and the objects were not only seen over Phoenix, but also initially in Paulden, then Prescott to Phoenix to Tucson.

The last sightings were from northwest Arizona around Kingman. Schnebelt summarized what Arizona residents observed: "Some witnesses describe the fleet of lights in a V formation; some say they were in a line; others saw a diamond shape. And the number of lights seen ranges from one to nine."

As they showed my video, Peter Davenport, director of the National UFO Reporting Center in Seattle, Washington, stated in a voice-over, "Another observer reported that when one turned they all turned together, as if by the same command."

I switched channels. There it was on KTVK NewsChannel 3. Anchor Liz Habib asked, "Did Arizona have visitors from another galaxy or was it a military exercise? Last night, people all over Arizona say they saw a UFO. People say they saw strange lights all over the state. A Paradise Valley resident caught these unexplained lights on videotape. Take a look at that. They appear to be near South Mountain. You can see three lights there and one by one they're going to disappear. See that? One UFO expert says those lights follow a pattern."

A MUFON field investigator stated, "What we're interested in is a multiple sighting by multiple people. And we have a time stamp as it moved down. We have three videos with different time stamps and they follow logically."

I changed channels again. The top story on the 6 P.M. ABC News affiliate, KNXV, called the sighting the most dramatic series of sightings in the decade.

At 9 P.M., KSAZ ran the following. First, an excited witness shared his personal experience, saying, "Pretty incredible what I saw. I didn't know what it was. I just saw lights in the sky in the shape of a big V and ran in and got my binoculars. It did not look like an aircraft. It was moving pretty slow . . . it was big."

Reporter Marissa Maggio elaborated: "Berry is not alone. This video was taken at ten o'clock last night by a Paradise Valley woman who would not go on camera. Three lights hover over Phoenix, then disappear. And this video [three objects in a triangle formation] was taken by an Ahwatukee man. *Arizona Prime* has been inundated with callers. Most say it looked like a fleet of lights in a V formation. A valley UFO expert says it's too soon to tell what the object was, but he doesn't believe it was flares from the military."

A MUFON investigator stated, "I'm assured by looking at this that the object is in front of South Mountain, but I have no take on what it is at this time. We haven't had enough time to study the situation."

The bemused witness added, "When it flew over us, there was no noise; it was completely silent."

All this media attention only confirmed that others statewide had seen samples of what I had been documenting for more than two years. On the 10 P.M. news, two more videos were aired along with mine. It seemed that hundreds of Arizona residents were outside on the clear night of March 13, 1997, checking out the Hale-Bopp comet. When these other mysterious celestial formations caught their attention, a few watchers captured the impressive sight on tape.

One of the videographers and firsthand witnesses, Bill Hamilton, explained what he saw for a 10 P.M. local ABC news broadcast. "These lights were sitting stationary. They just came on in place. They lined up in a formation. They did not look like flares, and they didn't move around at all like conventional aircraft."

The reporter, Paul Jonchich, added, "It's something UFO enthusiasts are calling a major sighting." He summarized the puzzling situation: "Now, if you just look at the videotape, you might wonder what's so unusual about three or four bright lights in the sky, what with so many planes coming and going from Sky Harbor. But the people who saw the lights will say the lights were orange, were bright and big, and were like nothing they have ever seen before. We checked with the FAA today, we checked with Sky Harbor, we checked with Luke Air Force Base, and there's been no official explanation of those bright lights last night."

That evening, I was so charged up I couldn't sleep. My mind was in overdrive. Was this a hoax, a military maneuver, or was it the unthinkable—a real Unidentified Flying Object? And what was I supposed to do with the other photographic evidence I had accumulated? I certainly had an opportunity to inform the media of my data, but I was hesitant. Frankly, I didn't know what to do, so I just waited to see what would happen next.

On the other hand, Richard, the field investigator, was thrilled about the recent events and called me three or four times that evening to relay the inside word he was receiving from his contacts and the media. He shared that he had gotten a report that Luke Air Force jets were sent out to intercept the objects, and when they got close to the lights, at about 5,000 feet above sea level, the objects just blinked out. His "reliable source" said that one of the pilots was pretty shaken up.

He then urged me to listen to the Art Bell *Dreamland* radio show. I had never heard of it. My background on UFOs and extraterrestrials was very limited. I enjoyed the movies *Close Encounters of the Third Kind* and *ET,* and my kids grew up watching the original *Star Trek* series, with its wonderful messages. But the film industry's rash of frightening portrayals of abductions and killer aliens kept me from getting into the subject. If anything, I shied away from it. But now, people throughout an entire state had witnessed something extraordinary and they were taking the unexplained sightings seriously. I was curious as to what others had observed, and since I couldn't sleep anyway, I went downstairs and turned on the radio.

The topic on *Dreamland* was what they called the Phoenix Lights. Residents throughout Arizona were phoning in to describe what they had witnessed the night before. I felt tempted to do the same, but didn't know where to start. How do you tell the radio audience that what took place wasn't just on March 13, that these strange objects had been lighting the Phoenix sky for weeks, and that I had pictures to prove it? I ended up listening to it well into the night, until I finally dozed off to sleep.

The following Monday, Richard phoned to tell me he had analyzed the scanned picture from 1995 and thought he could see some structure in the close objects. In his office, he showed me several kaleidoscopic depictions of the enlarged orbs. The colors were spectacular. Even though to the human eye and in the original photos there was a definite space between them, in his rendition there seemed to be some kind of colored energy connection. He pointed out the blotchy white row at the bottom of each object, which he claimed might be portholes. Portholes? I didn't know what to make of this, but one thing was certain: his computer copies of the "unknowns" were beautiful.

As he handed me two prints and a book by researcher Richard Hoagland on theories of a human-looking face and pyramids on the surface of Mars, I asked him about his own background. He shyly admitted that he had been interested in UFOs since his childhood when a neighbor had introduced him to the topic. Through the years he became a self-taught Ufologist and computer buff. I could imagine that for someone who was deeply into Ufology, this recent incident was a potential milestone. He also wanted to be on top of it, and graciously offered his camera with telelens so I could capture better pictures. Even though I sensed that whoever had done this had gotten our attention and probably wouldn't be back for a while, Richard didn't agree.

Tuesday rolled around and I was still baffled as to what to do with what I had. For some reason, I felt as if I were *supposed* to be doing something constructive with it. I just didn't know what. Maybe my friend Barbara could give me some unbiased insight. Her husband and mine have known each other since childhood. Both grew up in Philadelphia, were Boy Scouts together, attended the same high school, pursued medical careers, and settled in the Valley of the Sun to raise their families. Our trusting bond goes way back. I have to admit, though, that Barb's candid comment caught me by surprise.

"Lynne, if anyone can do something credible and professional with this, you can," she said. "That's what you do—educate others to the truth, to the reality of things. You of all people can get this going in the right direction."

It started sinking in. I had been disseminating the realities of vital health issues for almost 25 years, dedicating my professional life to community education. Was I supposed to educate the public about this vital issue as well?

While contemplating this challenging new perspective, I started leafing through the *Arizona Republic* for any mention of the uncanny event. After all the TV coverage for days, it was surprising that nothing had appeared in the state publication. As I turned to the "Valley & State" section, I was delighted that there was finally a brief account concerning the Phoenix Lights. Peter Davenport, director of the National UFO Reporting Center in Seattle, Washington, was quoted as saying, "Four days later, there is no clear explanation for the object, described as both a triangle and a straight line. Make no mistake about it, there was a dramatic event that took place in Arizona that night."[1]

Davenport said some callers stated that as the object moved south toward Tucson it appeared to send out a red beam. His best guess was that it was an "ultrasophisticated craft" that did not come from this planet. The National Weather Service couldn't offer any answers, nor could officials at Luke. Lieutenant Colonel Mike Hauser said, "We just know it was not one of our planes."[2]

I had to search out more information and turned to the Internet. Among hundreds of UFO websites, I found "Mass UFO Sighting in Arizona, March 13, 1997" and clicked on it. Its graphic report was the most comprehensive so far. The following is a summary of an article by Bill Hamilton, assistant state director of MUFON Arizona:[3]

(1) On March 13, Hamilton had an incoming e-mail message from a Joe Travors in the U.K. who had been receiving messages from another man named Steve. Steve lives in Ahwatukee, Arizona, just south of Phoenix and behind South Mountain. He reported that beginning March 10, he and his family had noticed and videotaped strange orange lights over the Gila River Indian Reservation.

Bill Hamilton met there with Tom King on the evening of March 13. Steve reported that he had been seeing the lights between 9 and 10 P.M. Then shortly before 10 P.M., one of the brilliant lights he had described just turned on. Within a minute, the group witnessed what Bill noted as six globes or orbs of yellow-orange lights appearing near and in front of the Estrella Mountains. He stated that they were extremely bright and formed a straight line at a slight slant. He added that the light on the left of the formation was divided into two parts (or orbs) as he personally observed these lights through a Celestron 500-mm spotting scope.

Two witnesses that Hamilton and King interviewed were demolition experts for the military and they stated that what they saw were not flares. One of those witnesses was MUFON member Herb Moran, who reported that on March 7, 1997, he sighted large amber lights over the Palo Verde Nuclear Generating Station for 35 minutes and another above the Estrella Mountains between 9:10 and 9:30 P.M. Moran stated that he was puzzled by this light, different from any he had seen in 48 years as an aviation industry worker and private pilot.

Hamilton mentioned in his report that the sight was unusual enough to even startle children. As one man put it, "It was huge. The kids got a little frightened, I suppose because we had no explanation for what we were seeing."

(2) A little after 8 P.M., another witness observed five bright lights, which appeared to be over Squaw Peak, in a single row and hovering. The anonymous pilot continued watching the formation travel to the southeast when the light on the eastern leg shifted slightly out of formation. Because there was no noise from rotors, the pilot did not believe that they were from conventional helicopters. He stated in the report that he was familiar with the police NOTARs, the Arizona Air National Guard, and hospital emergency response equipment that fly over his home regularly. He assured us that the lights he observed were not part of a typical aircraft, that there was no red or green to indicate left or right, no strobe lights and that the center three lights were too far apart and not aimed ahead like traditional landing lights.

(3) Bill Hamilton relayed that other witnesses from Glendale, which is located at the west end of the valley, were both ex-air force and well acquainted with aircraft and their characteristics. At about 8:15 P.M., Kelly and his wife saw a perfect V-shaped formation of seven lights, a lead light with three trailing lights on each side of the V formation. Kelly pulled the car off of 67th Avenue and shut off his motor. They both watched the event for several minutes, noting that there were no navigation lights visible and no engine sounds detectable. Kelly also stated that he was a former skeptic.

(4) A fourth witness, Bruce Gerboth, reported from Ahwatukee in the east valley that on March 13, 1997, at about 8:30, he viewed something in the night sky he had never seen before: five amber lights in a triangle formation. Gerboth had the feeling that the lights were connected to a single structure. He also observed those lights until they disappeared over the Gila Bend Indian Reservation. He saw the amber lights again about 9:30 P.M. and felt these were the same lights he observed earlier.

(5) Witnesses Don and his wife, Grace, reported to Hamilton that they

could observe structure on the triangular object. They described gray panels on the underside of this structure with seven orange lights. Suddenly one of the orange lights detached and went out to the right and then returned and redocked with the primary object.

Hamilton revealed that other reports from California indicated that these orbs had been seen leaving and remerging with some primary object or light.

(6) At 8:30 P.M., Chandler, Arizona, witness Mike Fortson believed that what he saw was a massive singular object that had a translucent surface, which passed between him and the moon. "'What the hell is that?' I remember saying. The massive V shaped craft we saw was under 1,200' altitude! I remember saying to my wife, 'That son-of-a-bitch is a mile long!' One thing that I remember the most is how this craft 'floated' approximately 30–40 mph. There was no visual means of propulsion and absolutely no noise. As the front of the V-shaped craft entered the light of the moon, this black chevron-shaped object became translucent in bright light! As the V-shaped craft exited the bright moon, it became a solid black object again. It never changed course, speed, or altitude. Just faded off into the night sky to the south of us. During the whole sighting, approximately one minute and 45 seconds, we never moved our feet. There was no question in our minds that what we saw was not of this Earth."

Mike Fortson could also make out a kind of "distortion field" around the object that seemed to "ripple" like waves through water. Another witness named Tim Ley also noticed this ripple effect.

(7) It's Hamilton's opinion that a later witness, a truck driver named Bill Greiner, gave one of the most impressive testimonies, but viewed a different event. Greiner witnessed two orange lights for two hours while he was driving his truck south on Interstate 17 from Verde Valley to a cement/gravel plant near Luke AFB.

When he arrived at his destination in the west valley, he witnessed three jets scramble from Luke to intercept the nearest of the two, now seen hovering one to two miles away to the southwest, while the other object hung at a position in the northwest. He described the objects as looking like toy tops or hot-air balloons without the gondolas, glowing a yellow orange from within and engirdled with a pulsating red-glowing ring of light. As the jets approached the near objects, the objects shot straight up and disappeared, with the jets passing through the spot where the object had been hovering.

A call to Luke AFB by Tom King received the answer that all jets had been bedded down for the night by 7 P.M. The witness volunteered to take a lie detector test, as he said that despite the air force denials, he knew what he saw.

(8) A report received from Tucson's MUFON director, June Sherrer,

revealed that a witness saw a diamond formation of slow-moving golden-yellow lights at around 8:45 P.M. in Saddlebrook, north of Tucson, and flying southward toward Tucson.

In his report, Hamilton stated that the sightings on March 13 were remarkable due to the sheer number of people calling in reports to local police, news stations, and the UFO Reporting Center, and the number of witnesses who recorded video images of their sighting. He summarized the reports by firsthand witnesses:

• a large V formation of six or seven lights

• a huge dark black triangle with structural details

• intensely glowing spheres or orbs of golden-yellow lights

• the description given by Bill Greiner of the large orbs hovering near Luke AFB

Hamilton revealed that, while a spokesman from Luke AFB said they received no calls from residents about the strange lights on March 13, Peter Davenport, director of the National UFO Reporting Center in Seattle, Washington, reported that some of his callers obtained his hotline number by calling the desk at Luke.

Hamilton ended his detailed account by stating, "It seems like the official statements made to members of the press and public by those representing our air force are, to put it delicately, on a course deviation from the truth."

From the looks of it, Bill Hamilton certainly had his nose to the grindstone. It was comforting to know that there were serious investigators compiling data. I found it noteworthy that, although similar, there seemed to be many variations in what witnesses observed that evening, at least their perception of it. Or were there a number of different things going on in different areas at about the same time?

Five days after the mass sighting, my sister-in-law's brother invited Frank and me to join his party in a private box at a Phoenix Suns basketball game. When we arrived, several of the guests were chatting about a project they were working on at Arizona State University (ASU) in cooperation with the National Aeronautics and Space Administration. What were they doing with NASA? Dr. Loveless, an ASU professor, was explaining his use of laser beam technology during dance performances to create original music.

We were introduced to Latti Coor, president of ASU, and his lovely wife, Elva. As the conversation continued about NASA, I couldn't resist asking Elva if she had seen the TV news reports about the UFO sightings. She was so captivated that I shared my experience with her.

As we were chatting, I noticed a few uncomfortable glances from other guests. It was intriguing to observe how different people reacted to questions concerning unexplained phenomena, including unidentified flying objects, and the possibility of other intelligent life in the universe. Even though we were only speculating, some of the guests were willing to explore the possibilities, while others scoffed at the mention of such gibberish. Through it all, I sensed that in the future I needed to be more discreet when divulging my experience. Remaining anonymous might be a good idea. . . .

The next morning, Wednesday, March 19, while surfing the Internet, I found Peter Davenport's account. It was the first data received via telephone by the National UFO Reporting Center in Seattle on March 13 and the days that followed. He stressed that every attempt was made to make the summary as accurate as possible, including only reports contributed by more than one observer. "Even though the night was very quiet, all of the witnesses emphasized that the object 'glided' through the sky and made absolutely no noise whatsoever, which contributed to the eerie nature of the sighting."

From the multitude of credible calls into the National UFO Reporting Center, the following two reports posted on the Internet caught my attention.

The first report was by a witness who experienced the event with his family while driving west on I-10 on the evening of March 13. He stated, "At approximately 8:20 P.M., my mother (age 69), my wife (age 33), my daughter (age 9), my son (age 10), and myself (age 34) were approaching the hills south of Casa Grande, Arizona, midway between Phoenix and Tucson, when the driver said, 'What the hell is that?'"

The eyewitness continued his detailed description by stating that the UFO did not appear to be very high because they could see it very clearly in front of them and finally above them. As the object got closer, they could see the definite triangular mass with the lights on each of the corners. He remembered it to be rather thin, yet the width of the triangle itself was huge, city blocks long. There was no noise coming from the craft at all. As it crept over their car, the witness laid his head back in the rear window and watched it go over them. He reported that it was a huge, solid black metal mass with a smooth underside, no windows, no bubbles, no flashing lights. He noted the enormity of this object and that it would not have been able to land on the interstate without its wings extending far over the fields on either side of the road. As this object passed them, the witness reiterated that there were no visible engines, flames, or lights, just the straight, distinct edge of the mass. After it passed, they could no longer see the lights they had seen as it was approaching. It appeared to have disappeared or blended in with the black night shortly after it flew over them.

The second report concerned five adults and a youth driving north on Highway 10 south of Prescott who observed a very large V-shaped cluster of lights that moved directly above them and hovered for several minutes. The caller reported to Peter Davenport that, based on his flying experience, he estimated that the object was not higher than 1,000 feet above the ground.

Davenport noted that the witness called both Prescott Airport and Luke AFB to report the sightings. The female operator at Luke AFB volunteered the information that their switchboard had been deluged with reports about the strange object. Later statements from Luke AFB alleged that they had received no calls about the object.

Peter Davenport concluded that the object was still unexplained, but that there were a few things that could be ruled out, based on the reports that had been submitted to him so far. Specifically, it could not be any of the following:

Conventional Aircraft: (1) Since it was witnessed by many people to hover silently; (2) because it apparently covered the distance between Paulden and Prescott, Arizona—not less than 30 miles—in approximately one to two minutes; and (3) the lights seen on it were not consistent with any sort of strobe lights or navigation lights on any type of known aircraft, either private or commercial.

Balloon: The object moved too fast to be a balloon.

Hale-Bopp Comet: The comet was clearly visible in the northwest sky.

Hence, the object remains unexplained at the time of this writing.

With regard to the alleged intercept of the object by USAF F15C fighters out of Luke AFB on the night of the sighting, Davenport elaborated that hours after the bulk of the reports had been received at the hotline headquarters, they received a lengthy telephone call from one or more parties who claimed to have been witnesses to a "scramble" of F15C fighters, which allegedly had intercepted the object over downtown Phoenix, photographed the object with gun cameras, and returned to Luke AFB. Davenport states that the sources went on to describe how the base had been "locked down," how the pilots of the fighters had proceeded in approaching to within one mile of the object, and how their targeting radar had been "neutralized" by the objects. Apparently, they provided copious details about the incident, citing precise times, the names and ranks of pilots, contents of radio conversations with the pilots while they were in the air, and many other aspects of the events of that night. Unfortunately, Davenport's staff was unable to corroborate any of the claims, despite the fact that the callers were stationed at Luke AFB.

Within a few days, Davenport received another call. This time, one of the sources reported that he was being transferred to Greenland.

The Phoenix Lights

All in all, the detailed descriptions by the witnesses were revealing. Hundreds of firsthand observers statewide had experienced similar unexplainable phenomena. People of all ages and backgrounds shared that they were astounded by the size, silence, and unusual behavior of the objects they had witnessed. Hundreds were compelled to call authorities, TV newsrooms, and investigators to report it. Obviously, something spectacular had happened on the evening of March 13, 1997, throughout Arizona. But what?

4. A Telepathic Message?

On the night of Wednesday, March 19, 1997, as we switched on the television, there it was again. My video of the three lights in a triangle formation over the city graced the TV screen. The news story was just commencing, only this report was different. It was an expose on other similar sightings—worldwide—complete with photographic verification.

KTVK NewsChannel 3 Reporter Mike Warren began, "One week after a triangular object was seen over Arizona, one valley man says while they are amazing, they are not uncommon. Here are those balls of light over Phoenix last week."

His guest enthusiastically continued, "When I saw this I thought . . . well, it's our fair city's turn. Phoenix is now in this global community of places where this incredible phenomenon is happening."

Mike Warren assured us, "Jim Dilettoso has been studying UFO sightings for 20 years. He showed us similar balls of light [in a triangle formation] seen across the globe. This one was taken in Belgium in 1992. This is in Russia in 1991, a light cluster photographed in the former Republic of Georgia. And this incredible video was shot by a news photographer in South Korea a year and a half ago. It shows one light ball gaining intensity, then actually breaking apart into a whole string of balls. Jim Dilettoso believes the Arizona objects are the same thing."

The guest stated, "They behave either like extraordinarily advanced Earth aircraft or like unearthly aircraft."

Mike Warren asked, "But what are these things?"

Dilettoso answered, "No proof exists right now about what it is or what it isn't. It's an extraordinary mystery."

Back on camera, Warren added, "Dilettoso will head to Washington, D.C., in a couple of weeks. He will testify before a congressional committee on UFOs."

Jim Dilettoso, a computer specialist and expert on analyzing UFO footage, seemed knowledgeable enough, but what got my attention was that the reporter mentioned that the computer lab Dilettoso operated was located in Tempe, Arizona. A UFO expert just miles away! Even before the report was over, I was confident that he was the authority who could authenticate and analyze my data. But I wanted to wait until he returned from Washington, so decided to hold off contacting him until April.

I usually fall into a sound, restful sleep within minutes of hitting the pillow. But that night I couldn't. I was tossing and turning for hours. I couldn't sleep. Even worse, I couldn't get rid of the pressing thought, *Take the negatives back . . . take the negatives back . . . there's something in the negatives . . . take the negatives back.* The notion kept repeating itself until early morning when I stepped out of bed, thinking, *Okay, I'll take the negatives back!*

I was convinced that I must take the blank negatives from both the February 6, 1995, and January 23, 1997, sightings back to the developer. I would never have thought to do this on my own. Something had influenced my thinking and my behavior. I felt compelled to investigate the blank negatives further, and I didn't waste any time. After retrieving all the negatives I could find of both sightings, I went to the film developer.

As I handed over the packet, I said timidly, "I believe there is something in these negatives, even though they look blank. Perhaps there is something that didn't show up the first time they were developed. Please try again. Darken or lighten them . . . do whatever you need to do. After all—they were only lights in the sky."

She started working on my negatives immediately. The minutes seemed to drag on. Finally, the clerk approached me with a faint smile. "We've got something here," she said, as she produced four new photographs.

Yes! Several photos did turn out after all. One picture (as you can see, first-hand, in the photo spread) showed my first January 1997 shot of six perfectly spaced lights in a row with three hovering beneath. You could tell by the landscape that the span was easily over a mile wide. The next was a photo of the array head-on, with five orbs across and two spheres underneath. The third looked like the formation was turning. It was a picture of a row of six amber balls curved on the right in a V formation. The last photo was a line of four amber lights in the same location over the city skyline. I assumed they were all from the January 23 sighting.

What did I have here? Nothing showed up in January and now, out of nowhere, exactly one week after the March 13 event, I was holding four photos from a previous sighting. There was also no denying that I had evidence that needed to be shared with someone who would appreciate it. By 5 P.M. that afternoon, I felt strongly that I must contact the UFO authority, Jim Dilettoso.

I nervously phoned him.

A male voice answered, "Village Labs."

I hesitatingly asked, "Is Jim Dilettoso in?"

"Let me check. Who can I say is calling?"

"Just tell him that I have some information concerning the Phoenix UFO incident last week."

Within seconds there was a click, "Hello, this is Jim."

"Hello, Mr. Dilettoso, I am the Paradise Valley woman who took the video of the three lights over the city that aired on the TV news programs last week."

"Oh yes," he said.

I continued, "I happened to see you on the news last night and thought it imperative that I call you. Especially now that I just walked in with four new pictures of an event that occurred two months ago. Even though I don't want to get involved personally, I thought you should know."

His voice was kind and appreciative. He tried to alleviate my fears by sharing that numerous luminaries had had the same apprehensions, including Jimmy Carter, Barry Goldwater, and several prominent filmmakers. "I've been in this situation a number of times before with other people. That's okay. We can handle this by mail and phone. That's fine."

He was so reassuring that I told him in detail about the sightings of January 1997, asking if he could explain the strange sideways trail that the air traffic controller had described coming from the six motionless objects on January 23.

"Well, it means that it is not to be considered plane or flare smoke, but ionization," he offered. "In other words, it's propelled as opposed to drifting. Please hold, I have a call coming in."

"Sure." I took a deep breath. I was thankful for a few seconds to gather my thoughts.

He was back in a moment. I started describing the incident that Frank witnessed the week before, of the strange cross formation of three orbs intersected by four.

He replied, "It's meaningful. The three, the six, the seven, and the nine. I have found things in the Qabbalah, the ancient Qabbalah with a 'Q,' not with a 'K,' that have these light patterns. The light formations have been seen in various places in the Middle East."

It felt wonderful sharing the details with someone interested in hearing them. "To start off, I photographed a close sighting two years ago," I said. "It was our first introduction into the mysterious world of UFOs. As far as my husband and I are concerned, it was something we couldn't imagine existing on Earth. We've heard nothing about this type of advanced technology in more than two years. I've also been searching for an explanation for the giant amber lights I've been filming the past few months. I figured there must be a logical one, but needed to confirm that with a professional. I started asking around until someone suggested I contact a MUFON field investigator. We planned to meet last Wednesday, but he called on Tuesday to cancel so he could attend the funeral of the mother of State Director Tom Taylor that morning. We rescheduled our first meeting for Friday. There I showed up on his doorstep with video in hand from the mass sighting the night before. I was just going to get the photo and footage analyzed by him. I had no clue that there had been a statewide event until I arrived. As it turned out, my video ended up on every news channel in town."

I didn't know if Jim was joking around or serious when he said, "It was all in preparation for that fateful night."

I paused to realize he wasn't kidding, and then continued. "When I originally tried to develop the 35-mm film from the big January 23rd sighting, nothing turned out. The photo shop told me that those particular negatives were blank. So I put them away. This morning I felt it was important to take them back to the developer for another try at it."

He asked, "They did find something?"

"Yes! I captured several spectacular photos of the formation of lights head-on and then turning into a V. It seems I may have documented evidence of something quite unusual."

His response was reassuring. "Yes, it is. In my research I have come to see a trend that certain people have the ability, we could say by coincidence, to be at the right place at the right time. But there's more to it than that. With these people, like yourself, it happens to them over and over. The phenomenon—and we have to call it a phenomenon, because traditional, physical rules in our science and vocabulary don't include some of these conditions—has been described for centuries. What I'm trying to say is that things that happen to you may not just be accidents or circumstances. If what you have photographed is under intelligent control, *they know* that you are taking the pictures."

Wow. I have always believed that everything happens for a reason, and many instances in my life seem too amazing to be happenstance. But this? The conversation was getting surreal. "I do a fair amount of community work, and something that touches my heart is getting the truth about vital issues out to the public to raise awareness. Education is definitely the best protection. So since I may have credible photographic documentation of something that seems incredible, I'd like to find out what it is before I consider sharing it."

Jim interjected. "By the way, I'm testifying in Congress in a few weeks about what I think is going on."

I asked, "What *do* you think is going on?"

He replied, "What if extraterrestrials are here and trying to teach us things about ourselves? Suppose that they are fascinated with the fact that we have free will, the potential for spiritual development, and individual growth?"

My call waiting interrupted his thought. I wanted to hear more, but I reminded myself that I had monopolized this man for over an hour. We said our good-byes and decided we should meet in person. I'd let him know when.

As the week progressed, my apprehension about meeting Jim Dilettoso started to dissipate. From all indications, he was the authority who could analyze my pictures and video on state-of-the-art computers and, it was to be hoped, give me an explanation for them. Was it military? Was it a hoax? Was it unearthly? I called to set up an appointment for after his return from Washington, D.C. I figured I had a few weeks to prepare myself mentally for this next crucial step on my quest for the truth. But when I called, Jim told me he had canceled his trip because of all the media obligations created by the mass sighting. By the time we finished our conversation, I was committed for the following Wednesday at noon.

The night before our meeting, I almost backed out. I was staring at the ceiling above our bed for hours, trying to decide if I should get involved at all. UFOs weren't my thing. Why was I drawn into this?

By 3 A.M., I couldn't lie there idle any longer. Grabbing my robe from the foot of the bed, I went out onto the balcony for reflection. Serene darkness covered the desert landscape. The tranquility consumed me. I inhaled deeply, the cool, fresh air filling my senses with the sweet scent of spring blossoms. Exhaling slowly, I gazed at the spectrum of glittering stars, their silent dances flickering in the evening sky. Closing my eyes, I reflected on questions that had filled my mind for days: *Why do I have what I have? Am I supposed to do something constructive with it? If so, what? And how? My privacy and credibility are paramount, so how can I get involved and still remain anonymous?*

An idea flashed through my brain. Maybe I could be myself *representing* the "anonymous couple" who witnessed and photographed the unknown lights. That would be the truth, anyway. I produced educational materials about the reality of things. What about this reality? If there was a logical explanation for what had been appearing in our skies, so be it. If the phenomenon was not military, we should also be informed—whatever it was. For some reason, I felt an urgency to help make that happen. *Please show me the way, lead me to what I have to do. Even though it may not be easy, I will do whatever needs to be done.*

As I took another sustained breath, I implored, *One more thing. Please give me a sign. Give me a sign so I'll know I'm doing the right thing, so I'll know this is real.* I then stepped inside and slipped back into bed.

Something happened that night, something both enlightening and reassuring. I drifted off to a sound sleep, waking the next morning refreshed and with conviction. I was supposed to meet Jim Dilettoso, take him into my confidence. I was supposed to do something productive with what I had—I was sure of it now. What happened during that night dispelled any apprehension I might have had about going forward with what had to be done. I was at peace.

When I walked into Village Labs that morning, an ultramodern complex a few blocks from the Arizona State University campus, a gentleman with shoulder-length grayish hair and a twinkle in his eye greeted me with a big smile and a warm handshake.

"Hi, I'm Jim Dilettoso."

There was an instant rapport between us as he led me into a boardroom and offered a seat across from him at a long table. I started to take out my photographic evidence as several other men walked in and introduced themselves. Then they left.

We were alone. Jim listened as I recapped events. I began showing him the pictures. He was startled and pleased. He asked if I would like to take a break and tour the labs. We entered a huge work area with state-of-the-art equipment including computers, monitors, and recording devices. Down a long hall there were other huge rooms filled with employees monitoring complicated technical workstations. At the back of the building was an immense warehouse area with a soundstage for rehearsals of his band. Jim pointed to exquisite artwork, paintings created by people who had experienced close encounters. A shiver ran through my body.

Several weeks before this meeting, about the time the amber lights returned in the distance, I had felt an urge to buy art supplies. All I wanted to paint were the memories of a profound childhood experience and the sighting of the three amber orbs outside our bedroom window; I thought it was silly and put everything away. The new brushes, paper, and paints were in my closet, unopened.

Now looking at these magnificent interpretations on canvas made me think maybe it wasn't so silly after all.

Jim had many intriguing anecdotes concerning the UFO realm and he seemed to possess great expertise in the field. I was fascinated. Suddenly, I realized I had been there for over five hours. It was getting late, so we set up another meeting for the following week, April 2, at 12:30 P.M. Before I left, he led me into his main computer room and displayed similar pictures of light formations from many different countries. I was amazed at his database of hundreds of authenticated sightings from around the world.

He then showed a promotional video of Village Labs. According to the tape, Jim lectures to MENSA (the elite IQ organization); he also helped develop movie colorization. His video showed dozens of important entities he had worked for from Walt Disney Productions and Turner Entertainment to NASA and the Voyager Project. Jim has also been involved in the computer technology of the music industry for many years, working with such legendary groups as the Moody Blues and others. His background was impressive.

After this enchanting meeting, I looked forward to our next. I was still keeping track of any reports on TV and in the newspaper about the mass sighting. One caught my attention on April 1. The Pentagon reiterated their official 1969 statement that "UFOs are not a threat to national security." I wondered why, out of the blue, they had chosen April Fools' Day to make this important proclamation.

The report continued on the *CBS Evening News with Dan Rather*. Not only did he bring up the unexplained lights over Arizona, he stressed that you didn't have to be in a cult or spaced-out to believe in UFOs. He declared that millions of Americans do, and believe as well that the government is somehow covering it up. Rather said they had asked the Pentagon and had been told it could not substantiate the existence of UFOs nor did it harbor the remains of UFOs. The air force quit investigating UFOs in 1969, he pointed out, but the results of its investigations into more than 12,000 sightings are in the National Archives.

Rather mentioned that one of the documents you can find there is the so-called MJ12 document, a 1954 White House memo summoning the Chairman of the Joint Chiefs of Staff to an extraordinary meeting of the National Security Council concerning UFOs. Rather assured us that, to UFO buffs, it's a "smoking gun," proof that the government has known all along that UFOs are real. "In last year's movie *Independence Day*," said Rather, "a thunderstruck president is taken to a top-secret base where the remains of a spacecraft and its occupants are preserved. 'Don't tell me you have had this for 40 years and you don't know.' Easy . . . to point out there is always a logical explanation for lights in the sky, but impossible to deny the belief in UFOs is widespread and real."

Chalk one up for Ufology. Now more than ever, questions raged in my mind regarding the strange events I had witnessed and photographed. After spending many hours with Jim Dilettoso, learning bits and pieces of this captivating topic the week before, my curiosity about Jim's impression of my data, and the unexplained sightings in Arizona and across the globe, was intensifying.

When I walked into Village Labs the next day, Jim was hurriedly passing by and assured me that he would be back in a few minutes. I waited patiently in the enormous lobby for him to return. I knew he was a busy man, but after all, we did have an appointment. It was way past lunchtime and no Jim in sight. A tall, dark-haired gentleman with a kindly demeanor approached me. I remembered meeting him briefly the week before, but wasn't quite sure of his position at Village Labs. He introduced himself as Michael Tanner, Jim's associate, and apologized for Jim's tardiness. "How about lunch?" he offered. I was famished, so we went to a quaint Mexican restaurant to chat.

Michael and Jim go a long way back. They had been friends, as well as business buddies for years, so I was pleased to get another viewpoint. From what Michael was sharing about the duo, they certainly did complement each other. Jim was the innovative scientist, with much of his knowledge self-taught; Michael was the businessman, apparently keeping things in order for Jim. They seemed to make a great team.

While I had this exclusive audience with Michael, I asked him about his own take on the recent events and what background information I should know now that I was going to be involved with the investigation.

Michael had been studying Ufology for many years, was very well read on the subject, and had some interesting views. In his opinion, these phenomena had been going on since biblical times, perhaps preceding them. He began by acquainting me with biblical interpretations of repeated encounters with what today would be called UFOs. I was trying to keep an open mind, but the Bible? There are dozens of references to clouds, balls of fire, wheels, and flaming chariots that bear a striking resemblance to unearthly objects seen today worldwide, he said. He quoted from Jeremiah 4:13, "Behold he (Yahweh) shall come up as clouds, and his chariots shall be as whirlwind . . ." and from Isaiah 19:1, "Behold, the Lord rideth upon a swift cloud . . ." and Isaiah 4:5, "And the Lord will create upon every dwelling place of Mount Zion, and upon her assemblies, a cloud and smoke by day, and the shining of a flaming fire by night."

Michael reminded me that the people who wrote these words had never seen or heard of airplanes, disks, or stealth aircraft, so would have lacked the vocabulary to express what they saw in modern terms. His examples were striking, particularly those of the prophet Ezekiel. On four occasions he had visions that some scholars believe are descriptions of extraterrestrial spaceships, recounted in Ezekiel, chapters 1, 8, 10, and 43. Michael quoted from Ezekiel 1:4, "And I looked, and behold, a whirlwind came out of the north, a great cloud and a fire in folding itself, and a brightness was about it, and out of the midst thereof as the color of amber, out of the midst of the fire."

He explained, "This could almost be a UFO sighting of today with swirling wind, a huge disk-shaped object with an intense amber glow. In fact, in the 1960s Joseph Blumrich, a senior executive at NASA's Marshall Spaceflight Center, actually reconstructed a 'spacecraft' Ezekiel saw. To add to the mystery, Ezekiel even describes the strange object descending from the skies with a likeness to a spinning wheel, driven by a powerful-looking being! Start looking in the Bible. You'll find many more examples."

Michael firmly believed the Arizona sightings were a benchmark spiritual sign. That it wasn't the UFO phenomenon itself, but the spiritual component that was paramount. Being in the medical profession and witnessing many so-called "miracles" myself has made me realize how important it is to trust in our own spiritual gifts. For example, my mother was told she would only live six months after metastatic colon cancer infiltrated her liver. But she wouldn't give up. And with the love of her family, combined with positive thinking and visualization, she lived seven more years in remission. When you see that happen, you know there is something within each one of us that can overcome almost any obstacle. Scientists tell us that we only use a small percentage of our brain. What's going on with the rest of it? Perhaps in the vast recesses of convoluted gray matter, our spiritual potentials lie dormant—waiting to be reawakened. Maybe that's what all of this is about.

While Michael was an expert eager to educate me in spiritual lore, I wanted to get back to the recent events. I had come to Village Labs and specifically to Jim Dilettoso because, according to the TV report the week before, he was well versed in analysis capabilities and other events of this caliber.

"Mike, haven't there been similar phenomena occurring worldwide?"

He assured me, "Oh yes, balls of light—very similar—in Korea, Germany, Belgium, the U.K., Russia, Japan, New York, Ohio, Nevada. But so far the Arizona event looks like the biggest event on record. Whatever it is, we should be informed about it."

I had to agree. "That's why I came to Village Labs. I have evidence of *something*. I don't know *what* it is—but I do know *that* it is. And it is affecting other people. Be it military or unearthly, I feel it's important that we are told the truth. Maybe that in itself will bring us all together."

Michael added, "And if it is in fact unearthly, wouldn't it be wonderful if people would pull together so that when the real arrival happens, it will be a welcoming event—from the entire world?"

Then, as destiny would have it, just days later I was invited to participate in a Passover Seder. Passover celebrates the escape of the Children of Israel from the Egyptian "house of bondage" and serves to remind everyone of the importance of continuing the battle for freedom in every generation. The Seder itself is a special Passover home service held on the first and second nights of the holiday.

As we each took a turn reading from a published Passover text, I happened to recite the following passage. It includes the words of Elijah, the great prophet and conscience of Israel some 30 centuries ago. According to tradition, Elijah did not die but ascended to heaven in a chariot and vanished. I read aloud: "Around 900 B.C.E., Elijah, the prophet from the village of Tishbi in Gilead, challenged the injustice of the king and overthrew the worship of Gall. He healed the humble sick and helped the widows."

In chapter 2 of the Second Book of Kings, Elijah crosses the River Jordan with his son Elisha; in verse 11, "it came to pass, as they still went on, and talked, that behold, there appeared a chariot of fire, and horses of fire, and parted them both asunder; and Elijah went up by a whirlwind into heaven."

It's interesting that at the end of his days on Earth, his disciple Elisha supposedly had a vision of Elijah being carried to the skies in a chariot of fire. Legend has it that Elijah returns to Earth from time to time to befriend the helpless and announce the coming of the Messiah when all mankind will celebrate freedom. His return has been anticipated by generations of Jews and will mark the advent of an age of harmony, peace, and understanding among all peoples and nations. Hence, he has a place in every Seder. A door is kept open so that he may enter, and a cup of wine is set to represent the final Messianic promise of freedom for all peoples.

As intriguing as exploring the hidden possibilities in ancient history might be, I felt that it was more important to concentrate on what was happening in the here and now.

The TV news reports had died down and there was nothing more in the *Arizona Republic* about the sightings or an explanation for what people had seen. So I went to the only public source left, the Internet, where I found the *Phoenix Lights Update* by Bill Hamilton. He reported that they had heard from a growing list of witnesses to the remarkable series of UFO sightings on March 13, and that all of the witnesses were consistent in their descriptions and easily recognized the testimony of other witnesses.

Hamilton pointed out that sometimes the formation (or huge object) traveled at "blimp" speed or hovered, and at other times must have been dashing through the sky to make its next destination. Golden glowing orbs were seen throughout the south valley after the passage of the formation.

They had also learned that a formation was seen over Las Vegas about 20 minutes before the Paulden sightings. At the same time, a man living in Bear Valley near Victorville, California, reported seeing a formation of yellow and white lights as large as a baseball diamond on the night of March 13. Several orbs had been seen in that area, including ones that drifted up to join a big hovering light in the sky over the desert west of Apple Valley.

Reminiscent of our own sighting in 1995, Hamilton stated that orbs seen close up, within 20 feet around Cave Creek, Arizona, appeared to be the size of a basketball and floated five feet off the ground. These orbs arranged themselves in geometrical configurations. They had also been seen hovering around the secret Lockheed, Northrop, and Douglas electromagnetic test ranges in the Antelope and Apple Valleys of California. They had been seen hovering near the Palo Verde Nuclear Generating Station in Arizona, about 50 miles west of Phoenix, and had been videotaped by Scott Montgomery.

Concerning military and government "official" explanations for the March 13 events, Hamilton summarized in his Internet article:

> A Colonel at Luke AFB, when called by Strange Universe producer, Arte Shamamien, replied that maybe some rogue pilot was flying over the urban areas with a light rig to fool people! Huh!
>
> The Governor of the State, mayor of Phoenix, and the local FAA office were called. "What was this now, uhhh, you say happened on March 13?" Our governor was not informed. Neither was the mayor.
>
> As for getting the tapes from Sky Harbor, by the time a Freedom of Information Act (FOIA) process is initiated, the tapes could be recycled, but then the tower said nothing showed up on radar . . .
>
> Also, South Mountain Park rangers are closing the park at early summer hours. This started the night of the 13th! The park affords an excellent view of the Valley in all directions.
>
> Signed,
> Bill Hamilton
> Assistant State Director of MUFON Arizona

5. The Witnesses

Even though the military and government were essentially in denial about the statewide happening, the news reports, televised interviews, and investigators' summaries were compelling. I was thrilled that hundreds throughout the state spoke out about what happened to them on the night of March 13, 1997. The eyewitnesses, after all, were the genuine truth-sayers.

The National UFO Reporting Center in Seattle and Village Labs in Phoenix continued to amass a plethora of impressive, articulate, and thorough personal accounts. While reading through them, I wondered if hearing it straight from the experiencer might give me even more insight. Mike Tanner had told me that a retired pilot, living in Scottsdale, had seen the giant triangle "up close and personal." I decided to give him a call.

After I described my own experience, I asked him about his.

He started right in: "One of the guys I was with outside said, 'What the hell is that?' As I turned around to look I saw a V formation of lights. We watched this thing for about 20 minutes. It only took about a minute for me to realize this wasn't like any airplane that I had ever seen because there were no anticollision lights or navigation lights or anything like landing lights."

I asked what color they were.

"Orange. Halogen type, just exactly the kind you were describing. The object went basically north to south, from about Carefree to Camelback, then it took a slight turn and went over the airport, down over South Mountain, and disappeared. We thought we could see some kind of structure to it as it went by perpendicular to us. One thing we were sure of, it was huge, at least a mile in area, and it was silent. I also noticed no movement between the lights, which means to me that it was not a formation of airplanes that we know about. You can't fly like that anyway. Not even the Blue Angels can do that. It was incredible."

Wanting to establish his background and credibility, I asked, "What was your pilot rating before you retired?"

He answered proudly, "I've got an airline transport rating. I've got ratings in 747s, B9s, 580s, DC9s, 727s, DC10s, and every little airplane there is. I've been flying since 1962, about 13,000 hours of flying."

That was enough credibility for me. Accomplished pilots, air traffic controllers, medical and postgraduate professionals, teachers, truck drivers, retired military, even children—all confirmed similar data. And every one of them would agree that what they saw was like nothing they had ever seen before. Something very significant indeed traveled throughout our state on March 13. Of that I was becoming more and more convinced.

Then on one of my weekly visits to Village Labs, witness Tim Ley handed me his own rendition. His nine-page report was captivating. He began by stating, "Until this event happened here in Phoenix on March 13, I was not a believer in UFOs." He continued:

My mind was searching for an answer that could balance these two different observations: the great distance between the lights; and the absolute integrity of their relationship to each other. They were coming straight at us, never altering course or altitude, for about 13 minutes. Where we live, up in this small mountain valley, we can hear the slightest engine noises from miles away. And now this object was almost upon us and we still didn't hear anything. Not even a dog was barking and this craft was close enough to hit with a rock. My first impression was that it was about 100 feet up in the air. My conclusion was that this object was traveling approximately 30 mph. At this point it began to dawn upon us that this was a real UFO. I told everyone to really pay attention so we could remember afterwards . . .

The outline of the structure of the object was so perfectly balanced, sharp-edged, and geometrical. I probably spent 100 hours sitting at my computer late at night focused on my memory of the event. When I look at that image, I experience all over again the actual feelings and perceptions of that night . . .

As we finally saw the shape of the structure against the stars, we were all totally astonished. It looked like something out of a science fiction story was about to pass directly over us . . . As it now approached, we had a brief moment of confusion, because one of the taillights on the eastern arm seemed to flicker in two, one above the other, and clearly separated from each other. Both lights took on a reddish-amber cast.

The length of the arm passing over us was probably 700 feet long. When it began to pass over, I felt a nervousness in my body, almost like stage fright. There was no logical reason to be afraid, because this craft stayed silently on its course, without deviation and without threat . . .

Somehow I was "feeling" the craft in my nervous system; and so was my family. It was as if there was some type of field extending beyond the edge of the structure, and we could sense it . . .

It was impossibly strange that there was no sound at all. There wasn't even a wind sound that you might expect from the motion of an object of such a size, or even a breeze from the air being displaced in front of it . . .

Finally, after about 13 to 15 seconds, the last light on the tip of the right arm passed slowly overhead perpendicular to the point where my wife and I were standing. I had been waiting for it to come by so I could get a good look at it from directly underneath. I was so focused that when this light passed over us, it seemed like everything slowed down and for a brief instant the light seemed frozen in time.

The diameter of the light was about 6 or 7 feet. The luminance [sic] was perfectly uniform. The light did not radiate out of the surface of the light well. We remained in the darkness below it without being illuminated at all. It was pure light, with such beauty that it's inexplicable within the normal human experience . . . It was super bright and yet not glaring. I could look directly at it without squinting my eyes. It was pleasing to look at. Even now, when I look at the light in my mind's eye, I feel soothed and pleased by its beauty. My wife experiences the same phenomenon. I have thought about that one light every day since the event happened. It's obvious that the function of the light has nothing to do with illumination . . .

The craft maintained its course and altitude, heading straight due southeast on a course that would pass just south of Squaw Peak.

Once it was out of sight, we continued to stand outside and talk. We were all excited because we knew we had just had the most unique experience in the world. This craft was not from this world. This craft was a reality. They deliberately allowed their technology to be seen and even videotaped by just everyday people for this reason. They are here to help humanity.

I certainly hoped so. But I had to admit that even though I could definitely relate to Tim's feeling of awe and his graphic descriptions—especially concerning the lights themselves—my prudent self begged for caution in jumping to any conclusions before the facts were in. The Phoenix Lights may have seemed benevolent, but we must wonder what the intent of such a happening really is. Besides, everyone brings a different perspective and perception into the mix. Our background, upbringing, religious beliefs, life experiences, and mind-set are thrown in for good measure when something extraordinary and unexplained is observed. I didn't want to come to any conclusions while all of this was still half-baked, so I decided that the best path was to let the data speak for itself and take it where it led me. And right on schedule, it led me to my fax machine as a newspaper article was coming through from Michael Tanner.

> One for X-Files? Strange Lights Reported
> Associated Press, Mesa Tribune, March 15, 1997
> Strange bright lights over northern and northwestern Arizona evoked a bevy of telephone calls but drew no official explanation. Law enforcement agencies said their phones began ringing Thursday night with questions from people wanting to know what the lights were.

The article went on to recount that one Valley man videotaped what appeared to be a string of nine lights hovering above the desert floor and that his video was highlighted on the TV news Friday evening. It acknowledged that the Arizona National Guard confirmed Friday that it had no earthly explanation, but added that a spokesperson for the guard had stated, "An Apache helicopter pilot told a Valley television station that the lights were caused by military flares sent up during a training exercise."

Flares? What was that all about? I called Jim Dilettoso immediately to clarify the article. He had already spoken to Captain Eileen Bienz, the head of public relations for the Arizona Air National Guard (AANG). She told him that an Apache helicopter pilot took it upon himself, without authorization, to call one of the TV stations professing that he was the spokesperson for the guard. He reported that the whole incident on March 13 was the result of flares. Captain Beinz confirmed that she, not the Apache helicopter pilot, was the official authority for the AANG, and that there was still no official explanation for what the lights might have been.

I followed up with a call to Captain Beinz. She verified what Jim had told me. I shared that I had documented similar lights before March 13. She was anxious to meet with me and see what I had compiled. I, on the other hand, was a bit apprehensive about having a personal military briefing, and declined.

It didn't take long before the national TV media arrived on the scene. They held a town meeting, which was covered by the nationally syndicated show *Strange Universe*. From the looks of it, the witnesses were not only intrigued by the phenomenon, but peeved with the military and government for ignoring the call for an investigation. Here are some of the issues raised by the witnesses present at the meeting:

• Whatever it was, no one has a logical explanation.

• Explaining this away as a flare is a cover story or all of us wouldn't be here tonight talking about this.

• Flares do not gain altitude.

• Either the government knows everything or they know nothing. They keep changing their stories.

• How can 10,000 people be crazy at the same time—mass hallucination caught on videotape?

• Possibly they're trying to protect the public against something they feel we're not ready to handle.

• There appeared to be air force jets actually going after these things, trying to intercept them. But as soon as the air force got near them, the orbs disappeared.

• If the military was launching some kind of operation, why'd they pick right in the path of Sky Harbor airport?

• If the authorities don't know what it is, they should say so. If they do know, they are accountable to the public.

The host summed up the official stance this way, "For the record, a spokesman for Luke Air Force Base says no jets were scrambled and nothing unusual occurred."

The witnesses were serious about what they saw. They wanted answers, not denials and excuses. They echoed many of the same feelings I was having. After the initial wonder or fear, the need to know what it really was only grew stronger. Having observed the strange phenomenon right before our eyes, no one could tell us that it wasn't totally unusual and not real.

I didn't want to be a conspicuous fixture at Village Labs while witnesses and media were crowding the facility, so I purposely didn't visit very often. However, the gnawing feeling that I was supposed to be doing something productive with what I had was growing with each passing day.

A month after the mass sighting, I visited Jim Dilettoso for some "expert" advice. I stopped by on a Sunday afternoon hoping the lab would be quiet. But as usual, it was a hub of activity. Whatever Jim didn't get done during the week, he continued on the weekends. I don't think he ever took a day off. He loved what he was doing.

I asked him how he got started analyzing UFOs.

"In the mid 1970s, I was involved with a noted UFO group called APRO, the Aerial Phenomenon Research Organization—the granddaddy of all UFO research groups. In 1977, they asked me to develop a procedure, a repeatable procedure, to test pictures, create a control group, and photograph models. I made a pie plate and photographed scale models of airplanes and cars, then real airplanes and real cars, and developed a procedure where I could tell the difference between the two. I did a controlled study first. It took about a year. I found the best hardware and software. I went to the manufacturers, went to the trade shows and trade associations, talked to hundreds of experts for their opinions on the procedures."

"Were you the first person to do that?"

"I was the first person known to publish a paper on how to test UFO pictures scientifically."

"When I bring my pictures for analysis, what do you actually do?"

"The procedure is to get these into the highest resolution possible, to get the image into the computer, so we can apply different filters and study the image for its edge and light characteristics. Using special software, I look at the signature frequencies of different lights—streetlights, airplane lights, flares. They all have different optical characteristics. Match the wave and you can tell what made the light. So far, the unknown lights are not like anything I've seen before. We can't get a match between the unknown and knowns that we have stored. However, with your orbs we can tell by our filters that they are light emitting—as opposed to light reflecting. They apparently don't light anything around them. They don't light up clouds, they don't light up the ground. And the light is diffuse, meaning it's more like a Chinese lantern where the light is inside the object. The light goes up to the edge of the object and stops right there.

"The quality of the light is a very pure, precise light. Even though these amber orbs happen to be bright, it doesn't appear that their mission, their goal, is to be a light. So it's an effect, not the result. With electric lights and pyrotechnics like flares, the result is that they are a light. These orbs are different. They are a cause/effect as opposed to cause/result.

"Maybe they *are* light as opposed to 'they have light.' Let's say that some of the descriptions in ancient literature about *light beings* are true. Just speculate for a moment that they don't have any choice about turning off their light. They *are* light. So they go away. They don't go off. They go to a different place—even another dimension—and you can no longer see the lights."

I commented, "Before 1995 I would have probably laughed at your suggestion, but after seeing the strange amber lights dissipate slowly before my eyes as if they were fading into another 'place,' not just disappearing, what you are saying makes some sense."

Jim agreed. "They weren't visible anymore, like a ghost. Sometimes you can see the ghost. Sometimes you can just feel its presence, but you don't *see* it. Why? Because it is dwelling in more than one dimension at the same time."

Ghosts? And other dimensions? Was Jim serious about this? It seemed that he was. As much as I wanted to disregard it, for some reason I understood what he was saying. After all, I had experienced it. I wanted to know more. "Is it some form of energy?"

"It's still mass and energy, and in this case the mass may be so tiny that we don't physically see it. Like we don't see the air. It's colorless, odorless, tasteless, but it does have mass. There are all kinds of things that we can't see in the air. Take the wind—2 mph, 5 mph, 50 mph. The wind has force. You take a picture and you can't see the wind. You step out into it and you can feel it."

The phone rang. As Jim answered the call, I surmised that these objects might act in the same way as air, as wind, to our human eyes. They are there right before us, but we can't see them—unless of course they want us to.

I had one more question. "Jim, I respect your opinion. You have a tremendous amount of background in this field. I also feel that you may have insight into what I should be doing with what I have. You know that my desire is to do something meaningful with this. I am overwhelmed just trying to sort out all that has happened in the past few months and would appreciate your honest appraisal as to where you think I should go from here."

Jim's cheerful demeanor transformed into a more serious one as his eyes pierced mine. "Write the book."

There was silence as thoughts raced through my brain. Wait a minute. Sure, I've written copy for my health reports, a few TV news scripts in my day, and even classroom curricula—but a book? "I appreciate the confidence, but I don't know anything about this topic. What's more, how do I stay anonymous if I write a book?"

He repeated those three words: "Write the book."

He turned away to scan one of the photos I had brought for analysis. I reflected on his suggestion. I couldn't deny my burning desire to do something constructive with what I had. It seemed important to help others understand the meaning and impact of what was happening, even though I didn't have a grasp of it yet. But that didn't seem to matter. My gut feeling was that whatever occurred, the truth needed to be told. I had no hidden agenda, no previous connection to anyone involved with the topic. If anything, I would never have chosen to be involved. But here I was in the middle of something mysterious, with too much hard evidence to ignore. I also couldn't ignore the fact that whatever this was, it was happening worldwide, not just in Arizona. If it wasn't military or a hoax, consider the implications for humankind. *Humankind?* Why would that pop into my head?

People approaching broke my train of thought. Jim was the center of attention, even on a Sunday afternoon. I was impressed that he never turned anyone away. He was always there for anyone who wanted to share what they had seen or experienced. I wondered how he got his regular work done with all the interruptions, and thought it best to let him get back to his other duties. As I thanked Jim for his precious time and advice, he handed me a fax from a couple living in Carefree.

At 21:30 on March 13 . . . stationary in the sky for over 20 minutes glowed a bright fiery orange ball of light. I was surprised to see a second light, about a mile away in the eastern sky.

We were both astonished to see the light on the right joined by six other lights, each one illuminated at one-second intervals. After only a few seconds, the lights went out, one at a time, starting with the last one first. My wife and I realized that what we had just seen was a ship lighting up only one side of itself. The light shining a mile away seemed very separate from the triangular ship. It looked like it may well have been a satellite to the triangular craft . . .

My feelings at the time were only of excitement and not trepidation. The ship was not acting in a threatening manner . . . If anything, it seemed to have an agenda that it wished to execute, as efficiently as possible. But its size, its spectacular shape seemed to resonate a heavy, powerful presence. The ship came across with an attitude that it had a job to accomplish . . . It was hovering near the nuclear plant.

This last statement, combined with the supposed peaceful yet purposeful nature of the sightings reported time and again by the multitude of Arizona witnesses, suggested that whatever the phenomena were, "it or they" were not out to alarm or harm us. At least, that was what it seemed. It was becoming apparent that whoever did this wanted to be noticed. But for what purpose?

I had decided three weeks after the mass sighting to go with the flow and trust in my guidance. I had to admit, in the two months that followed, it seemed as if things were just falling into place. Even though there was still no official investigation or explanation, public interest in the mass sighting was alive and kicking.

Then a lone councilwoman arrived on the scene to champion the cause. I first read about her on the front page of the May 10 *Arizona Republic:* "X-File Is Opened into Phoenix 'UFO.' Barwood Asks Staff to Investigate Lights."

" . . . Sculley—Sheryl, the assistant city manager, not X-Files FBI agent Dana Scully—has asked police to look into the sightings, at Barwood's request."[1] Councilwoman Frances Emma Barwood stated that, at the very least, city staff should check out the strange lights in the Phoenix sky. All she was asking was for the city council to find out if the lights were a hoax or otherwise. She claimed that, from what witnesses had told her, the lights were as big as a football field. The national UFO reporting center in Seattle drew hundreds of calls, even one from Las Vegas, and resulted in an inch-thick stack of written reports, UFO center Director Peter Davenport said.

When the reporters asked Barwood if she believed in UFOs, she said she was keeping an open mind. "Since God created the universe, why couldn't he have created others?"

Peter Davenport was thrilled to hear that a public official was taking the sightings seriously. He stated for the record that, as far as he knew, this was the first that a local or state body took an official stand. He was encouraged and heartened by Barwood's stance.

But after this article ran, the Arizona government and press weren't quite as enamored. They tore into Barwood, leaving snide remarks on the city bulletin board, and blasting her on the radio and in the paper for her inquiry. For some reason, no one in the government, military, or print media was taking her or the event seriously. Of course, that wasn't true of the thousands of people who had seen it.

Barwood was getting so much flak that I thought it might be important that she know that there were others out there who welcomed her veracity. I called to give her my verbal support. To hear her tell it, after she had been inundated by dozens of phone calls from witnesses, many her constituents, and then approached by a TV film crew, she innocently asked at the next council meeting for an investigation into the March 13 event. Something had alarmed the Arizona residents. She thought it was appropriate, as their representative, to pursue an explanation for something out of the ordinary, nothing more.

She was so sympathetic and sincere that I ended up sharing my own story. I think it helped strengthen her conviction that the Phoenix Lights should be investigated. She was most appreciative. Our lengthy conversation also put things into perspective for me. By the time I hung up the receiver, I was more determined than ever to get to the bottom of this mystery.

6. Reality Sets In

Almost three months had passed since the mass sighting and there was still no official explanation. Even with the witnesses, media, and now Barwood pressing the city and state officials, there was no formal investigation taking place. I had to wonder why, particularly since the witness reports were so credible. A number of our patients, who had for weeks after shared their accounts, were also puzzled why no one in the military or government was taking the incident seriously. Their concern and the reaction of many others prompted me to extend my own inquiry.

I arranged to have air traffic controllers who had witnessed both the January 23 and March 13 events meet at Village Labs for a briefing with Jim Dilettoso, Michael Tanner, my friend and science writer Paul Perry, and me.

One of the controllers, an FAA air traffic controller since 1982, has an undergraduate degree in geology and formal training in meteorology and climatologic studies. He also teaches meteorology at Mesa College in Arizona and made some impressive statements concerning the January 23, 1997 sighting.

In a serious tone he began, "It was so unusual. The alignment was spaced out exactly, amber and bright. It wasn't like an illuminating light like a flare light. These were like points of light. The points of light were so huge they appeared to be bigger than if an airplane were approaching the airport with its landing lights on. Just from the size of the light it couldn't have been a flare. And I didn't see any indication of a downward movement or parachute. They were all in a straight line, equidistant apart. We said, 'This is very weird.' I had never seen anything like this in my life.

"So I took a pair of binoculars out and looked at it. What I saw was not an object, but seemed to be an object with lights on it. I could see a trail, not going up or down like flares or a hovering object, but moving west to east, right to left horizontally. Then the trail hooked around like a 180-degree turn, not up or down. The other thing that got me is that the wind was going in the opposite direction that the trail was. This object was turning—whatever it was. There was no variation. Perfect alignment. The lights were about 1,000 feet off the ground, about 4,000 to 5,000 feet above sea level. After that turn, they seemed to disappear behind South Mountain."

The other air traffic controller joined in. He has been a licensed corporate and charter pilot for more than ten years and an air traffic controller since 1985. "I saw it the night of January 23 and then again March 13 when I guess the whole state saw it. There must have been five of us up there and we all saw these lights. None of us came up with anything. We've never, ever seen anything in that direction before and the level at which they were spaced apart, the uniformity, was very odd. And with that intensity. We were awestruck by the intensity of them. We saw them on both dates at the same location and they were the same basic color, the same basic size, and so on. They looked very much the same."

Both controllers denied ever seeing these phenomena before, only on January 23 and March 13, 1997. They also stated that the military doesn't do any training missions in the area.

One controller clarified, "When they're sending F16s or A10s from Davis to Luke, they are high, about 25,000 feet. So they're not even close to where these were."

The other confirmed, "Anyone who flies within five miles or lower than 3,000 feet has to call in and report it."

The first added, "Someone called the police helicopter at eight P.M. on Jan. 23 to report the three lights, but no one responded."

Since I have pictures that prove that the same thing happened twice, I asked if the exact formations could have been created by atmospheric conditions, weather phenomena, or flares on two separate dates, two months apart.

The air traffic controller with a background in meteorology answered, "That's impossible. It would take exact atmospheric conditions, an exact amount of water vapor, an exact amount of heat index to produce that specific kind of phenomenon. It's a very narrow tolerance for whatever it is that produces that. You wouldn't be able to get the exact same replication two, three months later. To me, a weather phenomenon or flares is out of the question on that. To me, they have not come up with an explanation for it yet."

The other controller added that he had talked to a number of military people who admitted that *they're* out there. "They've seen them [UFOs], and there's no disputing that. I guess people in power are sworn to secrecy, and I don't know how you would break through that veil of silence."

I was so pleased that these professional sky watchers took the time to share their own stories with us. It was clear that what they saw, as experienced and highly qualified professionals, was unusual, genuine, and unexplained.

That evening there was another meeting at Village Labs. Jim and Michael had set up a conference for Frances Barwood to view the evidence and to meet with a few of the witnesses. Even though I was eager to attend, I cautiously excused myself. The media once again converged on Village Labs. The nationally televised syndicated show *Extra* had set up a shoot to capture this important gathering. It aired that Friday night, May 16, 1997.

The anchor began. "First, an *Extra* investigation into an apparent UFO sighting over Phoenix. The government shrugged it off, until now. A city leader has demanded an investigation. And a pair of air traffic controllers have come forward revealing what they saw."

Air traffic controller Bill Grava, a pilot and a controller for 12 years who had duty that night at Sky Harbor International Airport, stated, "I never observed anything like this in my flying or controlling days."

Fellow air traffic controller Vern Latham added, "It's a sighting I can't explain, a sighting I've never seen anything like before or have the experience to explain . . ."

Barwood stated that, if it was military, we needed to know it was military, and also revealed that no other politicians would back her up.

According to *Extra*, nearby Luke Air Force Base officials would only say that the lights didn't come from there. And even though Latham and Grava saw the lights while on duty at the Phoenix airport, a spokesperson for the FAA, which oversees air traffic controllers, stated, "There were no unexplained radar sightings on the night of March 13."

Not surprising, said Latham and Grava, since the lights did not show up on radar.

On May 20, a story hit the Arizona newspaper, only this time it was in the "Valley & State" section and both the heading and content were a bit disappointing: "City Probe of UFOs Is Grounded. Phoenix Has No Air Force."

Not only did Luke Air Force Base officials state that they did not plan on investigating, but according to the article, the report from the City of Phoenix staff alleged that the police department received fewer than five contacts, "concerned residents, not aliens" (as the journalist phrased it), reporting or asking about the mysterious lights. They also stated that the city's aviation department only turned up a few calls. On top of that, the Federal Aviation Administration, which operates the Sky Harbor International Airport control tower, didn't report anything unusual that night.

Councilwoman Barwood said she wasn't surprised by the city's "ultra-brief inquiry," having expected the staff to brush the issue aside, but she was amazed that no one seemed that concerned about the event. Repercussions from her innocent query were another matter, however. As the article put it:

> She also hears the "Frances sees little green men" talk and the derisive laughter running through City Hall. "I know that Skippy and Scott Phelps [the Phoenix mayor, Skip Rimsza, and his spokesman] are having a field day over this."[1]

Barwood couldn't understand why such a fuss was made when she asked city staff to look into the matter. She felt the city should get to the bottom of what was flying around the Phoenix skies that night, noting, "It could have done damage to antennas or something."

You had to admire Barwood's fortitude. She was leading the way for people like me who were terrified to go public. I could only hope that when the day came for me to speak out, her valiant effort would have paved a road that would be free of skepticism and harassment.

All Barwood wanted was a thorough inquiry. Contrary to the article, she had received hundreds of calls from witnesses, many stating that they had also phoned the police, airport, and Luke AFB. So why was she getting ridiculed and mocked? It didn't make sense, especially after two separate sources confidentially revealed to me that an elected official, who was vehemently denying the incident, had actually seen it with his wife and another couple. He continued to blast Barwood for asking for an investigation.

But our own investigation was churning away. Village Labs had become the clearinghouse for both the witnesses and the media. Michael was gathering firsthand witness accounts and setting up radio and TV appearances for Jim. Jim was working on a computer-generated compilation of the multiple videos to simulate the triangular object's whereabouts across the state on the night of March 13. I was researching and compiling all the data I could amass.

Jim was also analyzing my 35-mm photos to see if the amber orbs fit into an earthly optical frequency. Besides comparing them to other light configurations in his computer base, he kept stressing that the unexplained orbs definitely did not illuminate anything—unlike flares, whose main function was to produce light to heat and illuminate an area. On May 25, Jim received a letter of confirmation ruling out flares entirely. Charles M. Byers of New River, pyrotechnical expert and president of the Accuracy Systems Ordinance Corporation, communicated affirming data.

> The "lights" did not appear to have any resemblance to any type of pyrotechnic flares that I am familiar with. As we discussed, there are basically two different types of aircraft flares: illumination flares and decoy flares. The illumination flares are designed to provide wide area lighting, whether for airborne photography or ground observation. These flares are normally attached to a parachute and burn with a white light for up to a minute or longer as they descend. Photo flares are basically a big flashbulb and go off with an instantaneous explosion and release of a brilliant flash of white light of very short duration (a few fractions of a second). Both of these flares normally produce significant amounts of white smoke that would be visible for a long distance. Decoy flares, on the other hand, are designed to "trick" infrared guided missiles into attacking the flare and ignoring the aircraft that dropped them. Ejected is a better word than dropped as most decoy flares are simply "burning bricks" of pyrotechnic material that are ejected from their launchers when a missile is detected approaching the plane. They typically burn for a few seconds at most.
>
> Since the lights that were depicted on your videos appeared to be both stationary and of long duration (with no visible smoke), it is my opinion that they were some kind of "artificial light" and not any type of military or commercial aircraft pyrotechnic flares that I am aware of.
>
> Something was definitely up in the Phoenix sky that night, and it did not appear to be any normal type of aircraft that I am familiar with, either civilian or military! Sorry I missed it . . .
>
> Good investigating,
> Charles M. Byers, President

(Captain Eileen Bienz, State Public Affairs Officer, Arizona National Guard received a carbon copy of the original letter.)

The Fox network affiliate backed up Byers' impressive communiqué in a May 26 televised report with a public statement by one of the lead MUFON field investigators, ruling out flares: "Talking to people who handle these ordinances—and two of our witnesses were either current or past military—the magnesium (illumination flares) that have the parachute will drift in a zigzag motion, and you will see smoke coming out of the top. None of the witnesses have described this and none of the pictures we looked at have this peculiar effect."

7. It Hits the Big Time!

On Monday evening, June 2, Michael Tanner called to invite me to the Labs the next morning to be interviewed for a documentary called "UFOs: The Best Evidence Ever (Caught on Tape)," featuring the Phoenix Lights. He thought it important to include my footage and story. I didn't think I was prepared to divulge my own tale and certainly not my identity, but I was curious about this venture so I decided to stop by. It would also give me an opportunity to meet the other March 13 key video witnesses: the Krzystons, Tom King, and Bill Hamilton. I was keeping a very low profile. After nearly three months of anonymity, I hadn't even met them yet.

When I first greeted Mike and Sue Krzyston, their soft-spoken demeanor and apparent sincerity impressed me. Mike is a low-keyed insurance salesman and Sue a professional artist. They had no interest in UFO phenomena other than a curiosity about the strange amber orbs that hovered close to the Estrella Mountain range periodically during the 17 years that they had been living in Moon Valley. They had captured on video the magnificent array of eight perfectly spaced lights plus one separate orb, which appeared to hover in front of the Estrellas a little past 10 P.M. on March 13. I was pleased that after weeks of hearing about the clandestine witness "Dr. X," the generic title Dilettoso and Tanner had chosen to preserve my true identity, the Krzystons were glad to finally meet me.

Then there were Tom King and Bill Hamilton. Tom is a handsome, outspoken construction worker who has been photographing strange objects in the sky for years. Bill is a scientist by trade and an avid Ufologist on the side. Both take the subject very seriously. When I shared my own experience and photographs, they were captivated. It was reassuring to impart my account to people who cared to hear it, without the fear of ridicule or reprisal. I took the opportunity to request a personal meeting with each of them.

Mike and Sue Krzyston were my first. Several weeks after our initial gathering, I visited their Moon Valley home to get a feel for their vantage point and perspective. Mike happened to be working on a new video camera when the major sighting occurred on March 13 and was able to capture it all. He also mentioned that when a crew from Mexico came to their home for an interview, the producer asked him the names of the two mountain ranges in the distance. "They're called South Mountain and the Estrellas," Mike answered. The producer then asked him how they got their names. Mike had no clue. The producer exclaimed, "Estrella means *star* in Spanish. Were these mountains named by the native inhabitants many centuries ago because they also observed these bright amber light orbs hovering near them, just like now?"

Then on June 18, after months of silence from the national media print scene, all hell broke loose. *USA Today* carried a full-page article in the "A" section, with the headline "Arizonans Say the Truth About UFOs Is Out There."[1] It featured a depiction of Tim Ley's V-shaped computer simulation, accompanied by the caption:

> Skies, Phone Lines Light Up Arizona
> . . . Unidentified: For 106 minutes on March 13, people saw something like this V-shaped object flying over Arizona. UFO? The only thing certain is that it still haunts them.

After an introduction, journalist Richard Price wrote, "So far there is no explanation, but the government is not investigating. Local and federal agencies disagree over who should pursue the report . . ."

Price asserted that the events of March 13 "may add up to the most contentious and confounding UFO report since the so-called UFO age was launched 50 years ago by the legendary crash of a 'spaceship' outside Roswell, N.M. The sightings come at a time when interest in UFOs borders on a nationwide obsession, saturating the movie industry, television, and literature." The article stated that a *Time* and CNN poll that month found that 22 percent of American adults believe that intelligent beings from other planets have been in contact with humans. In addition, Gallup polls found that more than 50 percent of Americans believe in UFOs, 72 percent think there is life on other planets, and 71 percent said they thought the U.S. government knew more about UFOs than it was telling. Don Ecker, *UFO Magazine*'s news editor and research director, acknowledged, "The fact is that more people are seriously interested in UFOs now than they ever have been. Convincing the government may be an exercise in futility, but it's not hard to find believers on the streets."

The article quoted Peter Davenport declaring that the incident over Arizona was the most dramatic he had seen, and stating, "What we have here is the real thing. They are here."

The reporter listed three things that witnesses generally agreed upon: (1) The phenomenon was enormous, with the most conservative estimate describing it as three football fields long. Computer analysis of the tapes showed the object to be 6,000 feet—more than a mile—wide. (2) It made no sound. (3) It cruised over Phoenix at 30 mph and hovered in place several times in the sky.

Price reiterated that even though air traffic controllers could see the lights, they couldn't help pilots in the region who asked them to identify the sight. Again the controllers confirmed that nothing showed up on their radar screens. The article quoted air traffic controller Bill Grava. "Weird, inexplicable," he said. "I still don't know what to think, and I have no idea what it was . . ."

The reporter shared the words of 31-year-old laser printer technician Dana Valentine. He was sitting in his Phoenix yard when he noticed the lights heading toward him. After he ran inside to grab his father, an aeronautics engineer, they both stared skyward as the lights passed directly above them at 500 feet. Valentine stated, "We could see the outline of a mass behind the lights, but you couldn't actually see the mass. It was more like a gray distortion of the night sky, wavy. I don't know exactly what it was, but I know it's not a technology the public has heard of before."

Price wrote that according to Jim Dilettoso and Michael Tanner, "Neither has anybody else." He described Michael and Jim as two of four partners who own Village Labs, a Tempe, Arizona, firm that designs supercomputers for the federal government as well as computerized special effects for Hollywood. He said they moonlight as analysts of UFO tapes. They told him that the lights overhead were dramatically unique—"a perfect uniform light with no variation from one edge to the other and no glow." So far they had ruled out aircraft lights, holograms, flares, and lasers as sources of the lights.

The article reported that while their work continued, Phoenix Councilwoman Frances Barwood was leading the cry for an official probe:

Barwood's path to an official answer, however, has gone the usual route of UFO investigations, which is a road to nowhere. One private organization has investigated, however. Arizona's state director of the Mutual UFO Network, a band of 5,000 investigators around the country, has proclaimed it a UFO. That's unusual. Only about 5 percent of UFO sightings earn that distinction from this group. "I can't vouch for it being extraterrestrial," State Director Tom Taylor says. "It could be military related, although I find it difficult to believe the military would let it fly around like that."

At Luke Air Force Base, beleaguered Lt. Col. Mike Hauser says the calls keep coming. People are angry and demanding. They want an investigation. They allege a cover-up. "They're calling us liars," he says. "I take great exception to that. I've answered every question. We have nothing to hide. But the fact is that we don't investigate UFOs."[2]

Price pointed out that Hauser acknowledged that F16 fighter jets were in the air that night, but had nothing to do with "funny lights in the sky." According to Hauser, the jets were on a routine training mission. Price added that Hauser will never convince cement truck driver Bill Greiner, who stated that one of the orbs was over the base when three military jets took off and veered right for it. "I know those pilots saw it. Hell, I'll take a lie detector test on national TV if that guy from the base does the same thing. I wish the government would just admit it. You know what it's like in this city right now? It's like having 50,000 people in a stadium watch a football game and then having someone tell us we weren't there."

The *USA Today* article hit a national nerve. More than three months after the fact, our sighting was big news. The national media converged on Phoenix. Every major TV station ran the story. ABC, NBC, MSNBC, CNN, Peter Jennings, Tom Brokaw, and even the morning shows offered reports and personal interviews. They couldn't resist the sensational announcement. I was thrilled that many used my video—gratis—of the giant triangle formation of three huge lights hovering over the city. What mattered was that others all across America and around the world were finally getting a glimpse at the extraordinary sight that we had witnessed in Arizona.

One of the most interesting interviews was aired June 19 on ABC's *Good Morning America*. The host, Charles Gibson, introduced the story. "Now comes what some call the most confounding UFO sighting since Roswell. Witness Mike Fortson, what were your thoughts on UFOs before March 13? What do you think now?"

Mike didn't hesitate. "I've been a mild skeptic. I always thought if I saw one it would be a small little saucer, never anything as immense as what I saw. Now

I'm pretty well convinced that this was an alien visitation craft. I'm sure it was interdimensional instead of interplanetary and I'm quite sure that our federal government and military knows what it was."

Mike Fortson's statement about an interdimensional rather than an intergalactic phenomenon hit home. Again, the only way I could interpret what Frank and I saw in 1995 was that the objects had faded into another dimension. And now a key witness to the Phoenix Lights on March 13, 1997, was reiterating the same strong feeling.

Perception of another dimension couldn't be denied. Was that also why so many witnesses visualized different things during the mass sighting? Could the object change form and appearance through some kind of interdimensional shift?

Sticking with the media blitz at hand, I started looking for other syndicated shows that might be carrying the story. From the looks of the TV entertainment news programs, it seemed that the *USA Today* article catapulted the mysterious Arizona event to national status in a very short time. That evening I caught *Entertainment Tonight*'s version and then *Hard Copy*'s, which told it like it was.

The show began with the anchor intoning, "If ever there was something in the sky that could shut skeptics up once and for all, it's these strange lights that appeared so ominously over Arizona. Thousands of dazed desert dwellers saw this UFO and they are bombarding authorities with panicked calls."

Witness Tim Ley relayed, "I had two kids who were with me, my 13- and 10-year-old. They started to jump saying 'Independence Day, Independence Day.' They were really scared. But then nothing happened."

Jim Dilettoso said, "At this moment we know that it does not behave like any known aircraft made on earth."

Tim Ley agreed, "I'm absolutely convinced that it's not from this planet."

After viewing this telecast, it was starting to bother me that our mind-set, particularly the mind-set of children, is a fearful one when first witnessing these strange phenomena. We have been so inundated with movies and books promoting scary, violent scenarios and terrifying monster aliens that as soon as something "otherworldly" besets our eyes we are unnerved by it.

As Tim Ley stated, "But then nothing happened." This last statement seemed important. I had heard it repeatedly in the preceding weeks. Those who were initially frightened by the low-flying, mile-wide marvel became comfortable, mesmerized, even "connected" in a strange way to the phenomenon as it slowly and silently glided overhead. Perhaps whoever was controlling the device was also helping us overcome our fears. An intriguing aftereffect to be sure. Should we begin to look at these visits from a new perspective? After all, *then nothing happened.*

8. Flared Up Again

More and more TV spots started airing after the *USA Today* article. One of the reports interviewed a self-proclaimed grassroots field investigator from the Arizona Mutual UFO Network. I'll call him "Martin." Even with all the confirmation to the contrary, suddenly, for some inexplicable reason, he was insisting that the unknown lights were flares. Only a few weeks before, in the May 26 TV news segment, MUFON reported that the unexplained lights didn't have any of the characteristics of flares at all. But now Martin was vehemently declaring they were definitely flares.

This seemed absurd given that when I asked him personally, Martin admitted that he had only viewed flares being dropped at one military base. Mind you, he never saw the unknown lights. So how could he make a definitive statement that the lights were flares, a statement that he would disseminate to the local TV and radio stations as fact? Why would he start pushing the flare theory now, almost four months later, without an official military or government investigation or announcement to back him up?

Since I was a healthy skeptic and was still searching out a logical explanation, on Tuesday morning, June 24, it was time that I got to the bottom of this.

My first call was to the Luke Air Force Base public affairs office. They made it clear that there was still no explanation, nor was there any intention of pursuing an inquiry into the mysterious Phoenix Lights.

57

In the words of the public relations officer, "We don't know anything. That's the bottom line. There was something there, but what it was, that's the question. No one knows. Until someone finds out what they were, God only knows. It definitely wasn't a Luke F16. It would have been loud and they show up on radar. These things were obviously very light because there was no motor sound, they moved very slowly, and the lights were equidistant and never dropped like a flare would drop. Helicopters are the only things that I know that hover and they're loud as hell and show up on radar. The warning lights are always blinking. All airplanes have them. I mean, it's just strange. A strange sighting."

I asked, "Are there any military or government agencies that do investigate these things?"

He answered flatly, "No. Because Operation Blue Book that did investigate these UFO sightings years ago stopped investigating in 1969. The only one who knows is God and whoever is doing it. I would love to know myself. So would lots of other folks. It's very strange."

Not that he would tell me anyway, but I had to ask, "I guess you would probably know if there was a secret mission going on?"

He responded succinctly, "We don't have any secret missions."

That satisfied my curiosity about Luke, but what about Davis-Monthan Air Force Base in Tucson? Did they know anything?

I was connected by phone to a lieutenant, who stated, "Specifically on March 13, we went back and checked our flying records and the last aircraft that we had land was at 5:50 P.M. and sunset was at 6:30 P.M. We do a lot of night flying out at the Goldwater Range and when we do, normally they do employ a lot of flares, at about 6,000 feet. And when they employ them it's not only one flare they expel from the aircraft, they'll employ a few."

Just to make certain, I asked, "Do flares stay in a formation?"

"The aircraft travel about 250 miles an hour—they're going to fall down and drift."

"That night, on the 13th, you say you did not have any planes out deploying flares."

"That's correct. All our planes were on the ground. The range is owned by Luke Air Force Base and Luke already confirmed that they didn't have anything out there. Besides, we never fly over populated areas. In fact, we're going to be training out there on the range tonight through Thursday night and probably next week in the evenings between 8 and 9 P.M. We don't fly them Friday, Saturday, or Sunday at night. As far as March 13, if something happened for which we had some responsibility, we would come forward."

None of the top-ranking military personnel would confirm that they, or anyone else for that matter, had sent off flares that night. They all denied any military maneuvers taking place on the evening of March 13, 1997. They also wouldn't address the video footage I had accumulated over the two months preceding the mass sighting. They did admit they were as stumped for an explanation as the rest of us. It seemed that they were all more interested in seeing my evidence than coming up with any logical explanation for it.

I had just finished talking with the lieutenant when the phone rang. It was Michael Tanner. "Hello Lynne. I'm here at KTAR News Radio and Jim is doing a show with Pat McMahon on the Phoenix Lights. I know you want to stay anonymous, but would you chat with Pat over the telephone?"

After coming up empty-handed after hours of phone conversations with the military, I was convinced that there was more to this story than just the March 13 events. By then my voice was raspy and hoarse. Maybe no one would recognize me anyway. If it was that important for Michael to ask me to do, I was glad to help.

I could hear the faint on-air conversation between the host, Pat McMahon, and Jim Dilettoso being broadcast across Arizona. Pat asked Jim what percentage of the extensive photo analysis, video analysis, and film analysis of so-called UFO sightings conducted by Village Labs turned out to be credible sightings.

Jim replied, "Five percent. Five percent are unknown objects without an earthly explanation."

Host Pat: "That's one of the reasons why we keep inviting you back. I have a guest that I have not met . . . [Long pause, probably because I actually had worked with Pat on the children's TV program, *Wallace & Ladmo Show*, relaying health tips for kids in the early 1980s, and Jim must have been making motions in the background] . . . I shouldn't say that, because I may have."

Pat addressed me then. "I don't know who this is other than the fact that Jim Dilettoso said that he would confidentially call you as long as I refer to you only as 'Dr. X,' which sounds like an incredibly melodramatic way to get somebody on the phone. But I understand you are a doctor, a physician locally. Tell me why Jim Dilettoso would suggest that I call you in the middle of the day during a show that we're doing on UFOs?"

I answered, "Fortunately or unfortunately, I have an abundance of evidence of strange lights on video and 35-mm taken over a period of time."

Host Pat: "Can you describe it to us please?"

"We live mountainside in the Valley and we have a panoramic view of the city. We've been living here for quite a few years and we know what planes look like, what helicopters look like, what other lights look like out there. Suddenly these large amber lights appear from nowhere, as we're staring out into the sky.

There are no planes, helicopters, nothing around them. They hover, most times one or two, sometimes more, for many minutes. They look like they're on the horizon, like they could be right above the mountain or right under the mountain ridge."

Host Pat: "And the most recent sighting?"

"March 13. They have not appeared since then."

Jim interjected, "And you also discussed with me that in addition to being on the horizon, there was one occasion where the lights came so extremely close that they seemed to be very near the house."

I replied, "Well, actually our first sighting was two years ago. I won't get into it too much, but it was literally outside of our window."

Pat asked, "Why are you being so cryptic, so guarded?"

I admitted, "Well, I'm hesitant because of the subject matter and because I'd like to remain anonymous."

He quipped, "And you don't want many talk show hosts calling you?"

"Not too many," I jested. "I'm really trying to stay away from that. But it is a big question in my mind, what to do with this information. I am an educator and feel obliged to share it with the public if it is something other than what we can explain."

"Well, I'm glad that you shared it with us. I appreciate your time, Dr. X."

Witness Mike Fortson then imparted his experience. "There were three huge, big, bright lights. If you would take your hand and make a peace sign, 1960s peace sign, then bring it horizontal, that's the craft I saw. No matter what they say about this—and you wouldn't believe some of the people I've been up against on some of these shows, but I tell people what I saw—this was the greatest visual thing ever. This was the genuine mega-Kodak moment."

Jim added, "You would expect that I would listen to every word they would have to say, that I would investigate all the evidence that there is available, and then separate the wheat from the chaff for you. Because if we don't do that, who will?"

After the radio program, I continued my thorough "military" inquiry. My next call was to Captain Eileen Bienz, State Public Affairs Officer for the Arizona Army and Air National Guard. She once again refuted the *Mesa Tribune* article and verified "Martin's" inappropriate insistence that the lights were flares. I requested she send me a fax explaining the error in the *Mesa Tribune* and confirming her stance. I received her explicit communication on July 2, addressed to Dr. Lynne. She reiterated that I had asked her to send me information "in writing" as it related to the Arizona National Guard regarding the lights of unknown origin that many people saw on the night of March 13, 1997.

As she had told me on the phone, her involvement started because one of their Apache helicopter pilots called a local TV station and told them he was flying that night and that he thought it was a combination of training flares at the Gila Bend range and a formation of military aircraft flying in a wedge formation. They (the Apache helicopter pilots) were flying using their FLIR (forward looking infrared) system, which picked up the "heat," and they made the assumption that it was due to flares and aircraft. They were flying down in the Picacho Peak area at the time.

Captain Bienz confirmed in writing that the TV station started reporting this as: "An Arizona Army Guard spokesperson said . . ." She called the station and asked them for the name of their source and they finally gave it to her. She also asked them to restate what they had been running as: "One of our pilots said he thought he saw . . ." The Associated Press picked up the statement and ran it the next day. She pointed out that she never sent out an official statement to the press on this issue—she simply responded to queries.

She ended the fax by expressing the hope that the written communication would assist me in my efforts and kindly added not to hesitate to contact her if she could be of further assistance.

Even with this official military confirmation, our mischievous "Martin" was still forcing the flare issue, sending derogatory written communications to all the local TV and radio stations, in which he criticized Jim Dilettoso's analysis. His letters were belligerent and defamatory. He even called in to Art Bell's national radio show, *Dreamland*, dismissing all the hard-core evidence and the serious investigation, harassing Jim publicly, and almost divulging my identity.

When I discussed the situation with Jim and Michael, they recommended that I contact one of the leading UFO investigators in the U.S. (who wished to remain unnamed for this book) to get a better perspective from a true insider. It was time to share my story with a key player in the Ufology realm. He was thrilled that I called. Once I got started, we ended up speaking on the phone for an hour and a half, talking on and on about the event. And then he switched to the topic of the Mutual UFO Network. Out of nowhere, he volunteered his distrust for MUFON. Even though I can attest for many MUFON investigators being diligent and sincere, according to this respected expert, some were apparently not as responsible. This is an organization that is supposed to support the UFO effort and investigate the facts, without bias. But from what he stated, "They had lost credible witness accounts and refuted data that they had previously confirmed, and there was infighting in the ranks."

I certainly didn't want to be involved with any of that. It all seemed so unprofessional. However, this information prompted some interesting speculations as to why "Martin" was so insistent on pushing the flare story. Whether his motivation was personal or otherwise, perhaps his aim was to confuse the public, or even worse, to discredit the witnesses and investigators.

Due to these questionable personalities popping up on the scene and growing animosities between factions of UFO believers and nonbelievers, I was happy to keep my identity concealed. The only thing that was important to me was to continue the investigation and to uncover the truth about the mysterious phenomena, quietly and meticulously.

Even though Jim Dilettoso referred to the undisclosed key witness as Dr. X, I presented myself to the visiting media at Village Labs as Dr. Lynne, of Health Education Learning Programs, representing the anonymous couple who filmed the video of the V formation of three lights over the city on March 13. It worked like a charm. No one ever questioned my cover. And what was more amazing and wonderful, those friends who did know I was the witness—and there were many who did—kept it confidential. I will forever appreciate their kindness.

Now back to the investigation. I had already spoken to the Arizona National Guard, the Marine Corps, and the Davis-Monthan and Luke air force bases— without getting any answers. If they did know something, anything, they certainly weren't sharing it with me. I was happy to learn, however, that Davis-Monthan AFB was going to be deploying flares in the coming week. That would give me the opportunity to check out the skies and compare sightings.

As clear as the evenings were each night, we saw nothing. No amber orbs, no amber light formations, no amber arrays. For the record, I watched the skyline for two weeks, my video camera on ready, waiting for the flares as the lieutenant had promised. But they never appeared. Even if the air force was flying at different altitudes, we probably would have caught at least one flare being dropped over a two-week period. Logically, from all indications, our experiences in February 1995 and January through March 1997 seemed to be of something other than flares.

The week of July 4, 1997, we, the inhabitants of Earth, landed a successful probe on Mars. What timing. Think about the irony. While some people scoffed at the possibility of beings of greater intelligence coming to visit us on our faraway planet, we had actually reached another planet ourselves. From the photos relayed back to Earth, NASA scientists were indicating remnants of past floods on the planet's surface and postulating that there could have been life on Mars— and still might be.

While reflecting on the possibilities, I came across an intriguing article in the Sunday, July 13, 1997, *Arizona Republic,* written by Thomas Ropp. I had just seen the movie *Contact* and was ruminating about how art sometimes imitates life, or is it the other way around? Ropp addressed Hollywood's treatment of UFOs, specifically the point of view presented in Carl Sagan's book *Contact* (on which the movie was based). While Sagan debunked UFOs as such, believing instead that contact with extraterrestrials might occur through radio transmissions, Ropp cited the scholarly works of professors J. Allen Hynek and Stanton Friedman. Hynek coined the term "close encounters" in his 1972 book *The UFO Experience: Scientific Inquiry.* Friedman, an esteemed nuclear physicist and former classmate of Sagan's at the University of Chicago, presented the "ubiquitous home video camera" as a legitimate tool for UFO investigation.

Ropp concluded his article by stating, "Like love and God, it's quite possible that UFOs can't be defined empirically. There is one particularly ironic twist in *Contact*, when [actress Jodie] Foster, [who plays] the scientist, can't explain the most significant event in her life with science. At that moment she discovers a new science—faith." (See appendix A.)

My own faith in our trusted military was again challenged. On Thursday, July 17, 1997, a disappointing front page article by Chris Fiscus appeared in the "Valley & State" section of the *Arizona Republic*, entitled, "Air Force Won't Probe UFOs."

It seemed that the Arizona UFO probe was going to be grounded for good. The air force told Councilwoman Barwood that they were sorry they couldn't help. She replied, "It's like a hot potato; no one wants to touch this. Do we have a bunch of wimps that are afraid to look into this?" It was baffling to her that there wasn't the normal human reaction of curiosity or, at the very least, concern for public safety.

Air Force Lieutenant Colonel Patricia Fornes explained that in the foreseeable future the air force was not likely to get involved because of steadily declining budgets. She added that no UFO reported, investigated, or evaluated by the air force was ever an indication of threat to our national security.

The article cited Barwood as wondering whether the military thought that if they ignored it, it would all go away. "Or was it that they knew what it was and didn't want to say?" she remarked.

I immediately got on the phone. I had to meet personally with a U.S. senator, either Jon Kyl or John McCain from Arizona. After viewing my own confidential evidence, I hoped they would push for a much-needed inquiry.

The first person I contacted was the past president of the Arizona State Senate, Senator Bob Usdane. This well-respected man had worked on several state medical boards with my husband, but didn't know much about my background. We met for several hours, discussing my professional endeavors and the curious events surrounding the Phoenix Lights. After my presentation, he made a statement that touched me deeply.

"You know, Lynne, if this had happened to just about anyone else, it would have probably been wasted."

I hoped he was right. I also hoped he would be able to connect me with one of the top elected state officials.

But after weeks of trying, no one in government responded. I surmised that for someone who depended on their constituents for votes, the topic was too controversial, particularly for McCain, who at that time was eyeing the presidency. Councilwoman Barwood remained the only ally to the cause.

It was Thursday afternoon, July 24, more than four months since the mass sighting and nearly five weeks after the *USA Today* article ignited a tremendous international media blitz. Representatives from U.S. and foreign media had converged on Arizona, hounding the military and government for an investigation and explanation, yet it was still quiet on the southwestern front.

I was discussing the lack of response with *Extra* reporter Cindy Huback when my call waiting interrupted our conversation. I told her I'd call her back.

It was the public affairs officer for the Air National Guard. "Hello, Doctor. I wanted you to know that I just finished a call with a reporter from the *Arizona Republic*. We finally figured out what the lights were over Phoenix back in March. Nobody thought to look at the log of visiting Snowbirds. We just realized today that the Maryland Air National Guard was in town the first two weeks of March and ran an exercise called Operation Snowbird along the Barry Goldwater Gunnery Range on March 13. They flew eight A10s and dropped a bunch of high-intensity illumination flares on their way back to Tucson. The lights that people saw could have been those flares."

I was flabbergasted. When I told her about the same formation in the same location that I had caught on film two months before the Maryland Air National Guard (MANG) even got to town, she exclaimed, "You never told me that!" and quickly excused herself for an incoming call.

Disheartened and confused, I hung up the phone, after thanking her for letting me know. Sure, the MANG may have been in town, and they might have sent off flares, but their flares weren't the things we saw or photographed. As I had learned repeatedly from my conversations with the military, flares are not amber but white, they don't hover or stay in an equidistant line, and they certainly don't travel across an entire state. After all the pressure for an answer, was this new "official" explanation a flagrant excuse for something they couldn't ignore any longer?

My growing suspicions were further validated when I called my sister-in-law in Delaware an hour later to wish her a happy birthday. The first thing out

of her mouth was that the TV newscasts were all promoting the MANG statement as fully explaining the UFO sighting in Arizona on March 13. How
strange. They got the news back East before we did. The wire service carries news
items across the country quickly and the media is always looking for something
to fill up their newscasts, but it seemed unusual for this questionable explanation to gain such momentum so fast.

It was close to 6 P.M. and I didn't have time to dwell on the surprising development. I was running late for my first in-depth meeting with video witnesses
Bill Hamilton and Tom King. By the time I got to Bill's home, they had already
received a call from the captain and were dwelling on it themselves. Actually,
they were furious at what they felt was an obvious cover-up by the military and
the dissemination of confusing information to the public, information that
would most assuredly cloud the issue.

Once they calmed down, I seized the opportunity to clear up some questions I had. Bill has an extensive background in chemistry and physics, as well as
Ufology, so I asked him for his educated take on where he thought these things
come from.

"First, I believe that some of these objects are extraterrestrial vehicles. In
other words, they are interplanetary spacecraft. Second, I think some of these
objects are what might be called extradimensional. They're coming from some
extra dimension of space and time. Third, maybe some of the vehicles that some
people are spotting, at least these days, could come from the Earth. In other
words, some advanced technology development that's going on with aerospace
contractors. I do believe that they have been working on this technology from
the 1950s. I think the Roswell incident did involve an extraterrestrial vehicle that
crashed. Yes, I do."

"You're saying that we obtained advanced technology from that?"

"From that and other incidents, not just Roswell. There have been other
crash retrievals. Not as well investigated as Roswell."

I asked again, "And as far as the March 13 incident—what is your conclusion?"

"My conclusion right now is that the objects seen on March 13 were unconventional, they're unidentified, and they're from an unknown origin. I do not
believe that they are our own advanced technology aircraft of any kind, even
allowing for field propulsion."

I interjected, "The pictures I took of both the January 23 and March 13
events seem to be appearing over the same location, between the South
Mountain and the Estrella Mountain ranges."

He agreed, "That's right. There's like a window, a gateway between dimensions, between one frequency reality and another. It seems that somebody has

learned how to cross a bridge from that one to this one and when they come into this one, they have density and materiality and energy."

An interesting hypothesis, one that seemed to be substantiated by my photos and footage. They in turn shared a video of amber balls of lights videotaped by a Rainbow Valley couple during the day, one month after the mass sighting. The footage confirmed once again that the lights couldn't have been flares.

Bill and Tom urged me to remain anonymous, elaborating on their own disconcerting experiences since going public, including ridicule, misquotes, televised statements taken out of context, and their copyrighted footage shown without permission.

On the ride home, I ruminated about how people connected with the sighting fared after going public. For the time being, I was content to stay behind the scenes. Until I was convinced that what was going on was real but unexplained, I didn't want anything—media, skeptics, or public opinion—to influence or disrupt my primary objective: to seek out the truth behind what I saw.

I tried to sort out the day's events, visualizing what the front page of the *Arizona Republic* was going to look like the next morning. I wasn't too far off for July 25, 1997: "Air Guard: Valley's UFOs Were Our Flares. Air Guard Unit Dropped Flares on Night Valley Saw the Light."

Reporter Richard Ruelas reiterated that on March 13, Valley residents reported seeing a V formation of lights, that the military bases continually affirmed that they had nothing in the air that night, that attention and speculation on the Phoenix Lights mass sighting developed in the following months, and then how, on Thursday, it was learned that on March 13 a visiting Maryland National Guard was dropping flares.

Ruelas explained that Captain Eileen Bienz purportedly started a one-woman investigation into the mysterious luminaries. Military officials said that on that legendary night they flew eight A10s along the Barry Goldwater Gunnery Range, southwest of Phoenix, and dropped many high-intensity flares on their way back to Tucson. Ruelas elaborated:

> What Bienz found out about was Operation Snowbird, which brings in aircraft from bases in the northern United States from November to April, hence the name. A flight schedule from Davis-Monthan AFB shows that a squadron of planes from Operation Snowbird left at 8:15 p.m. on March 13 and returned at 10:30 p.m. A spokesperson for Luke Air Force Base confirmed that the Maryland planes were authorized to use the Goldwater range from 9:30 to 10 p.m. on March 13.

If the reporter had delved further, he would have discovered that Operation Snowbird is one of the code names for a diversionary, covert operations tactical maneuver, specifically used by the military during UFO sightings. In addition, Luke AFB, who owns the range, had already confirmed that there was no one using it that night. When we followed up after this news release, the Maryland Snowbird unit's public information officer at Davis-Monthan AFB, Lieutenant Keith Shepherd, stated that an eight-plane squadron of A10 fighter bombers from the 175th Fighter Wing, based in Baltimore, Maryland, returned from the Phoenix area to Davis-Monthan at approximately 8:30 P.M. on March 13—not at 10:30 P.M. So where did the reporter come up with that time?

To her credit, Captain Bienz stated in the article that the Snowbird maneuvers didn't explain everything spotted that night, and that the planes did not match up with reports of lights coming in from the north, passing over Phoenix, and showing up again near Kingman. But even though Lieutenant Shepherd reported to us otherwise, Captain Bienz indicated in the article that Operation Snowbird might account for the lights seen in the west about 10 P.M., the sighting that produced most of the footage seen around the country.

The article quoted a Captain Drew Sullins, the Maryland Air National Guard spokesman. He stated that after their mandatory military exercises the A10s still had a number of flares left to eject. According to Sullins, Davis-Monthan doesn't let planes land with flares on board. He added that he didn't know the logic of that rule, but imagined that it was a safety issue. Strange that they were suddenly worried about safety. He said that as the Snowbird unit was leaving the range, the planes jettisoned their flares at 6,000 feet.

The article mentioned that Jim Dilettoso was at a loss for words when told of the news. Jim confirmed for the reporter that the optical analysis of photos and videotapes showed that the lights couldn't be flares and that a computer simulation matching witness accounts placed the lights nowhere near the gunnery range. He was keeping an open mind that they could be flares, but there was no evidence of that being the case. Ruelas added that the Maryland Air National Guard was also keeping an open mind. Its spokesman, Sullins, said they had aircraft in that area doing night illuminations; they were there, they could prove it, and whether people wanted to believe that it was the mysterious lights or not was up to them.

For those of us who had experienced these phenomena, the military's new explanation didn't seem credible. Is it plausible that while the military was being inundated by inquiries for more than four months from witnesses, media, investigators, and Councilwoman Barwood, neither Captain Beinz nor anyone else involved with the gunnery range ever took a look at the log before July 24? To us, it was an obvious ploy, and a smart one at that, designed to get the attention away from the real phenomena.

Luckily, most of the local TV news stations that had been covering the story were on top of it and questioned the validity of this new explanation. To make the point, the local ABC affiliate, KNXV, introduced the fourth couple who had videotaped the mysterious lights of March 13, Chuck and Karla Rairden.

The news reporter questioned the dubious announcement. "The Air National Guard out of Maryland is saying that this is only a possibility, perhaps a possibility of what some of those lights that people saw were."

Chuck Rairden said, "The video doesn't do it justice . . ."

Then curious footage emerged on KTVK NewsChannel 3:

Anchor: "This new video was taken from the far west valley. It shows the same group of (unknown) lights. But then the photographer looked farther south towards the gunnery range and got this, a more elongated shaped light, what Dilettoso says are the real flares."

Jim Dilettoso: "It accounts for the National Guard flares being dumped and at the same time two lights that match the characteristics of the unknowns that were shot elsewhere in the Valley."

It was comforting to know that at least the people of Arizona were being informed of the developing details. But what about the rest of the nation? My thoughts were answered. *Extra* came through again.

Their host stated that the March 13 Phoenix event was by then being called one of the most significant UFO sightings in years and that demands for an explanation had become so great that national news programs picked up on the story. Video snippets followed, including one of Tom Brokaw declaring, "Weird happenings in the skies over Phoenix." The *Extra* host then announced that, after five months of no comments and unanswered questions, the government was now saying that it might have solved the mystery.

Spokesman for the Maryland Air National Guard, Lieutenant Colonel David Tanaka stated: "Those flares that were seen could have been our flares."

The host quipped that the story was over—mystery solved. Or was it?

Dilletoso, on the other hand, stated in the *Extra* program that there was just one problem with the military's new explanation about flares. It ignored the scientific facts! And witnesses attested that the geography was all wrong. They saw the lights directly over downtown Phoenix. Then there was the question of how the lights appeared to defy gravity, just hanging there in midair. Veteran munitions and flare expert Chuck Byers showed pictures of known flares falling to the ground, and as the viewer could clearly see, they did not stay in a straight, steady line. The show ended with the host stating, "I don't know about this one."

Was the military deploying flares as a last-ditch effort to distract curious eyes away from the real UFO and disorient the public? Was our National Guard aware of what was going on statewide? Sources reported that they were, and for days before the mass sighting. Then on March 13, after hundreds of alarmed witnesses started calling Luke AFB, police stations, and the news media, they sprang into action. Feasible, but that still doesn't answer why they waited so long to announce it. Or how the perfectly spaced light arrays that we saw and photographed could have possibly been flares that the military admits descend haphazardly to the ground. Tom King's videotape clearly shows that the arrowhead light formation seems to be attached to "something." If anything speaks to the reality of the unexplained phenomena, the documented footage does.

We surmised that, after nearly five months, the National Guard looked at what had surfaced as credible evidence. Since the giant triangle craft was too dark to photograph in the night sky, as many witnesses statewide had reported, there were no 35-mm photos and only one fuzzy video of the earlier event. So the military didn't have to worry about explaining that phenomenon.

What they could debunk was hearsay and a handful of videos showing lights in different equidistant arrays photographed around 10 P.M. As Chuck Rairden indicated, the footage doesn't do the lights justice. The unknowns appear smaller, whiter, and flicker in every video—similar to what flares look like. Since they needed a scapegoat for this documented event, one that was videotaped by several witnesses gazing southward at about 10 P.M., the military could make a case for the similar-looking flares being sent off near Tucson. The witnesses, however, were adamant that the strange lights were over Phoenix, close to South Mountain and the Estrellas, and were definitely not flares.

Let us not forget about the traveling orb parade throughout Arizona for the preceding two hours. It certainly seemed that whoever did this had the perfect scenario in place. Thousands of people living along the most populated corridor in Arizona had their watchful eyes fixed skyward, looking purposely at the clear heavens for a glimpse of the Hale-Bopp comet. Were *the lights* trying to get our attention? If so, *they* succeeded.

The investigators and key witnesses felt that the military was probably hoping that now that they had made their official announcement, the inquiries would fade away. They didn't. Quite the contrary. We were actually becoming more convinced that the massive low-flying craft and amber orbs were not our own.

After enduring five months of put-offs and now a dubious explanation, the next step for me was to verify scientifically the position of the lights in the videos taken around 10 P.M. through someone outside the Ufology realm. I contacted an Arizona State University geological surveyor who graciously agreed to triangulate the videos to confirm where the light arrays might have been positioned. When Fred (a pseudonym) had visited our respective homes, however, he realized it would be impossible to do. Since each of us had taken video at a different time, over a 20-minute period, there was no way anyone could triangulate the exact position of the arrays around 10 P.M.—not the military, not MUFON, not even Jim Dilettoso.

The plot thickened, and the publicity continued, far and wide. The story of the Phoenix Lights was fast becoming a special event in the annals of Ufology. Michael Tanner handed me a featured article, entitled "Arizona Lights. Massive UFO Hangs Low Over Phoenix, Arizona," from the North American edition of *UFO Reality,* with comments by Jilaen Sherwood. It seemed that people outside our state had done their own investigative work and were much more candid about the obvious inconsistencies of the Phoenix Lights story than our local papers were.

The article said that even though some witnesses were from military backgrounds and others were pilots, no one could identify the flying object. Some witnesses who saw the object in Casa Grande said that it was large enough to land airplanes on. The reporter asserted, "In other states people are seeing lights like this and there always seems to be some kind of cover-up story involving flares. More debunking perhaps."

According to the article, John Greenwald, a noted researcher of government UFO documents, submitted a request for FOIA (Freedom of Information Act) documents to be released from Luke Air Force Base. Luke replied immediately, but said they had no response to the lights over Phoenix. In addition, they stated that they don't fly their aircraft at night. The reporter said it is obvious that they do fly their aircraft at night as was admitted by Lieutenant Colonel Hauser from Luke AFB, who said that the F16s were on a "training mission" on the night of the sighting. She added, "They obviously lied in the Freedom of Information Act report."

A crew for an hour-long TV special, devoted to our statewide event, was coming into town on July 28, 1997, to begin shooting. They were calling it "UFOs Over Phoenix: An Anatomy of a Sighting," to air on the Discovery Channel in November. It got me thinking. With all the conflicting explanations being tossed about by the military and the media, perhaps it was time to do an anonymous interview to set the record straight. At the very least, the public should become aware that there was more to the story than just the March 13 events. Sharing my confidential photographs and account would help the viewers make up their own minds.

I met with the producer and voiced my desire for anonymity. I also stressed that it seemed important to relay what I had filmed before the Phoenix Lights mass sighting and what I had discovered since. With apprehension, I agreed to a "shadowed" interview, but only if I didn't have to focus on the March 13 event. The producer consented, adding that the military stated officially that the lights were flares anyway. He remained convinced of this, even after I showed him my dramatic pictures of the same equidistant V formation in the same location almost two months prior to March 13.

When I mentioned this to Jim and Michael, they pooh-poohed it, assuring me that the film company was producing an unbiased anatomy of a sighting, not an investigation into the Phoenix Lights. I didn't feel comfortable. Something wasn't right. But I had already committed and they were putting the finishing touches on the set for my interview.

After they took a half-hour adjusting the backlighting so that my identity was obscured, the director bombarded me with questions concerning the March 13 event. He was unrelenting. I didn't want to be rude, but he wasn't getting it. As diplomatically as I could, I insisted that the reason I was doing the interview was to inform the public that the mass sighting wasn't the whole story and that similar events were occurring worldwide. He kept pressing me about the March 13 event.

After the interview, I wondered what they would edit from my statements. What if the producer had a particular slant in mind? He had promised that the program was not focusing on the March 13 event. But after my interview, I wasn't so sure. I was also taken aback by the producer's conviction that the sightings were just flares, ignoring my evidence. The tense interview itself left me with an uneasy feeling.

On the other hand, that very evening one of the most candid TV programs revealing the existence of global UFO phenomena aired nationally on FOX. "UFOs: The Best Evidence Ever (Caught on Tape)" displayed a montage of unexplained objects and lights documented in many different countries, including ours.

As they showed my video, the voice of *Star Trek*'s Jonathan Frakes narrated, "What you are seeing may be the most credible UFO footage shot . . . Phoenix, Arizona, 1997. It began March 13 . . ." They shared Tom King's astounding recording as he related, "If you look at it, you know that is not an aircraft. We were perplexed the whole time trying to figure out, what is this thing?" Host Frakes continued, "As the tape rolled, five lights blinked on in sequence, offering an outline of a flying object as it hovered near the mountains."

Sue Krzyston elaborated on the individual orbs, "They were large, larger than any light in the city." Mike Krzyston urged, "Take a look at the footage. I'm not telling you what they are. If they're an alien spacecraft, there's something out there that they can't defend us against."

Frakes continued, "Amazingly, a third video [mine] was shot simultaneously, showing the lights going out in order. National newspapers *[USA Today]* soon carried front-page stories of the enormous V-shaped object seen over Phoenix. But the local military bases did nothing to calm the fears of the 10,000 residents who were startled by what they saw. Phoenix Councilwoman Frances Barwood has called for an investigation into the strange incident."

Barwood admitted openly for the first time, "There are people who were active [in the] military [who] were afraid to say publicly what they saw because they were told it would be the end of their career." Investigative journalist George Knapp argued that the military was lying, that they have had an interest since the very beginning of the UFO era. He expressed the opinion that there are people who operate for our government or their emissaries to scare people who get too close to the truth.

After treating the audience to impressive UFO footage, taken at home, abroad, and in outer space by NASA's own cameras, Frakes clarified that even presidents are interested in UFOs. "Before he was president, Jimmy Carter saw a UFO and reported it to authorities. Subsequent presidents have also expressed their concern about visitors from outer space." They showed President Ronald Reagan at an international meeting stating, "I occasionally think how quickly our differences worldwide would vanish if we were facing an alien threat from outside this world."

Then astronaut Stori Musgrave strongly insisted, "I think the public is ready to accept any information. I think the public is ready to know if anyone has visited us. They can accept that and they want it."

Acclaimed Mexican investigator Jaime Mauson made a stunning statement of encouragement. "We the people are going to prove that this is truth—not the scientists, not the authorities, not the military. We—hundreds, thousands with cameras in our hands—are going to be able to produce the evidence that is going to be seen around the world, and are going to prove that this is real."

That Friday night, August 1, 1997, a KSAZ-FOX TV news report surfaced revealing the April 12 daylight sighting that Bill Hamilton had shown me weeks before. Reporter Jim Schnebelt shared his findings and the remarkable footage with the public:

> One light blinks out and another one appears jumping around, while a third object streaks across the top of the screen at a very high rate of speed. Even UFO critics have a hard time explaining this sighting as bombing flares over the Barry Goldwater Range. For one thing, this sighting was made in the daytime when flares aren't used. And

for another thing, this sighting was made in this direction towards the Estrella Mountains.

From where Schnebelt was standing in Rainbow Valley, the Gunnery Range was far to the left. In other words, Rainbow Valley was in between the Estrellas and the Barry Goldwater Range.

The anchor, John Hook, announced one more startling fact, "And this is getting even weirder. Because people near Rainbow Valley also say they frequently report seeing black helicopters in formation and some sort of mysterious law enforcement group wearing black uniforms marked as the *Arizona Police.*"

Days later, a local TV news broadcast announced, "Now a new theory emerges concerning the origins of the mysterious lights over Phoenix, that supposedly our own government has knowledge of mysterious balls of light visiting us from other galaxies. Jim Dilettoso claims he was paid a visit by the 'real men in black,' men affiliated with the jet propulsion laboratory and NASA."

The reporter said NASA might be interested in UFOs because of recent UFO sightings from the space shuttle. The broadcast showed a video of three spheres lining up in a triangle formation over the Earth taken from STS 80, a shuttle flight the previous December. "Other shuttle missions have made similar sightings. Could these be similar to the balls of light seen over Phoenix?" The station ran my footage of the three spheres in a triangular array.

Dilettoso said, "It's very interesting that NASA personnel have the courage to circulate documents like this."

The reporter told us that Jim was allegedly given two technical documents on hyperdimensional travel written by one of NASA's top scientists. The paper describes how in quantum theory it would be possible to generate balls of light in a distant galaxy and send them hurling towards Earth faster than the speed of light, using tiny black holes and the forces of gravity.

The reporter commented, "It's the stuff Einstein theorized about."

After the piece aired, Jim shared with me that he was impressed that impartial scholars, including NASA's Breakthrough Propulsion Consultant Dr. Hal Putoff, not only acknowledged the incident, they were theorizing an explanation for it. Also exciting was that after Dilettoso reviewed the detailed memoranda, he believed the photos I took might prove that there was a gateway between South Mountain and the Estrellas. That would put it over the Gila Bend Indian Reservation, sacred ground and the area where numerous witnesses had reported viewing the unexplained orb phenomena over their heads for many years. Like Bill Hamilton, Dilettoso felt strongly that the objects were coming in and out of another dimension or space-time continuum. This hypothesis seemed to explain why the same amber light formations might have appeared at the same location two months apart.

Fall was upon us and the November airdate for the Discovery Channel special was fast approaching. We were all hoping that this important venue would lead to an open and thorough recap of the facts. As it turned out, "Anatomy of a Sighting" was professional and well produced. The hour-long look at the Phoenix Lights reiterated the multiple witness testimonials, and rehashed the response by the media, air traffic controllers, military, government, and UFO investigators. It also shed some light on how the "flare" explanation was likely "launched."

The Discovery program stated that on June 25, 1997, one week after the major national media blitz initiated by the full-page *USA Today* article, a convincing explanation for at least one of the events emerged from the local NBC TV station affiliate. They showed that one of their cameramen had recorded illumination flares being deployed at the Barry Goldwater Range. The KPNX News reporter (who happened to be the same NBC reporter who had ignored my firsthand account and photographic evidence the morning after the mass sighting) stated emphatically for the TV audience, "When we saw those lights pop on in the sky, to us they looked exactly the same. The photographer looked at it and said, 'Well, there's your lights.' It looked so similar to us it had to be the explanation—although we didn't know who could have dropped the flares that night."

A female voice-over maintained that air force officials initially denied that any of their aircraft were involved in maneuvers in that area that night. "But oddly, after the KPNX broadcast, they reversed their statement." She then explained the subsequent admission that, on the night in question, the visiting Maryland Air National Guard had conducted night maneuvers, which had involved the use of illumination flares. But despite this "overwhelming evidence," she stated, the many witnesses remained unconvinced that illumination flares were the cause of the 10 P.M. phenomenon.

Witness Bill Hamilton confirmed once again that when he looked through his telescope he could see no suspension apparatus—no parachute or balloon. He emphasized that the unknowns had no vertical descending motion, they did not drift together or apart as flares usually do, and they maintained a fixed relationship between themselves. He noted that he could see that they were round lights of some kind, like orbs, pulsating at a high frequency.

KSAZ-FOX TV news reporter Jim Schnebelt agreed. "While they look similar, they don't look the same as flares. Flares flicker and illuminate what's around them and these lights over Phoenix didn't do that."

The host explained that shortly after the Air National Guard announcement, Jim Dilettoso reanalyzed the videotape. Jim said when he compared the optical characteristics of the unknown objects and those of the flares, they didn't match. "They're so different from each other that it's not even close."

The host said that not everyone agreed with Dilettoso's conclusions or the accuracy of his methods. A MUFON investigator argued that the videotape does not have the resolution you need to perform those types of tests. He stressed that videotape is very limited in use for investigating UFO incidents, that the camera overloads from the brightness of the flares. They'd rather see film, motion picture, or actually 35-mm, which gives a greater dynamic range and much more resolution than videotape.

Well, no one in MUFON had any idea that I did have 35-mm photos of the identical January 1997 unknowns—integral evidence that could be analyzed. Jim had preserved both my identity and this vital proof throughout the entire inquiry, something I am sure wasn't an easy task under the circumstances.

But the host didn't stop there. She stated that, according to the Maryland Air National Guard, the illumination flares were deployed, fell, and disappeared from sight behind the mountain range seen in the video. However, many eyewitnesses claimed that the lights they observed were in front of the range and therefore could not have been the same flares.

In an attempt to settle the crucial debate, the producers of the program allegedly gave the video shot by one of the witnesses to Dr. Leonard Rudin of Cognitec, a California imaging firm.

Dr. Rudin claimed that he superimposed Krzyston's original tape with another video made during the day from *approximately* the same location, with the camera pointing in *approximately* the same direction. Rudin stressed that the intricate process took several hours. Even though this procedure didn't prove what *they* were, his conclusion was that the lights disappeared behind the mountains, supporting the contention that the ten o'clock event was the result of illumination flares being dropped behind the distant ridge.

The host admitted that the controversy surrounding the V formation seen earlier that evening was far from over. In other words, a definitive explanation for the Phoenix Lights had still not been established, though it was apparent that this program pushed the flare theory. They even tried to prove it. More baffling still, the video they used in their comparison did not look like Krzyston's footage.

I wasn't the only one disappointed in the program. Although it didn't blatantly accuse the witnesses of overreacting, it left the TV viewer with tremendous doubt as to the validity of the UFO claims. After the first airing on

November 2, 1997, and even more so after it had aired numerous times through-out the following years, including prime time on Thanksgiving 1999 and Christmas weekend 2000, many people across America bought into the program's ordinary explanation for an extraordinary event. When the national public is told that the lights were probably flares, over and over again, with no rebuttal that questions the validity of that conclusion, more and more get convinced that the Arizona mass sighting was just that—flares.

It was fascinating to me that so many non-witnesses, even in Arizona, just accepted this explanation as an answer to the entire event, disregarding the extensive and credible verbal documentation concerning the massive V-shaped phenomenon. It was as if that remarkable aspect of the sighting wasn't worthy of addressing after an apparently sensible conclusion had been drawn concerning the 10 P.M. videos.

After viewing the program, I was happy that my own shadowed interview had not been included. Besides the push to prove that the flare theory was the answer to the Phoenix Lights, it concerned me that there wasn't a mention of other similar unexplained phenomena occurring worldwide. Wouldn't that be important to acknowledge?

The next day I started my own probing, trying to locate Lieutenant Colonel Tanaka, the spokesperson in the program from the Maryland Air National Guard. But it wasn't an easy task. Tanaka was nowhere to be found. After numerous referrals, I was finally connected to a captain, the head of public relations for the Maryland Air National Guard—in Maryland—and the apparent PR person for the Phoenix Lights event.

Our conversation was riveting, at least for me. Both the captain and another officer, a Major "M," stated that the Maryland Air National Guard Snowbirds had been in town for only two weeks, March 1 through 15. They were flying A10s at about 15,000 feet, not 6,000 feet as had been reported. According to the captain, during their last maneuver the night of March 13, eight jets were sending off multiple flares. I wanted to find out exactly what time that took place and where. I also wondered how many flares they supposedly sent out that evening.

The captain stated, "Under each wing there is a pod of eight. So that night in question they could have dropped eight times eight, which equals 64 flares."

To back up my own sightings prior to March 13, I asked, "Do they ever drop just one or two?"

He answered emphatically, "No. They usually drop three to four of them at least because they're trying to string out a distance and illuminate it."

Just to make absolutely certain, I asked, "And what color are they?"

The captain answered without hesitation, "They always look white to me."

I pressed, "And what time did you say they dropped them?"

"I'd have to check," he answered bluntly.

I requested, "Could I speak with Lieutenant Colonel Tanaka? He would probably know."

He replied curtly, "He won't talk to anyone."

I thought that was odd, but persisted. "Is there anyone else who would have exact information?"

The captain answered flatly, "He's the full-time officer. He's the only one."

"So how can I get in touch with him?"

He snapped, "You're talking to the contact. He'd refer you right back to me as the public affairs officer."

So I picked the captain's brain a little more. "Do you know if they dropped flares on the preceding nights? And where? How many each time? What time? Maybe Tanaka would know."

He started to chuckle. "The funniest thing is that Tanaka wasn't even there. He was the spokesman for the wing, because he was the operations officer."

When I finally got back on my chair, I replied, "Thanks for your time. That was all I needed to know."

Fascinating. After trying to get information, any information, from the Arizona Air National Guard, Davis-Monthan AFB, and Luke AFB for two days, the only one who would even talk with me about the details of the March 13 event was in Maryland. On top of that, he and the TV spokesperson, Lieutenant Colonel Tanaka, had not been in Arizona when the mass sighting event took place.

My next call was to the producer of the Discovery Channel special. I wanted to find out what scientific analysis they had done to determine that the lights in the footage were flares. If they had that capability, I wanted them to analyze my pictures for authenticity.

The producer must have thought I was calling about my absence from the aired program because as soon as he picked up the line he stated that the reason he didn't use me in the piece was because "new facts may have confused the public."

I assured him that I was pleased that he hadn't included my interview and asked if he would be kind enough to explain the analysis of the lights by the independent lab in the program that aired. He revealed that they hadn't really analyzed them. The lab did him the favor of lining the video up to a daylight photo to see if the lights went behind the mountain. As he put it, "And they did, so the lights were probably flares from the Barry Goldwater Range."

I was taken aback. That was the extent of their analysis, the expert testimony that had led to a supposed well-informed conclusion? I pushed him further. I wanted to see if he actually had the resources to scientifically analyze the photos. I welcomed a backup to Jim's assessment. He replied that that would happen only if someone funded a follow-up program. Hmm. I began to wonder who had funded this one.

For the military, pressured for an answer, and for the public, understandably wanting a logical explanation for the event, this could fly. But it didn't for the witnesses. And it certainly did not for the investigators at Village Labs, Bill Hamilton, or TV news reporter Jim Schnebelt.

Schnebelt had been following the story since March 13 and happened to be at Village Labs when I dropped by. He had witnessed the mile-long craft that night and was convinced something extraordinary was going on. He was following the story with the mind-set of an investigative journalist. I couldn't resist sharing what I had experienced, divulging the photos I had taken of the 1995 and January 23, 1997, incidents, even though I made it clear that they were not for publication—at least not yet. He understood. Like me, he wanted to get to the bottom of the mystery, a stance common among the witnesses. We had been profoundly touched by something and wanted desperately to find out what that something was.

The more we talked, the more questions we had:

1. If the Maryland Air National Guard was only here in March, who created the same formation in the same location two months earlier?

2. If spokesman Lt. Col. Tanaka wasn't even in Arizona to witness what occurred on March 13, then why was he the spokesman and not someone who was here?

3. What was the silent mile- to two-mile-long formation/craft that traversed the state, and why had this aspect of the sighting essentially been ignored by the military, media, and public?

4. If all military planes were grounded by 8:30 P.M., how do they explain the photographs of lights at 10 P.M.? Flares had never been deployed at that time and altitude before *(or after)*. If the "Snowbirds" did perform diversionary maneuvers, why on that particular night and so late?

5. Why had witnesses felt strongly that the lights were close to Phoenix?

6. Why had all four videos of the spectacular finale around 10 P.M. been filmed on the north side of the Estrella Mountain range, and not one on the south side where the Goldwater Gunnery Range is located?

These blatant inconsistencies were confirmed by a fax I received on November 14, 1997, from investigator Bill Hamilton, now the executive director of Skywatch International. He had broken off from the Arizona MUFON group because of alleged infighting and unprofessional behavior in their ranks. I was thrilled that someone with an extensive background in the sciences and Ufology was investigating independently. He verified many of our conclusions, and more (see appendix A).

Bill also acknowledged that the unexplained phenomena were just that, unexplained, even though certain people were trying to persuade the public otherwise. The witnesses and investigators were searching for anything substantive that could prove the dubious military explanation false.

One local TV news reporter answered our prayers with an enlightening report that aired that Sunday evening, November 9, 1997. He stated that Mike Krzyston believed that the strange lights were not over the bombing range beyond the Estrella Mountains, because he could clearly see the mountain, and the lights were lower than the mountains.

The reporter mentioned a one-hour TV special that aired on November 2, 1997, on the Discovery Channel, in which a California optics lab compared Krzyston's nighttime video to the same scene taken during the daytime and concluded that the lights seemed to disappear over the bombing range—which would support the flare theory.

Krzyston watched the program and questioned its conclusion, believing that the lights were lower than, and in front of, the mountains. So the reporter tested the footage by using daytime and nighttime video, both taken by Krzyston, using the same camera.

A video specialist at the TV station assured us that it was the first time he had seen this and it didn't take long to do at all. (Unlike the hours that Dr. Rudin reported it taking in the program that aired.) He matched the shots up on camera, going from one to the other. "The lights are in front of the mountain," he confirmed.

The reporter asked why there was a discrepancy in the results, and Krzyston answered that Dr. Rudin had changed the position of the lights so that they would coincide with a certain peak. Apparently shocked, the reporter inquired, "He actually altered the footage?"

Krzyston answered, "How else could he do it? This light [to the left of the foreground tree in the Discovery Channel's aired video] was always here [on the right side of the tree in the original footage]."

Within days, the word was out that the courageous reporter was getting some major heat. I wanted to help. My similar photographs from the January sighting, before the Maryland ANG was even in town, might just do the trick. This additional evidence could help challenge the questionable explanation of flares and assist the dedicated reporter in his quest for the truth. That in itself made it important for me to act.

After the professional developer had stated in 1995 that only one photo was printable and that there weren't any other photos of the February sighting among the negatives, I disposed of some, never thinking that there might be images on them that didn't turn out at the time. I put the remaining negatives with dozens of photo packages in our den cabinet. After discovering the four additional photos among the blank negatives, one week after the mass sighting, I became much more cautious. Now that others had seen what I had been documenting, I wanted to make certain that the evidence was in safekeeping. Into the bank vault the negatives went and there they sat, untouched, for over nine months.

Upon retrieving them, I started looking for the negative of the four amber orbs hanging in a row over the city. I couldn't find it. As I searched through the series of January photos, which began with six equidistant amber orbs hovering over the three, I realized the series ended with the V formation of six lights. The next two negatives were of gorgeous Phoenix sunsets, taken days after the sighting. I then remembered that I had stopped snapping pictures and run into the house to call the *Arizona Republic* as the bottom lights began disappearing so they could witness the giant array on top. I had never photographed just four amber orbs during that sighting. Then when had I taken that picture? I had assumed all this time that the particular photo was from January 1997, but looking at the negatives I realized that would have been impossible.

I meticulously inspected the rest of the package, coming upon negative #8, the only photo that had turned out from the 1995 sighting. I began searching through the strips of blank-looking celluloid with a flashlight, just in case there was something I had missed. There, in negative #5, I found what I was looking for. Four lights in a row over the city skyline. But wait, on closer scrutiny there was something else in the foreground—two large orbs. Was this the first picture I had snapped from the close sighting in 1995? Did I have another piece of evidence that would have remained buried had it not been for the Phoenix Lights mass sighting?

I called Jim Dilettoso to give him the news. He asked me to print and enlarge the negatives so he could do a thorough computer analysis of them. While comparing the data, we realized that the row of four lights was in almost the same location as both the January 23 and March 13, 1997, sightings and that two orbs were in the same location above the city in negative #8. We had thought that those lights were just part of the city landscape.

It started to sink in. These photos seemed to substantiate that a similar orb array was disappearing in the distance above the city while Frank and I were focused on the phenomenon closer to us. (Check it out on page 103.) Dilettoso confirmed that the lights in the foreground and on top of the city skyline matched the unique optical characteristics of the unknowns.

Back to the reporter. I felt confident that I had done everything I could to verify that I had documented true UFO appearances two years apart. It was time that the public became aware of it. But when I tried to reach him, I was told that he no longer worked for the station and had moved back to Minnesota with his family. In December, in the dead of winter? When I asked for a forwarding address or telephone number, they had none. I tried for months to contact him, but in vain. I'm still wondering what happened that made him leave Phoenix so abruptly.

9. They're Back

Disappointed at the loss of a true ally, I began looking at the whole picture with a new perspective. The turn of events was unnerving, but I felt it must have been for a good reason. Perhaps it wasn't time to reveal my own evidence just yet. After seeing what was happening to others who went public, I wanted to make certain that when I finally did I was prepared, not only for the skeptics, but with my own thorough knowledge of the subject. It was becoming increasingly evident that I had just touched on the visible tip of the iceberg. There was a great deal more lurking under the surface of this cryptic topic, much more I needed to learn and understand. I also wanted my photographic evidence authenticated by an outside source, someone other than Jim Dilettoso.

After all, I'm a physician who believes in a second opinion, and I was certain my detractors would as well. Jim was the only one analyzing the evidence. That would be the first thing the skeptics and hard line debunkers would focus on. I figured there had to be someone else of repute who could substantiate what I had, so I started making calls.

My first was to the University of Arizona optical sciences department in Tucson. I was thrilled when the head of the department, Dr. Richard Powell, took my call. He is one of the leading authorities on laser technology, having worked on the military's "Star Wars" project. I was told that university-based professors, particularly someone of his stature, wouldn't touch this topic with a ten-foot pole, but Dr. Powell was open and intrigued by the exclusive information I was sharing over the phone. He asked if I would like him to gather a team of specialists in the field to meet with me at the university in Tucson. Their department is one of the finest optical sciences departments in the world, so I was delighted by his generous offer.

Dr. Powell invited four prominent professors from the optical sciences center and computer departments to join us. It was an exciting prospect to share my photographic evidence for the first time with noted scholars. I was looking forward to their expert opinions and technological analysis of my data.

Dr. Powell had touched base with Jim Dilettoso the week before the meeting, at my insistence. As I had anticipated, the first thing the group brought up was Jim's credibility. Dr. Powell stopped the discussion short. He strongly supported Jim's efforts, stating emphatically that he understood the analytical approach Jim had been taking all these months. He assured everyone in attendance, including myself, that Jim was "top notch." He even checked out Jim's past association with University of Arizona faculty members. They all agreed that Jim was a brilliant and trustworthy scientist and scholar. That was the good news.

After my presentation, Dr. Powell stated that they couldn't do anything more than what Jim had already accomplished. He did suggest that in the event that the lights returned, I should procure a special filter lens for more definitive photographic imaging. Unfortunately, even with improved pictorial documentation, they weren't sure they could identify what it was anyway. I was disheartened that our meeting hadn't led to a viable conclusion.

Dr. Powell was more philosophical. "I have a feeling they'll be thinking about this long after you leave."

I could certainly relate to that. But I couldn't understand why these professional academicians had neither the expertise nor the equipment to analyze my photographic evidence. I was thankful for their time, but disappointed that this fruitful source ended up to be barren after all. I did receive a kind follow-up letter dated December 16, 1997.

Dr. Powell thanked me for coming and for sharing my photographs, video, and details of my observations of lights in the night sky over Phoenix. He stated that those at the meeting found my information to be very interesting. "Your research on this subject appears to be very thorough with respect to collection of photographic data and interviews with observers. From what you told me and from my conversation with Jim Dilettoso, it appears that he has done everything possible in performing a computer analysis of the photographic images."

The consensus of his group, however, was that there was not enough conclusive scientific information available to determine the source of the lights that were observed. As far as they were concerned, the origin of the lights that were seen remained an interesting mystery.

He reiterated that if they appeared again, it would be helpful if they could be photographed with a spectral dispersive filter in front of the camera, and photographed from below so that the shape of an object (if any existed) could be clearly seen. He apologized that they could not be more helpful at the present time.

My work was cut out for me. I had to investigate other areas of expertise. It was essential that I have a second opinion, and even a third and a fourth. Dr. Rand Molnar, Dean of Graduate Studies at the Brooks Institute of Photography in Santa Barbara, California, concluded that after extensive optical analysis of my photographic collection, "the lights were self-luminescent and did not cast any light on the surrounding area. The phenomena did not follow the laws of physics that we are familiar with, and are certainly unexplained." After this tape-recorded verification and authentication, I knew it was time to share my story, in confidence, with other accomplished UFO investigators. Their opinions and guidance were now integral to my case.

The more I eventually imparted to these learned professionals, including Dr. Bruce Maccabee, Linda Moulton Howe, Dr. David Jacobs, Dr. Kenneth Ring, astronaut Dr. Edgar Mitchell, Steven Greer, M.D., John Carpenter, Dr. Roger Leir, D.P.M., Dr. John Alexander, and Dr. Richard Haines, the more confident I became that what I had experienced and documented was important—and real. It was reassuring that every UFO investigator I spoke with was supportive and encouraging of my effort. The next meeting was no exception.

World-renowned UFO researchers Brit and Lee Elders were bringing Jaime Mauson, the acclaimed Mexican journalist and respected UFO maven, into Phoenix to meet with Jim Dilettoso. What a stroke of luck for me. I was at the right place at the right time, able to visit with these Ufology icons personally. I proudly showed them my video. Jaime was impressed with my evidence, stating that this was how it had started in Mexico City years ago, assuring me that we were in store for a lot more.

I took the opportunity to ask him, "Jaime, you are entrenched in the UFO realm in Mexico. Please give me some background of the UFO phenomenon from your viewpoint."

"This has been going on for a long time," he said. "Look at the Mayans. The Mayans were so accurate in their knowledge of the eclipse. They knew exactly when an eclipse was going to happen somewhere around the world. They knew that this eclipse that we had in 1991 in Mexico happens every 676 years and that this one was a very important one. They considered the eclipses were the beginning and the end of eras and that this era was going to be very special. It would be the time of the meeting with the Masters of the Stars. There's another prophecy. This is Aztec, probably 500 years old, that says that in this era that started after the eclipse on July 11, 1991, everything buried and hidden would be discovered.

"But the truth is that after this eclipse, probably because we look up to the sky, we discover many strange objects. Not only around Mexico City, but all around our country. My participation was to organize people to record these UFOs.

"The U.S. intelligence [agencies], not the government or the people, declared war on these *beings* back in 1947 because they were flying so close to very sensitive areas. The Los Alamos nuclear plant, for example. And from that moment the whole idea around this incredible phenomenon changed. For many years the U.S. has been trying to decide how dangerous they could be. I think that's what marks the difference of what's happening in the U.S. compared to the rest of the world, which is much more open to UFOs.

"I think the important thing at this moment is that they are sending signals. You remember the movie *Close Encounters of the Third Kind* by Spielberg? They made this connection through music, sound, and color. And when both [aliens and humans] understood what it meant [that] is when we got connected. I think that's the right idea. When they know we understand, when they know we are trying to connect, [that] is when we will really communicate. They won't present themselves until we do communicate. Or until the governments openly accept their presence. At that moment they will come closer and closer."

His reasoning sounded so logical that I asked him what he thought about our own mass sighting.

He stated emphatically, "It's a sign. What you saw here, what you will continue seeing here, are signs. They are trying to attract our attention, slowly. They don't come here accidentally."

I had to share my own impression with this endearing man. "It's funny that you say this. Since the March 13 incident I feel *they,* whoever *they* are, know they got our attention. Now it's up to us to do something about it."

Jamie smiled and nodded his head in agreement.

While I had this international authority within arm's reach, I took the opportunity to ask, "Could you analyze my evidence? Jim has certainly tried to cover all the bases, but I think it's important to get a second opinion, especially from another country."

"Sure. But even though they analyze them [sic] at the University in Mexico, I don't think anyone is going to make a better analysis than Jim Dilettoso. He is from here. He knows the area. He knows the mountains. He knows the directions. He has heard many, many witnesses. He knows exactly what happened. But I will be happy to help."

I thanked him and asked, "In the meantime, what else should I be looking for?"

"When it's cloudy, they come closer. They use clouds a lot. They like to use clouds to hide, especially during the day. We now know . . . through many videos [that] they camouflage themselves."

"And my own pictures from 1995, of the close objects and the same line of lights in the background as this year. Are they proof of real UFOs?"

His eyes widened, "Yes. Pretty heavy. You keep on observing and you're going to see more things. I think the more important things are coming. Of that I am absolutely sure."

Almost one year had passed since the statewide sighting and nothing remotely close to the unusual amber orbs or colossal triangle craft had since appeared in the skies over Phoenix. Even so, because of the March 13 event, my own life had changed dramatically. I had pushed my career aside to pursue the source and meaning of what we had seen and experienced. My own photographic evidence and the vast amount of collaborating documentation from witnesses statewide were overwhelming. My journal was growing each day. If I were actually going to take the next giant step and publish it, I thought it might be a good idea to meet with local authors to get some feedback and advice.

While TV channel-surfing, I happened on an accomplished writer, a stately, charismatic astrology expert named Noel Tyl. He had published 14 books on astrology and was prophesying that by the year 2005 extraterrestrials will have made contact with Earth and our lives will change for the better. I found his words intriguing. It was mentioned that he lived near Phoenix, so I contacted him. I gave him no clue as to my purpose or intent, only that I wanted to arrange a meeting. Before we hung up, he asked for the date, location, and time of my birth.

I have never been interested in this realm of science, being a bit skeptical if anything. Nevertheless, I was curious to learn what this authority on the subject had to say, considering the past year's events and all.

As I entered Tyl's lavish home, I was struck by the man's stature. His full blond mane fell neatly about his face while his giant physique emitted a confident, almost overbearing, aura. In a low, melodious voice, he asked me to sit down on the opposite side of his carved hardwood desk. As my eyes wandered around his cozy office, I noticed his extensive library filled with encyclopedias and books on astronomy, astrology, and paranormal topics. Other than this substantial collection tucked away on shelves, one would never have known this was the home of a metaphysical specialist. I felt comfortable right away.

As he pointed to the papers in front of him, I reminded myself that he had no idea why I had come to see him. He began by translating what appeared to be my astrological chart. What it indicated, according to Tyl, was the characteristics of a natural-born public spokesperson, with a tremendous amount of positive humanistic energy. In his own words, "Your chart shows an overwhelming potential as a human being destined to be some kind of world humanitarian, social leader."

I had been so busy researching since the mass sighting that I never stopped to think about the whole picture, or what my role might ultimately be. I could only stare at him for a moment before replying, "When I share why I came, I think you will understand."

He quickly added, "I appreciate that. I'm extremely taut about perceptions in this matter because my reputation is riding on it. I travel the world doing this. I have to have this clarified. Whatever it is, it strongly relates to *love*. This was all written down before you came in here."

By the time he finished describing my astrological chart and I had imparted my own story and photographic evidence, he was on the phone with his publisher setting up a phone appointment for the next morning. He assured me that what I had in my possession was important and needed to be disseminated.

That weekend had been eerily foggy, a rare occurrence in Phoenix. You could not see one light beyond our own street. I even joked with Frank that *they* could be right there watching us and we wouldn't know it. By Monday evening, January 12, 1998, a thick haze blanketed the city skyline. Frank arrived home from his busy day and joined me on the upstairs balcony for our evening chat. I was glowing, bursting to tell him what had happened that day. The breeze was pleasantly cool as we gazed at the muted backdrop of faint city lights.

"Frank, all of this is just incredible. It seems that since I stepped out here three weeks after the mass sighting and decided to go along with the flow and trust in the guidance, everything has just been falling into place. It's as if this were all planned, as if destiny were playing out its beautiful melody . . ." I didn't get to finish my sentence.

Staring at us in the distance, at the same location, were two huge golden lights, one on top of the other. They were amber, motionless, and in a formation. We looked at each other, as Frank whispered, "Are they back?"

I quickly ran inside, grabbed the video camera that had been lying in a corner of the bedroom for nearly a year, and plugged it in. Stepping out onto the veranda, I focused the lens to capture the sight.

Was it them? The thick mist muted their brilliance, so to be on the safe side I decided not to get everyone excited, just yet.

The next morning I felt wired and impatient at the same time, as if I should be doing something. I just wasn't sure what. I picked up the *Arizona Republic* and my eyes settled on the headline: "Barwood Pushes UFOs in Bid for State Office."

The accompanying article by Chris Fiscus explained that Barwood was announcing her run for Arizona secretary of state based in part on a pledge to get answers to "such seemingly paranormal events" as the Phoenix Lights. The article quoted a written statement from her:

> This is a public safety issue of state and national significance which should not, in good conscience, be ignored by a responsible candidate for high office. We need to get back to what's really important, like our constitutional rights and our state rights. We have to have someone who's willing to stick her neck out to protect our freedoms.

This new turn of events gave me an idea. After the mass sighting, it was very difficult to get any answers from the military. Either they weren't saying anything, were denying everything, or were more curious about what had been documented than interested in providing answers for what it was. With the Arizona National Guard announcing, almost five months after the fact, that the lights were flares, I figured this time I'd check it out before anything else happened.

After an hour on the phone, trying to get information concerning military maneuvers being performed over Arizona, I realized I was getting nowhere fast. Everyone I contacted from Luke Air Force Base in Phoenix to the Davis-Monthan base in Tucson was evasive about giving out any information, repeatedly asking me my name and why I wanted to know. I couldn't even get through to Captain Eileen Beinz at the Arizona Air National Guard. After numerous referrals, the only bit of information I finally did get was that the Battle Creek, Michigan, Air National Guard was at Davis-Monthan for a couple of weeks.

It was interesting that in the Tuesday morning paper they acknowledged that the heavy fog had created havoc at the airport. The headline read, "Going Nowhere," with the subhead "Throwing about 120 flights off schedule" under a large photo of grounded Southwest Airlines commercial planes.

After reading this front-page appraisal, I was curious how the military would explain the Monday evening sighting. Had they been on maneuvers in the dense fog? And if they were, could we have possibly seen their flares being deployed near Tucson, about 90 miles from us, through a thick haze? I'm no meteorologist, but I doubted that was possible. On the other hand, could what Jaime Mauson said about UFOs hiding in clouds be true? As the article remarked, "heavy fog is indeed a rarity in Phoenix."

It was late morning and my patience was wearing thin waiting for the military to return my calls. I felt compelled to do something and remembered that Dr. Powell had recommended a special dispersive filter lens to capture a better-quality photo should the lights return. Since I had given back Richard's high-end equipment months before, I knew I would have to do some serious shopping for the right accouterments if I was going to be prepared for that evening. So I set out to get them.

After searching for most of the afternoon, I ended up purchasing a top-of-the-line Pentax camera, a giant telephoto lens, and a dispersive star filter. I was ready to go—that is, if the lights came back. I had a strong feeling they would.

Right on schedule, they did, even though it was still foggy, at about 9:40 P.M. Frank and I started capturing three separate sightings on video and 35-mm film. By the third sighting, we were convinced they were the same lights as in January and March.

With the new roll of photographs proving there were three similar sightings from the night before, I felt obliged to find out what was going on with the military that week.

At 9:30 A.M. Wednesday morning, I reached a lieutenant colonel, head of the Battle Creek, Michigan, Air National Guard unit that was down at Davis-Monthan, a two-hour drive south of Phoenix. When he first got on the line, he was very open and informative, apparently not briefed on the March 13 sighting or the Maryland Air National Guard's explanation of it. He told me their unit had been sending off illumination flares the whole week before and the present week as well. Nothing unusual, just ordinary flare illumination maneuvers over the designated range.

When I asked if they had been deploying flares the last couple of days in the fog, he hesitated and under his breath whispered, "Oh man." Then it seemed as if someone was feeding him information in the background. He said, "Well, we don't fly in the fog. Are you calling from Phoenix?"

"Yes," I replied.

"I don't think you can see flares that far down there anyway," he remarked with conviction.

I was writing down every word he said. I wanted to make certain I was clear about the facts. I also wanted to make certain of the number, so I asked, "How many flares all total do you think would be going out each night?"

He stated, "A dozen. We're off the range by 8:30 P.M. heading back to D-M [Davis-Monthan]."

Not only did he confirm that they finished their maneuvers over an hour before our sighting that began at 9:40 P.M. the night before, but he denied that they ever send flares out in special arrays.

"Why would we ever do that? How could we anyway? After leaving the jet, they just fall where they fall, depending on wind, air current, and atmospheric conditions."

At least now I knew the Michigan Guard was in town and, according to the lieutenant colonel, nothing special had been going on that week, except for the fog.

After hanging up, I drove to the film developer. It was exhilarating to see how the pictures from the three Tuesday night sightings turned out with the new camera and high-tech photo lens in place. The images were awesome. It was time to share them with everyone at Village Labs.

I walked into the lab at 2 P.M. for a meeting, which had been prearranged the week before. I was aglow with excitement and they noticed. I couldn't wait another moment. Pulling out the spectacular pictures (one is included in the photo layout on page 107), I smiled in anticipation as I handed them to Jim and Michael. From the pleased looks on their faces, they were thrilled as well, especially since they were already being inundated by calls from curious witnesses and the news media concerning the strange lights in the sky the night before.

I asked them to help me coordinate an effort with the other March 13 video witnesses so that we were stationed at different locations (north, south, east, and west) in case the mysterious orbs returned that night. Again, I had a feeling they would.

When I arrived home late Wednesday afternoon, there was a telephone message waiting for me. "This message is for Dr. Lynne. My name is Lieutenant Colonel ___. I'm the commander of Snowbird at Davis-Monthan AFB. I understand you have some questions about flares that were dropped from a deployed unit here at Snowbird. If you need further information, please give me a call. Here is my work number or you can call me at home. That's in Tucson. Bye."

At home? I thought it was odd for a lieutenant colonel to leave a stranger his home number. It was too late to call him at work anyway and I didn't want to bother him at home, so I figured I'd follow up the next morning.

As I approached the kitchen table, I noticed the bold heading on the front page of the *Arizona Republic* "Valley & State" section: "UFOs Invade Barwood Race." Even though the article the preceding day concerning Barwood's run for secretary of state had been benign, some of the other reporters weren't going to let this one pass without some hometown cynicism.

Reporter Michael Murphy made the point that Councilwoman Frances Barwood was going where no politician had gone before, even in Arizona, where we are known for our offbeat politics.

> The former Phoenix vice mayor emerged Tuesday as an international poster girl for the UFO crowd by vowing to become the first candidate ever to push the issue that the government is concealing evidence that alien beings have arrived on Earth.

Murphy bantered that even though Barwood didn't have any firsthand experience with ETs, that wasn't stopping her from championing the cause of those who believed that alien ships had visited Earth. "And carted off a few humans on their way out," as the reporter put it. But Barwood stood her ground and made the public plea, "Whatever it is, I want to know, and I want a reenactment."

The journalist quipped, "Barwood is a Republican, but the state's GOP establishment is likely to treat her as if she just arrived from Neptune."

The *Arizona Republic* reporters had a field day. One of their most respected political writers, Keven Willey, wrote that after covering politics in Arizona for so long, she thought she'd seen everything, yet now former Phoenix City Councilwoman Barwood had announced that she was running for secretary of state on the "UFO platform." She couldn't understand what that had to do with the largely clerical nature of the secretary of state's office, but admitted that it got Barwood front-page headlines, and that maybe that was the whole idea. Willey concluded, "I'm sure SOS Betsey Bayless is quaking in her boots for the GOP primary. I wonder if she'll embrace the OSOR platform—Only Sane One Running."

What should Barwood have done, as a dedicated public official, when confronted with a plethora of inquiries from her constituents? It would have been much easier for her to turn her back on this bizarre incident, but she didn't. She was simply asking *why* the government wasn't being forthright and addressing this question. You had to wonder why they weren't investigating something that was a valid concern of the very people who trust in their leadership.

But there was another mystery. If the sighting had become such a major issue for many Arizona citizens, and now Barwood was running for secretary of state to get to the bottom of it, why hadn't the military done something to prove it was them? If the lights were flares, as they had been contending since the end of July 1997, perhaps they would reenact the March 13 incident now that they were being challenged publicly on the front page of the daily paper to do so. We'd have to wait and see.

About 7:45 that evening, while chatting on the phone with my son, I noticed two huge amber lights appear high in the southwest sky. I raced outside and took three snapshots before the lights blinked out. I then called Village Labs to alert them. Within seconds the lights reappeared. They hovered in a fixed position for several minutes, then disappeared. Two new brilliant orbs popped up right where the large January 23 and March 13 formations had occurred. They stayed in place for close to six minutes.

Since most of the sightings had been in "threes," I was preparing to take the photo equipment inside when two more lights appeared. They seemed much farther away and to the west. Something made me call Village Labs again. Michael Tanner answered.

I breathlessly announced, "Mike, something is going on. There was just a fourth sighting. There was never a fourth sighting before. I have a strange feeling that something is about to happen. Please call everyone else to get their cameras ready."

And he did. The Krzystons were already outside filming. Tanner then contacted Chuck Rairden and the couple from Rainbow Valley as well. Unfortunately, Tom King's phone line was busy.

But there were four of us at four different vantage points: Paradise Valley (north); Rainbow Valley (south); Ahwatukee (east); and Moon Valley (west). We were all recording a spectacular grande finale as glittering amber globes filled the Phoenix skyline. In synchrony, we captured a 20-minute array of formations spanning 40 miles and higher than they had ever been before. There were two huge diagonal mirror images (40 miles apart), then four lights in a row, hovering above the Phoenix landscape. The stationary lights would fade away for only a few seconds and then reappear in the same exact spot. Suddenly, an amber orb blinked on over the two far southwest spheres, forming a small triangle that just hung there, motionless.

Since Frank was in the backyard with the dogs, he was unaware of this display, only visible from the front of the house. I, on the other hand, was switching from the video to the 35-mm camera trying to capture this spectacle on film, bouncing from one viewfinder to the other to make certain I was getting the shot. It must have been a comical sight. Even so, I was determined to document it all.

The lights were up there for so long that after the third roll of film, I grabbed my high-powered binoculars for a closer look. While the camcorder continued videotaping, I gazed at each round, pulsating orange ball. Then, over two spheres to the east, I noticed one golden orb blink on, higher than the rest. A gigantic triangle sparkled in the evening sky for 40 seconds.

Just as Jaime Mauson had suggested, this light show reminded me of the movie *Close Encounters* when the alien spaceship answered the humans' musical call. Whoever was creating this exhibition seemed to have a purpose. It was as if *they* knew we were waiting. *They* knew we were ready. They also knew they would catch everyone else off guard, especially the military.

When the last light blinked out at 8:46 P.M., I was shaking with disbelief. Something had occurred that could finally verify our suspicions and clear our doubts. I had been told that morning by the lieutenant colonel of the Battle Creek, Michigan, Air National Guard Unit that the military couldn't possibly create formations with flares, let alone triangles and diagonal mirror images 40 miles apart. Then who did this?

As I was calming down from the experience, I turned on the 9 P.M. TV newscast to see if there was any mention of it. They were interviewing Senator John McCain.

Reporter: "Even Senator John McCain has been getting calls about these new mysterious lights."

Senator McCain: "I don't know any good answers to it except to say so far we have found no evidence of any black helicopters or alien invasion or anything of that nature. But, there has been an inability to explain reports that some have made about the presence of lights."

Reporter: "They have called everybody, the National Guard, the FAA; no one has an idea what these lights are right now."

It was time to phone that lieutenant colonel at home. Keeping an open mind, I was curious to hear what he would say about the sightings, particularly since this panoramic light show was far different from what had occurred on March 13, 1997. He was the head of the Snowbirds, so if they had carried out this exercise he should be aware of the aerodynamic maneuvers displayed above the city. His wife answered and said he had just left for a meeting. I could only guess what that was about.

The first thing Thursday morning, I called the base. I was prepared for an official statement like, "We put on a show for Barwood" or "Did you see the reenactment?" But when the lieutenant colonel got on the line, he didn't mention a thing about the night before. No Barwood. No reenactment. Not even a reference to any special deployment. When I asked, he stated that the Guard was out doing maneuvers as usual the night before, nothing out of the ordinary.

I couldn't hold back any longer and divulged that something unusual had popped up across the skyline, and that it was witnessed and photographed by a number of people in the Phoenix area. He wasn't sure what to say. So I asked for the wing commander of the Battle Creek, Michigan, unit with whom I had spoken the day before. When the lieutenant colonel got on the line, he immediately began changing his story from the preceding day. Instead of the routine maneuvers he had described, now it was that they had deployed dozens of flares. Since I hadn't described any specific characteristics of the light show, when he stated that the aircraft was capable of shooting a string of flares at the same time, I wondered if he was trying to cover himself in case we had observed an array of lights similar to those seen on March 13. But of course we hadn't.

He started to become flustered as one of the pilots, a major, who had supposedly flown the mission the night before, got on the phone to answer specifics. The major was much more assertive. Yet the story was changing once again.

"We're leaving on Friday, so we had to make sure we got all of the flares off. And due to some considerations in terms of how we were flying our planes, we didn't get as many as we thought early in the week, so we had to get a lot of them off last night. So I think some guys went ahead and expended as many as possibly six or eight. You've possibly seen eight flares, you know, in formation right next to each other, possibly."

Funny, that was the same number captured on video on March 13. This scenario kept popping up in the conversation. But, as I knew, that formation definitely didn't happen the night before. I asked, "Did you hear about the event that occurred last March by any chance?"

He stated, "Yes, when those three or four lights were over Tucson. Oh yes, the rumor when we got here, we were told, was that another guard unit was out here and they had gone ahead and expended their flares higher up in the 20 thousand, 22 thousand range that had actually caught the jet stream. So these things got blown over towards Phoenix and that was probably what it was."

That was a new one. The story had changed once again. And this one made my photographs of the identical January 23 sighting even more incomprehensible. If what he was professing was true, then two different Air National Guard units would have performed the same unprecedented maneuver and had the same jet stream conditions two months apart! I had heard enough and interrupted, "Are you going to be deploying flares again tonight?"

He answered, "I think we have nine left. One of the aircraft has eight of them and the other one I think has one. So if you see anything, you may see one and then you might see a group of them. That then will probably be us. If it's something else—ha ha ha—I don't know, it would be something that we couldn't answer for. Heck, who knows?"

Why did he add the rider? And if they were leaving on Friday, why would they deploy so many flares on Wednesday night, leaving only eight or nine for Thursday night?

Even with all the obvious holes in their stories, I was still open to a logical, military explanation. Over the past year I had remained open to any common-sense scenario. Finally, here was the military's chance to set the record straight, to prove it was them once and for all, to put an end to the year-long controversy.

In the meantime, Jim Dilettoso satellite-fed some of my footage from the Wednesday night event to the producers of *Extra* early Thursday morning. They aired a special report on the 20-minute "return of the Phoenix Lights" at 6:30 P.M. Did the military, which had already announced to *Extra* and the Arizona media that afternoon that the lights were their flares, watch the report and wring their hands, knowing they couldn't duplicate the formations I had photographed? Or would they be out there creating a light show of their own to prove it was military in origin?

I was prepared at 7 P.M. for the showdown, and so were the others. I had alerted Village Labs of my conversation with the military and we were all waiting with cameras ready. As I sat there looking out at the vacant night sky, an idea entered my mind. *If you are unearthly and you can hear my thoughts, don't come back. If nothing happens, what will the military say about their scheduled flare drop—or lack of one—for that evening?* I can never prove that anyone received my silent message, but as I sat by my camera from 7 P.M. until 10:30 P.M., there was nothing. Nothing in the Phoenix skies save a few commercial airlines flying in and out of Sky Harbor.

When I called Davis-Monthan Friday morning to inquire about their slated flare maneuvers, they told me that the lieutenant colonel was in a briefing meeting. He never returned my call.

But I didn't have to wait to hear from the other video witnesses. Mike Krzyston was particularly confident in his description of the "new" sighting. He stated, "Lynne, whatever caused the lights on the 13th of March, 1997, caused them on January 14, 1998. My astronomical telescope is so sensitive that if I look at the moon with it I have to adjust the telescope every 35 to 40 seconds because the moon is traveling that fast out of the screen. When I put my telescope on one of these lights and came back a couple of minutes later, it was at exactly the same spot as before. This light was totally fixed in that position. There was no aura being generated by these lights, no reflections, no parachutes, no rays, no smoke trail. The edges were smooth like a ball. It was like a dot of bright orange light. It looked like there could have been a swirling to it."

By the weekend, the TV news stations in and out of town were on the story. One particularly good report surfaced on the nationally syndicated show *Hard Copy* on January 20, 1998. Both the Krzystons and Rairdens shared their impressive new footage with the public. The show included the following statements.

Jim Dilettoso: "It's the most important sighting in 50 years."

Frances Emma Barwood: "Here is something that has invaded our airspace and we need answers."

Reporter: "For a while it seemed that they'd finally gone. But now, suddenly they're back."

Jim Dilettoso had viewed this sighting himself and confessed, "It makes you feel like you're in the presence of something really powerful."

Chuck Rairden explained, "The lights go off and on and the final thing is the triangle shape."

Host: "And like many others, the Krzystons want some straight answers from authorities. The military and the Air National Guard are sending out a message of their own—that the UFOs are just flares, some of them being shot off in the sky by the local sheriff, Joe Arpaio. But when we caught up with Sheriff Arpaio he seemed mystified."

A surprised Sheriff Joe Arpaio said: "I never heard about that. Is that called passing the buck? I never heard about flares. I think I would have known about it."

Jim Dilettoso: "This is not a flare. We have gone to extremes to determine whether or not it was military aircraft, a covert military operation, or flares. And it's none of those."

The media frenzy continued. Coincidentally, the anniversary week of the mass sighting was approaching. For Jim Dilettoso, it wasn't a good week. In fact, it was devastating. A local free press magazine printed an offensive personal attack attempting to discredit both him and Barwood. Those involved with the investigation were convinced that someone wanted Jim and Village Labs out of the picture. Were they right? Was Jim too tied into the media and getting too much information out to the public, information that someone might not want divulged?

Unfortunately, the attacks worked, causing Jim to lose a number of important contracts, and Village Labs in the process. He had been so absorbed with the Phoenix Lights that he had neglected his investors and paying clients. By the summer of 1998, there was no longer a clearinghouse for the evidence nor a place for witnesses to share their sightings.

Since word had gotten out that the article was being published in the next issue of *New Times*, I called the reporter and offered a meeting to enlighten him as to what had been going on behind the scenes. But he was more interested in his deadline than in speaking with any of the photographic witnesses or viewing their evidence firsthand. I was saddened by this irresponsible journalism. Not only does this sort of public derision stop others of credibility from coming forward, but it puts a black cloud over the investigative process. It reminded me that this is exactly what debunkers want.

I called Steve Wilson, one of the most esteemed columnists at the *Arizona Republic*. I figured if I could share my evidence with him, he might be able to set the record straight. A confidential meeting with a newspaper columnist was a first for me. I was thrilled when he said that he was keeping an open mind. As I had become increasingly aware, that was the first important step. I began by telling Steve that as a scientist I deal with facts. But I also knew that something unusual was going on and in good conscience I couldn't ignore what I'd compiled. I had been trying to convince myself that it was nothing, but I couldn't any longer. I told him I thought that disregarding all the evidence would be irresponsible. Then I presented the composite video of edited media clips and footage that I had assembled. He was impressed.

Wednesday morning, March 11, 1998, I ran out to grab the *Arizona Republic*. The title of Wilson's column alone was proof that someone in the local print media was starting to head in the right direction: "Phoenix Lights' Witnesses Credible, Hard to Dismiss."

Then two days later, on the one-year anniversary of the March 13 event, an article in the *Arizona Republic* embellished on a provocative and recurring aspect of the sightings: "Phoenix Lights, Plus a Year—Alien or Not, They Lit Up Some Lives."

In the report, Richard Ruelas wrote that the Phoenix Lights, which had appeared a year ago that day, had a definite impact, whether their origin was ordinary or out-of-this-world. Several documentaries had been made, more were on the way, he said; books and a CD-ROM were in the works and the lights were gracing T-shirts and talk radio. They pushed a relatively unknown former Phoenix city councilwoman into the national media spotlight and prompted a bizarre news conference by Governor Fife Symington, who trotted out an aide dressed in an alien costume. The lights also cost two investigators a business relationship with a "Spam millionaire."

For believers, a clubhouse had emerged: Village Labs. The lab had been set up five years before, with designs to enable other companies to access a planned Nebraska supercomputer. According to Ruelas, instead of finding investors,

Dilettoso and Tanner told him they spent the bulk of their time investigating the Phoenix Lights. Tanner said he spent countless hours interviewing more than 300 witnesses while Dilettoso became the media's expert on the lights. Jim Dilettoso mentioned that he was courting companies such as US West and TRW for support, but they backed off.

"When you're dealing with companies that big, you can't say, 'Sorry, I missed the paperwork deadline because I was working on some UFO video last night,'" Dilettoso said.

Gordie Hormel of Hormel Foods fame had recently yanked his funds from Village Labs, saying he couldn't wait any longer for the computer project that was supposed to return him millions of dollars. "It was all legit, there was nothing fake about it," said Hormel, who estimated he put $2 million into Village Labs. "It just never got the financing it needed."

But there did seem to be an optimistic result of the sighting for a number of witnesses, including Nannette and Mike Fortson, also mentioned by Ruelas. The lights had rekindled their marriage. Since the event, they had spent every night outside looking for a repeat show.

"Other than the hand of God coming through space, nothing could have been more profound," said Mike, a safety products salesman. Not only did they tear out a gazebo so they would have a clearer view, but they purchased a $900 video camera that's on the ready and a high-beam flashlight "in case any craft want to communicate." But according to Mike, the main benefit seems to be the passion that has been brought back to their 25-year marriage.

What fascinated me most about this article was Mike Fortson's personal story. He was obviously deeply affected by the sighting, just as other witnesses had been, and he made no excuse for it. The still unexplained event had changed his life for the better—a positive aftereffect for experiencers that I would certainly have to explore.

Incidentally, after all the months of unrelenting posturing to the media about his "flare" theory, shortly after this article appeared, the belligerent investigator "Martin" quit MUFON and seemed to fade into oblivion. I had the feeling that since we now had more photographic proof from the recent sightings that he was not involved with at all, he was out of the loop. Besides, he got what he wanted anyway, which was to discredit Jim Dilettoso.

Since the mass sighting was still unexplained, I agreed to an anonymous radio interview to celebrate the first anniversary of the Phoenix Lights. As I turned on KTAR radio to set up an audiotape to record my first in-studio interview, I caught the tail end of an expose by Tim Crawford, president and founder of UFO Central in California: "The consensus of opinion is that the Phoenix

Lights was definitely some form of extraterrestrial craft. No military activity, such as flares, could produce the effect witnessed by thousands; nor could any private company come close to creating a craft capable of the maneuvers that were observed and recorded."

I had met with radio show host Pat McMahon twice the week before to brief him on my evidence. Since Pat knew my family, he was shocked and thrilled when he first walked into the conference room and found out that I was "Dr. X." After my thorough presentation, he was overwhelmed by what I had accumulated and excited to interview me live for the anniversary show. I was excited to be there.

Pat began, "This is an historic moment. The only time that *McMahon* has been narrowed down to one subject. The subject is the Lights over Phoenix. McMahon or Mulder? You decide. And to do that we have gathered Dr. X, who happens to be a local physician, a Phoenix Lights observer, chronicler, videotaper, and the person who has been on the spot and can tell us firsthand experiences with the lights over Phoenix, one year ago today. Jim Dilettoso, president of Village Labs, UFO investigator, and the star of a recent article. Dr. Paul Cook, a professor and senior lecturer in the English Department at Arizona State University, and a science fiction writer."

The following is some of what aired that day.

Dr. Paul Cook: "I've published six novels and I have a seventh coming out in February of 1999. My take on all of this is a reasonably conservative one. That is to say that I believe that people, normal, rational, level-headed Americans and other people around the world, are seeing something—a genuine phenomenon of some kind that, very clearly, our government chooses to stonewall. They won't comment on anything or they basically try to debunk things. My interest is in taking seriously what people are seeing, trying to make sense of it. Something's going on out there . . ."

Jim Dilettoso: "I take a similar approach as Dr. Cook. I enter into this open-mindedly, first of all trying to find out what evidence and data there is, from the people's point of view. People who could testify in a court of law on any other subject and put a man in jail for life. But an eyewitness can look and see the lights in the sky and be dismissed. That alone is an interesting curiosity to me."

Pat: "People mess up on their observations all the time, much less things in the sky that none of us understand."

Jim: "You're absolutely right. But what if five people standing outside describe seeing exactly the same person, same height, same jacket, everything. We have five witnesses. If that situation happens in a UFO case or in the Phoenix Lights case, all five of those witnesses are dismissed."

Pat: "Okay . . . Thirty seconds. Was it a solid body or separate lights, in your opinion?"

Jim: "I think it was in between the two. Because some witnesses said it had a solid structure and others said it had no structure. And if we compare all of the evidence—not being on radar to having photographs and all the conflicting data from the official sources—we have something that can either cloak itself and not be on radar, or balls of light with a field between it."

Jim then mentioned several coincidences: The government had gone into DEF-CON 3 alert on March 13, 1997, and President Clinton disappeared for hours to an undisclosed location; the battery on an important satellite that detects incoming missiles went dead; and in July 1997, *Scientific American* had a multipage story about how on March 13, 1997, bursts of gamma radiation entered our atmosphere, source unknown.

Host Pat: "All the shows, *Sightings, Extra*—they always come to Jim Dilettoso. Paul Cook is a science fiction writer and academician at Arizona State University. But the most intriguing person we have here in this studio is Dr. X. Please tell us the *Reader's Digest* version of your experience with lights you couldn't identify."

Dr. X: "Actually I should call myself Dr. Y, because I have so many *why* questions."

Pat: "I thought you were going to say chromosomes and I didn't even want to get into that."

I finally had the opportunity to describe my 1995 and 1997 sightings in detail.

When I had finished, Pat asked: "Why is it that the only sighting that's gotten so much press is the one a year ago today?"

Dr. X: "That's curious to me also. There are other sightings occurring worldwide that are very similar. I think that's very important to note and for people to become aware of. I just became aware of it all this year myself. If it was military, why did they pick a clear night when people were outside looking at the Hale-Bopp comet with cameras in hand? Or did some kind of craft traverse over the sixth largest city in the United States to get our attention? Either way, I'd like to know why."

Pat challenged my statement: "If it's a military thing, they have no obligation to tell you."

Dr. X: "People were really rattled by it. Wouldn't that be important to address? If it was military and it concerns the Arizona citizens, do you think they should be obliged to explain the phenomena openly?"

The media interest surrounding the first anniversary of the mass sighting continued. At the end of a two-hour *Sightings* program called "100 Years of UFO Cover-Ups," which aired on the Sci-Fi Channel in March 1998, they reported on our Phoenix Lights.

Jim Dilettoso is quoted: "Why would anyone believe the flare story? It's someone's duty; it's someone's responsibility to say that it was flares, it was hot air balloons, it was a mistake, it was a hoax, it was an accident, it was nothing. The Phoenix Lights has created an entirely new 'confederacy' among UFO investigators worldwide that see that now there is something tremendous that's happening—without a logical explanation."

The host stated that for Ufologists, the Phoenix event was particularly important because it fell in line with very similar craft seen in Great Britain, North Africa, and Japan.

As they showed a 1970s government declassified "top secret" picture of a huge V-shaped object with multiple lights down each side, the host asked, "Is this the shape of extraterrestrial craft to come? The saucer is dead. Long live the triangle. And Ufologists aren't waiting around for the government to feed them information. They're stockpiling sophisticated computers, software, cameras . . . mobilizing more and more scientists and average citizens. The new millennium of Ufology is born."

Karl Pflock, former deputy assistant in the Department of Defense, admitted, "In my gut and in my heart I am firmly and absolutely convinced that we have indeed been visited by alien beings from another world. Now we need to bear down and see what we can do about getting the proof."

Jerome Clark, author of the *UFO Encyclopedia,* said: "The UFO question is not going to be solved until science takes it up and treats it as a science question. This thing doesn't have to be a mystery forever."

I hoped he was right. So many times in the past year I had heard the official refrain, "The military and government do not investigate UFOs." Why not? And that "UFOs are not a threat to national security." How do they know? Maybe they do know. Maybe they *can't* investigate these seemingly benevolent, intelligent phenomena. Maybe what I had uncovered during my research thus far was true—that every time the military scrambles to intercept them, either the aircraft instrumentation goes haywire, the electrical circuits turn off, or when the jets get too close the unexplained phenomena blink out, or take off at tremendous speeds.

Maybe our military doesn't investigate because *they* won't let them. Maybe, just maybe, *they* want *us* to investigate—not the military, not the government—but us the people. And now *they* know that *we* have finally begun.

View from our balcony of unexplained phenomena sighting area above the basin between South Mountain Range and Estrella Mountain Range.

Driveway lights   Car lights   House skylights

February 1995. Three unexplained amber orbs, in a triangle (pyramid) formation, hovered over this private desert area just yards from our property.

First and last photos from 02/06/95 sighting of two close amber orbs that began in a triangle (pyramid) array of three amber orbs, just yards from our home. Then they disappeared one by one. There are also distant orbs in a line above the city skyline disappearing as well.

Note: In the first photo there are FOUR distant amber orbs in a line array above the city skyline. In the last photo that night there are TWO amber orbs above the city skyline.

First and last photos during 01/23/97 sighting two months before the Arizona mass sighting. I caught six photos in a row of the unexplained phenomena head-on and then turning into a "V" formation. The sighting was confirmed by air traffic controllers the next morning.

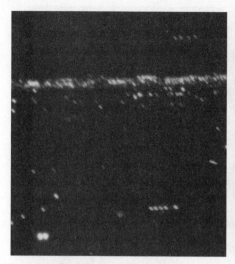 

Cropped first photo taken 02/06/95 of sighting close to the house.

Cropped last photo taken 02/06/95 of sighting close to the house.

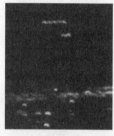 

Cropped first photo of sighting 01/23/97.

Cropped last photo of sighting 01/23/97.

Since I only captured video on 03/13/97, I am including a 35-mm shot of an unexplained sighting almost identical to the 03/13/97 mass sighting. Three amber orbs (three points of light in a triangle formation) hovered over the city skyline in the same location as the array at 10:00 P.M. on 03/13/97. Below is a cropped version of this photo, which was taken on 09/16/02. This sighting was witnessed by myself, Frank, and our son, Daniel.

Dense fog blanketed the Phoenix landscape 01/10/98 through 01/14/98. This photo was taken on 01/13/98, the morning after the return of the Phoenix Lights.

One of three sightings taken on 01/13/98 as seen through the dense fog with a telelens and star filter. Note that the hovering orbs are in the same location as in the 02/95, 01/97, and 03/97 sightings.

40-mile-wide sighting during 01/14/98 event photographed by four witnesses (N, S, E, W)

Giant triangle finale in the same location during the 01/14/98 sighting. This photo was taken off the videotape.

Krzystons' photographs of unexplained phenomena formations hovering above the city, behind a foreground ridge near their home in Moon Valley (NW) during the 01/14/98 sighting.

Note: The four amber orbs in a row and the three amber orbs forming the giant triangle finale are bigger than any city light. They are also in front of the Estrella Mountain Range, which lies beyond the city landscape.

10. Ufology—A Brief History

It was time for me to delve into the history of UFOs and the verifiable evidence of other similar unexplained phenomena as reported worldwide. It seemed integral to my investigation that I be as informed as possible. So I started combing the library and Internet. Not only was I overwhelmed by the abundance of reputable references on the topic, but I soon realized that from the dawn of civilization humankind has told stories of flying objects and strange, mystical visitors. The more I explored, the more I discovered that detailed accounts of unexplained phenomena had been documented since humans began keeping records. Many of these instances were reported as actual cases, not myths.

For example, consider the discovery in Pakistan of an authentic Stone Age cave painting picturing a helmeted figure complete with antenna emerging from a classic saucer-shaped vehicle. One wonders how a "caveman" could have imagined this scenario—or was it documentation of an actual event as sketched by a witness?

Twenty to thirty thousand years ago, the primitive inhabitants in what is currently northern Spain and southern France painted presumably accurate cave drawings of animals long extinct. In their rudimentary renditions, they also depicted disc-shaped objects. How would these prehistoric peoples have known what flying saucers looked like if they hadn't seen them?

Ted Peters of the Center for Theology and Natural Sciences in Berkeley, California, explained that the UFO issue was even debated in ancient Greece.[1] Philosophers argued that there are many worlds, that all worlds have their organization, that reality is plural.

Astrophysicist Dr. Jacques Vallee wrote that in the ninth century the Archbishop of Lyons, France, reported ships sailing through the clouds and referred to a land called *Magonia*, from which they supposedly originated.[2]

There are possibly renderings of unexplained aerial phenomena in medieval art as well. In a monastery in the former Republic of Yugoslavia a fresco painting portrays a person who is sitting in a pointed airborne object that has three fiery jets protruding from its posterior.

At the end of the twelfth century, William of Newburg wrote about terrified monks in North Yorkshire, England, who witnessed a flat, round, silvery disc flying overhead.[3] A painting found in one of the oldest Russian churches illustrates two discs hovering above the crucifixion, complete with onlookers. Again, they seem to have depicted what they saw.

The possibility of life beyond our own planet took a giant leap forward in the sixteenth century when Copernicus discovered that the Earth was not the center of the universe. This meant that maybe there were other celestial bodies like our planet out there, and perhaps other life as well.

At the beginning of the seventeenth century, our worldview changed once again when Galileo Galilei first used the telescope invented by Hans Lippershey. Galileo accepted Copernicus's theories that Earth revolved around the sun, not the other way around. He also discovered that four satellites were orbiting the planet called Jupiter. Galileo's discoveries put him in the lead as the most important scientist of his time. But because of his unorthodox revelations, he spent his final days punished under house arrest.

In the nineteenth century, American astronomer Percival Lowell announced that he had detected artificial canals on the surface of Mars, contending that this meant there was evidence of intelligent life on that planet. His influence as a scientific pioneer in creating an interest in the possibility of extraterrestrial life is still felt today.

There are many more examples, but let's jump to the end of the nineteenth century, when miraculous inventions, including the telephone and automobile, were unleashed. Yet thousands of people also saw something that did not yet exist—an airship.

In April 1897, the *Chicago Times Herald* printed a story about a 70-foot airship with "moveable head lights." The *Chicago Record* reported that 10,000 people saw a great black airship in Kansas City. It hovered over the city for ten minutes. After flashing white, blue, and green lights, it shot off to space. Throughout that April, people in Canada, Washington, and California witnessed lights. After that, there were no more sightings of airships. That is, until six years later, when the Wright brothers invented the first aircraft built by humans.

In 1945 the atom exploded, as did the age of UFOs. Sightings increased tenfold after World War II. Humankind had developed a force of galactic significance—nuclear power. Were these otherworldly entities keeping tabs on what was now going on down on Earth?

According to UFO researcher Donald Keyhoe, they were. And the air force knew about it. They were officially analyzing the motives of possible visitors from space and admitted it. Keyhoe related a direct quote from an official air force report: "Such a civilization might observe on Earth that we now have atomic bombs. We should therefore expect to behold such visitations."[4]

Objects similar to the amber balls of light seen throughout Arizona were documented in the 1940s. The Germans, Americans, and Japanese each thought the other had some sort of intelligently guided amber "spy" spheres flying around their aircraft, just checking things out. Air force pilots in each country have verified this fact. It wasn't until after the war that each side realized that no one had this advanced technology.

Richard Haines, Ph.D., a research scientist and world-renowned UFO investigator, said of UFO sightings during the war, "There were sailors on ships, there were GIs on the ground, in artillery battalions, there were German soldiers on the other side of the line. People from all sides of the war were involved and reported the same thing."[5]

These mysterious phenomena were spotted across the globe. They became known as "foo fighters," from *feu*, the French word for "fire." Robert Leroy, a "foo fighter" eyewitness and member of the 11th Airborne in New Guinea, explained, "Suddenly I saw this ball about three feet in diameter following this Japanese Betty Bomber and it started changing colors. I thought I'd seen a new secret weapon. I had to agree with the rest of the guys because that's what they thought it was. They didn't know any better and nobody had ever heard of a UFO in '44."[6]

According to Dr. Haines, who has done extensive research into the phenomena, "Pilots would report glowing luminous balls of light . . . often orange or red, anywhere from one foot to six feet in diameter, that would accelerate up to their altitude, level off very quickly and then stay beside the airplane. They would fly singly or in pairs or in trio, oftentimes in rigid formation, which is important. And all of these flight dynamics point in one way or another to a fairly high intelligent level of guidance."[7]

Were these the same objects that Frank and I witnessed in 1995 hovering in a stationary triangle formation outside our bedroom window?

As maintained by intelligence sources, services for both Allied and Axis forces were hard at work trying to figure out where the UFO or foo fighters came from. Dr. Haines contends, "There's a possibility that 'foo fighters' could have been and still are guided, controlled, created, produced by an advanced intelligence—not of this planet. But that is a difficult thing to prove, clearly."[8]

By 1947, the U.S. government believed the UFO phenomenon was genuine and might be an advanced secret weapon. It prompted an official but secret investigation.

General Twining, head of the Air Material Command, declared that the phenomena were real and that UFOs the size of aircraft were being observed. General James Stamford, air force public relations officer, stated publicly: "The air force interest in this problem has been due to a feeling of an obligation to identify and analyze, to the best of our ability, anything in the air that may have the possibility of threat or menace to the United States."[9]

Even though people had witnessed UFOs before 1947, the sighting in that year by accomplished rescue pilot Kenneth Arnold set the stage for the next 50 years. This sighting became public knowledge. What's more, the respected aviation specialist first coined the phrase "flying saucer" on June 24, 1947, while he was flying over Mount Rainier in Washington State. Arnold was alarmed when he saw nine boomerang-shaped vehicles flying in formation at incredible speeds. He described his own observation to a radio reporter several hours after his sighting: "I can see them only plainly when they seem to tip their wing or whatever it was and the sun flashed on them. They look something like a pie plate that was cut in half. They seem to flip and flash in the sun, just like mirrors in such a way it almost blinds you . . . As I was looking at them I kept looking for their tails, but they didn't have any tails."[10]

Arnold timed how long it took the unidentified objects to fly between two peaks, and estimated their speed to be 1,200 to 1,500 mph, twice the speed of the fastest conventional craft of that day.

During the two weeks following Arnold's sighting, there were over 1,000 reports throughout the country. Did the fact that America now had atomic weapons mean that perhaps the "checking out" was getting closer to home or could this advanced technology possibly have been ours? The U.S. government disclaimed any connection to the objects.

Then just weeks after the Arnold sighting, "something" crashed near Roswell, New Mexico. The crash occurred in close proximity to the 509th bomb group, the only squadron in the world that packed a military arsenal of atomic weapons.

Within months, the U.S. Air Force created the top-secret project "Sign" to investigate UFO reports. What began as top-secret projects—Sign, Saucer, Redlight, Grudge, Magnet, and Snowbird—became a public study by the air force known as Project Blue Book.

General Twining's public conclusion, as announced by General Stamford, was: "We have received and analyzed between one and two thousand reports that have come to us from all kinds of sources."[11]

He also said, "From this great mass of reports we have come to adequately explain the great bulk of them as hoaxes, erroneously identified friendly aircraft, as meteorological or electronic phenomena, or as light aberrations."[12]

But according to a TLC documentary, "The U.S. started investigating aerial phenomena on January 2, 1948. From 243 cases studied, a report entitled *An Estimate of the Situation* by the Air Technical Intelligence Center concluded 'flying saucers are probably real extra-terrestrial spacecraft.'"[13]

The public didn't hear that part of the story, because General Hoyt Vandenberg, air force chief of staff, said this conclusion was not acceptable, and ordered the air force to find a more admissible "earthly" explication for these unidentified flying objects.[14]

The government realized how simple, and maybe necessary, it would be to explain away any unusual sightings. After all, in 1938, Orson Welles proved how susceptible Americans were to misinformation with the radio broadcast dramatization of H. G. Wells's fantasy *War of the Worlds*. The public panicked. It showed how easily we could be misled, and how vulnerable we were to media pronouncements and propaganda.

American authorities weren't the only ones worried about these unexplained aerial phenomena. In the late 1950s and early 1960s, the Supreme Headquarters Allied Powers of Europe (SHAPE) noted a large number of UFOs on radar, apparently flying at great speeds and at high altitude above central Europe. The technology was far more sophisticated than anything the Russians or anyone in the West had at the time. SHAPE began a three-year probe to solve the mystery. Their conclusion still remains classified.

To confuse the issue, John Pike of the Federation of American Scientists recently stated, "It's certainly the case that in the 1950s and '60s the CIA knew many UFO reports were in fact sightings of classified balloon and aircraft programs, but they didn't do anything to dispel the public confusion. The public was seeing a lot of classified programs in the '50s and '60s that looked like [unidentified] flying objects. The intelligence community knew they were their own projects and just didn't tell anyone."[15]

Even though some UFO sightings may have been triggered by secret projects, General James Stamford, the director of air force intelligence at the time, made a public statement in connection with the 1952 sightings over Washington, D.C., "We can say that the recent sightings are in no way connected with any secret development by any secret agency of the United States."[16]

The UFO wave continued. Those behind these unexplained phenomena even tried to make contact with the heads of our own nation. On July 21, 1952, the *New York Times* reported that on July 19 and 20, formations of glowing objects hovered over the capital in Washington, D.C. Startling photographs were taken of the event.[17]

According to the Associated Press, "The air force disclosed tonight it had received reports of [an] eerie visitation by unidentified aerial objects, perhaps a new type of 'flying saucer,' over the vicinity of the nation's capital. For the first time, so far as has been reported, the objects were picked up by radar. Speeds of 7,000 miles per hour were clocked by radar operators. One week later [July 26 and 27] the objects returned. The air force claimed that it was caused by unusual weather patterns or a meteor shower, but the public demanded an investigation."[18]

In January 1953, a secret air force memo directly confirmed the existence of UFOs, stating, "If the speed and maneuverability are accurate, then the objects had to be from another world."[19]

The public only became aware in 1952 that the air force had launched Project Blue Book. Sightings that were difficult to explain disappeared from the report, while those that were easily defined were included, debunked, and even publicized to pacify the public. It was officially stated that the government would investigate these phenomena to find out if they were "a threat to security or [represented] technical advances that could be used for warfare."[20]

Robert Friend, director of Project Blue Book (1958–1963), has admitted, "As the program grew and additional sightings were investigated they suddenly decided that there was the possibility that these things were from extraterrestrial origins."[21]

Then on February 27, 1960, retired admiral Roscoe Hillenkoetter, first director of the CIA (1947–1950) and member of the board of governors of the National Investigations Committee on Aerial Phenomenon (NICAP), a UFO investigating group, was quoted in a NICAP news press release. He broke his silence in a statement published in the *New York Times:* "We declare that it is time for the truth to be brought out in open congressional hearings. Behind the scenes, high-ranking air force officials are soberly concerned about the UFOs. But through official secrecy and ridicule, many citizens are led to believe the unknown flying objects are nonsense."[22] He charged that "to hide the facts" the air force had silenced its personnel through the issuance of regulations.

Still nothing changed. Six years later, on March 28, 1966, U.S. Representative Gerald Ford sent a letter to the Armed Services Committee: "I strongly recommend that there be a committee investigation of the UFO phenomenon. I think we owe it to the people to establish credibility regarding UFOs and to produce the greatest possible enlightenment on this subject."[23]

The congressional hearing on unidentified flying objects began in April 1966. One of the most important figures in the investigation of UFOs was Dr. J. Allen Hynek, the respected Northwestern University astronomer and scientific advisor to Project Blue Book. As a senior government official between 1952 and 1969, he dismissed all UFO sightings as conventional aircraft, swamp gas, temperature inversions, or mass hallucinations.

There was another study, called the Condon Report, supposedly conducted by the University of Colorado between 1966 and 1968. In reality, the project was solely authorized by "scientific director" Dr. Edward U. Condon; there was no committee. Moreover, when the Condon Report was released in 1968, the American scientific community seemed to accept its negative conclusion concerning evidence for extraterrestrial visitation. In *Analysis of the Condon Report,* however, Peter Sturrock, a distinguished plasma physicist at Stanford University, details the many discrepancies between Condon's dismissive summary and the actual data.[24]

Sturrock documented that Condon took no part in the investigations and indicated the conclusion he intended to draw *before* the data was examined. Out of 63 cases investigated, 29 percent remain unexplained to this day. Even so, the National Academy of Sciences endorsed the report after an unusually rapid review. In addition, the air force quickly used the report as a justification to terminate any further public involvement in the topic of UFOs.

Project Blue Book, the U.S. government's only acknowledged study of UFOs and extraterrestrials, closed up shop in 1969. While our astronauts walked on the moon and our young men were fighting in Vietnam, the Pentagon announced that after extensive investigation, it had established that UFOs were not a threat to national security.[25]

UFO investigator Don Berliner maintained: "There was fear initially that they [the UFOs] might be Soviet. By shutting down Project Blue Book, until today the air force hasn't said anything beyond 'we've studied the subject, there's nothing to it, we've lost interest.' I don't believe it. Since the air force has a responsibility of protecting our skies, if something is flying around they better know what it is."[26]

It's intriguing that four years after the 1969 announcement, Dr. Hynek founded the Center for UFO Studies. But the denials continued.

For example, in 1976 the Viking probe mapped the surface of Mars, revealing objects resembling pyramids and a humanoid face. These findings and others continue to be ignored or debunked by the military, including a covert committee that was supposedly formed in late 1947 to deal with wreckage recovered from the UFO crash near Roswell, New Mexico. Twelve highly accomplished military and civilian personnel, comprising Operation Majestic 12, were to analyze and determine the motives and intentions of the occupants of the Roswell crashed spaceship. In keeping with the secrecy established, the government denied and continues to deny the existence of Majestic 12.

But some of the major players have come forward. In 1985, shortly before his death, Dr. Hynek disclosed that Project Blue Book had intentionally misguided and misinformed the masses. "I was there at Blue Book and I know the job they had. They were told not to excite the public, don't rock the boat. I saw it with my own eyes. Whenever a case happened that they could explain, and that was quite a few, they made a point of that and let it out to the media. Cases that were very difficult to explain they would keep the media away from them. For they had a job to do, whether rightfully or wrongly, to keep the public from getting excited."[27]

Pilot Graham Shephard confirms the silence: "If pilots see something that is unusual and very strange, the chances are very high that it won't be reported. So my opinion is that there is a huge resource of experience and sightings that have never been reported. My certainty is that what I have seen represents a technology that not only can fly in our planetary environment outside our normal aerodynamic envelopes, but by implication must be able to fly outside the planetary environment well beyond our dreams and expectations."[28]

Mexican air traffic controller Enrique Kolbeck concedes, "These kinds of things exist because they are flying, the pilots have visual contact with them, and sometimes they register on radar."[29]

Although sightings occur frequently, Mexican pilots and air traffic controllers admit that they are rarely spoken about in public or are the subject of official reports. "I don't know what it is. If it belongs to the Earth it is breaking all the rules, and that is very dangerous because nobody knows [of] anything like these that fly," Kolbeck admitted.[30]

It seems that now, many years later, concerned military and aviation professionals who were personal witnesses to extraordinary events during their duty are starting to share their harrowing experiences, and they are looking for answers.

One report that caught my attention recounted an incident that took place at two nuclear missile bases in Montana within a 12-hour period on March 16, 1967. Someone or something back then intentionally tampered with our nuclear arsenal.

Retired USAF Deputy Crew Commander Robert Salas was one of a two-man team inside one of the missile control bunkers at Malmstrom Air Force Base in Montana, 60 feet underground, when missiles equipped with nuclear warheads were switched off for several hours. As he described it, "There was a UFO hovering just outside the front gate and it was glowing red. It was a saucer shape. Within a minute or two the missiles started shutting down and going off alert."[31]

Just 20 miles away and 12 hours later, launch commander Lieutenant Colonel Don Crawford experienced a similar shutdown. Thirty seven-ton Minuteman missiles under his command also turned off. "There is no command in the capsule to turn [the missiles] off. There is no switch—no off switch. They do not break. And I never saw an off alert missile in the three and a half years I was a crewman."

After three hours of stunned silence, with little they could do at either facility to rectify the matter, the missiles came back on. It was as though nothing had gone wrong in the first place. Crawford said, "It just started back up normally like they had installed it from the factory. And so they found no broken pieces, no broken cables, nothing like that. It just started back up."[32]

What makes this story captivating is that neither Lieutenant Colonel Crawford nor Deputy Crew Commander Salas was ever informed about the other's incident. It took a *Sightings* program, 30 years later, to get them together to compare notes. They had both filed official and top-secret reports. But neither was told exactly what happened.

In a now declassified air force document, "Strategic Missile Wing History," we learn that security guards questioned stated that no unusual activity or sightings were observed.

Salas adds, "I know that I briefed my commander on the UFO incidents. The ECHO flight crew not only briefed their commander but had to brief the headquarters on the entire incident. And they had logs. So I know for a fact that those statements in that historical document are false. Certainly if the UFO, whatever it is, has the capability of shutting down our missiles as they did, it's in the public interest to make this an open debate as to what it all means."[33]

I found that the most impressive testimonials of sightings similar to ours in Arizona were from professional pilots and air traffic controllers. Up until recently most reports of this type were kept classified. But now many experiencers, particularly retired ones, are speaking out about their encounters.

In December 1978, there was another unexplained sighting in Wellington, New Zealand, witnessed by pilots and recorded on radar. An air traffic controller verified: "The objects were moving on radar in the same direction as reported by the pilots. They were flying in a tight formation and were related to each other. We hadn't been notified of any craft. They would have had to have clearance from me to operate."[34]

It seems that all efforts to identify the strange objects failed. Then two other separate aircraft spotted unidentified objects on that same night. Pilot Vern Powell said, "We had no idea what it was. This large orb was just a light hanging in the sky. The hairs on the back of my neck were standing. But I realized that we weren't being attacked at all. It was just out there."[35]

The target radar tracked it for 40 miles in the same position in which it was first seen. Then the object disappeared. As the crew prepared to land at 4:30 A.M., they noticed a very fast blip on their radar screen from right to left, far quicker than any aircraft. They realized it must have been going 15,000 kilometers an hour. The Wellington airport radar operators couldn't believe what they were seeing. One said, "I'm a trained pilot. I've been flying for many years. This light I saw on that particular night is like nothing I've ever seen before."[36]

News of the sightings leaked to the press, and Australian reporter Quentin Fogarty rushed to cover the story. He actually went up in an aircraft to check things out. As he described it during a TV reenactment, "When we got into the flight deck we saw this string of lights—three or four, sometimes as many as five lights. It started as a small pinpoint of light and grew into this large pulsating glow with tinges of red and orange. It would keep that shape for a time and then go back to a pinpoint. I just sat there transfixed." The pilot said, "It was moving with us. It appeared to be under some form of control."[37]

The announcer on the Discovery program that aired this report stated that "skeptics claimed that the images came from everyday objects on the ground or out at sea. But all of the witnesses are adamant that none of these explanations add up." In the air traffic controller's words, "If you look in the sky on a starry night and you say we're the only ones alive in the universe, I'll call you the biggest egotist ever."[38]

I discovered that since the 1980s, an increasing number of sightings described as discs, silent mile-long triangular craft, and stationary amber balls of light have been reported worldwide, particularly above sensitive military installations and nuclear bases in Argentina, Belgium, China, the U.K., Russia, Germany, Australia, Mexico, Japan, Israel, Africa, and Canada, as well as throughout the U.S. Of course the most interesting to me were documented reports of global sightings similar to the Phoenix Lights.

Beginning in 1983, the residents of the Hudson River Valley in New York and nearby Connecticut witnessed unidentified objects described as "larger than a football field." The objects seemed to take on a boomerang shape. One sighting was reported by at least five thousand witnesses including police officers, scientists, and people from all walks of life. As in Arizona, the spectators indicated that the silent, slow-moving UFO was something that they had never seen before and could not identify.

Strikingly similar phenomena were also documented in Belgium. The biggest difference was that the Belgian government acknowledged the sightings.

From October 1988 through 1993, hundreds of reports of lighted objects, frequently described as triangular in shape and enormous in size, were recorded in Belgium. Air force supersonic F16 jets chased these strange objects, which were simultaneously tracked by airborne and ground radar. Among the thousands of witnesses were many military and police officers, pilots, scientists, and engineers.

The Belgian government cooperated with civilian UFO investigators, an action without precedent. The sightings were documented by the Belgian Society for the Study of Space Phenomena (SOBEPS), a private organization in Brussels, which published two thick volumes on the UFO incidents of strange aircraft, similar to the ones witnessed by thousands in Arizona on March 13, 1997, and those in the Hudson River Valley sightings.

Auguste Meesen, professor of physics at the Catholic University of Louvain in Brussels, Belgium, and a scientific consultant of SOBEPS, summarized the cases, "Most witnesses described seeing massive dark, triangular objects with white lights at the corners and a red light in the middle. Many of the objects were said to have hovered, with some of them suddenly accelerating to a very high speed . . . and made no sound."[39]

The Belgian UFO wave yielded volumes of credible cases along with many videos and photographs. The phenomena still remain unexplained even after numerous attempts at analysis, including a thorough computerized study at the Royal Military Academy of Belgium.

Even though nobody found a definitive answer, one of the most poignant statements came from Major General Wilfred De Brouwer, deputy chief of the Royal Belgian Air Force: "Not a single trace of aggressiveness has been signaled; military or civilian air traffic has not been perturbed or threatened. We can therefore advance that the presumed activities do not constitute a concrete menace."[40]

Reminiscent of our own sightings, UFO investigator Timothy Good, author of *Beyond Top Secret*, confirmed that during the Belgian UFO flap, "there were several thousand sightings, some of them at low levels, of triangular shaped objects over Belgium. Not just [by] ordinary civilians, but [by] highly qualified observers, such as military pilots." Good explains that unlike our own air force, the Belgian air force is very open to the phenomena. They even disclosed that they had flown against flying triangles and released cockpit radar film showing an F16 intercepting the triangle. They also demonstrated the terrific acceleration of this triangle from a stationary position. "In many cases they went from zero to say 900 knots/hour in a matter of seconds. They dropped from 10,000 feet to 500 feet in a few seconds. They were performing acrobatics that no human pilot could have withstood the G forces," Good reported.[41]

To add to the mystery, Leo Delcroix, the Belgian minister of defense at the time of the UFO wave, wrote: "Unfortunately, no explanation has been found. The nature and origin of the phenomenon remain unknown. One theory can, however, be definitely dismissed since the Belgian air forces have been positively assured by American authorities that there has never been any sort of American aerial test flight."[42]

Hundreds of eyewitnesses, including airline pilots, have also been watching and videotaping huge triangular V-shaped objects in the skies over England. Again, these enormous craft, with large glowing lights at each corner, travel only a few hundred feet above the ground and make no sound. They can glide slowly, hover motionless, or accelerate to a tremendous speed.

Since the 1950s, the defense ministry policy of Great Britain has been to deny, divert, or discard evidence of all UFO sightings. As revealed in a 1952 document to British Prime Minister Winston Churchill, UFOs were routinely explained away as anything from birds and balloons to psychological delusions and inclement weather. This uniform dismissal of UFOs changed in 1991, when Nick Pope, a new appointee to the government post of UFO Ministry of Defense, took office. Pope told a reporter that when he started the job he didn't know what he was letting himself in for. He was a skeptic with very little knowledge of what it was all about. But then things took an interesting turn.[43]

"I'd been doing the UFO job for a year or so when a case came along which really changed my perception on the whole UFO mystery," said Pope. "It occurred on the 30th and 31st of March 1993 and it was without a doubt one of the most major waves of sightings that Britain had ever seen. At 1:05 A.M., March 31, 1993, radar did not detect a massive triangular UFO in British airspace. There were military and police eyewitnesses and impeccable documentation. There were dozens and dozens of witnesses all over the country. These UFOs seemed to be targeting military bases and were impossible to trace. I certainly believe that some of the reports are extraterrestrial spacecraft. That simply, elsewhere in the universe other intelligences have evolved and are doing after all what we ourselves are beginning to do—to go out into space and to see what's out there."[44]

An Air Argentina pilot agreed. On July 31, 1995, a huge UFO appeared over Argentina. An unexplained power outage ensued. According to Captain Jorge Polanco, his aircraft was in the thick of it. Their worries began when they saw what he described as "the light." They immediately consulted the control towers, but were told there were no other known craft in the area. Captain Polanco recapped what happened next: "The first impression was shock from the people inside the plane. The lights of the object were well defined. There was an orange light on top of it and the solid part of the object was dark. Because of the 'blackout' the lights on the runways at the airport were gone. I noticed that the crew was starting to get nervous."[45]

There was no electricity at the airport, so the plane started to make an escape maneuver. When they went up, the object to their right shot up at a 90-degree angle at incredible speed. When the aircraft banked over a lake toward the airport, they saw the object again waiting for them in their trajectory. The UFO disappeared below them once they finished their turn towards the airport.

Polanco landed his aircraft and filed a report immediately. His initial fear turned to frustration. He never received an explanation from airport investigators or the military. As with other similar events experienced by professionals, however, a riveting aspect was forthcoming. Polanco explained, "What I always ask myself is how they could know the maneuvers and if the object knew what I was thinking? I had the impression that this object could foresee what I was thinking. This is an experience that has changed me for the rest of my life."[46]

I, too, had entered this inquiry as a skeptic, but in all of these cases the logical explanation eluded me. Reasonable proof that this wasn't a military ploy of some kind was becoming increasingly apparent. With each additional sighting report, my doubts that these were true UFOs were slowly evaporating. There was clearly something unknown occurring in the skies worldwide, not just in Arizona. Who was behind these events and why weren't most governments around the world addressing the phenomena?

I found out that some were. Not only was another superpower studying the UFO question, with military assistance, but they had come to some startling conclusions.

Due to the unexplained nature of many UFO sightings, the then Soviet Union had established an official inquiry into the phenomena in the 1980s. Their military and the prestigious Moscow Academy of Sciences joined efforts.

According to astrophysicist Dr. Yuli Platov, "The Soviet Union began this project because of the huge amount of sightings and strange phenomena. Most of the time we were unable to give any convincing explanation. A directive was issued to all units of the Soviet armed forces to officially report what it was that people were seeing and send it to Moscow."[47]

Dr. Felix Y. Zigel, professor of mathematics and astronomy at the Moscow Aviation Institute and known as the "father of Russian Ufology," acknowledged publicly on November 10, 1967, on Moscow Central Television that "observations show that UFOs behave 'sensibly.' In a group formation flight, they maintain a pattern. They are most often spotted over airfields, atomic stations, and other very new engineering installations. A considerable list of these seemingly intelligent actions gives the impression that UFOs are investigating."[48]

General Abexeyev, who was in charge of space communications, was ordered to review all reports on UFO incidents in the secret military region. He declared: "This investigation was carried out by our military forces, with the assistance of the Academy of Sciences, and the secret services. It took place at one of the areas, the military region in the Volga Steppe, where the phenomenon was frequently seen. It was proved conclusively and also reported that in the end, no . . . secret weapon tests were taking place.

"They were not yet that far advanced, which leaves the question as to what all this could be. Despite the fact that there was a great deal of apprehension about using this phrase, the officials who were responsible for this high level commission felt obliged to report that in the end there probably was an alien civilization present. The commission came to this conclusion, even though it was realized, at this time, that it would be a difficult idea to put forward."[49]

Researchers say that the report Abexeyev alluded to was never publicly released. It could be that, like the Americans, the Russians were exploiting the UFO phenomenon to cover up their most closely guarded military secrets. Then again, the general confirmed several times that he supported the opinion that these objects appeared to be of an extraterrestrial origin. He pointed out that in 1988 his country published 500 cases over a 12-month period. These reports supposedly document the best-recorded sightings in recent times.

One of the latest Russian accounts stands out because it was not only similar to our own, but it occurred only one month prior to the Arizona event. On February 19, 1997, a series of mysterious lights appeared in the sky over St. Petersburg in Russia. Multiple witnesses captured video recordings and air traffic controllers documented the event. Captain Pavel Syrchenko, a Russian naval officer and military UFO investigator, officially investigated the St. Petersburg incident. The Captain stated, "It began at 7 P.M. in the evening. At 7:30 they suddenly began to see the UFO at McKlover Airport. Air traffic control[lers] that were monitoring the runways saw it from the control tower where they were working that night."[50]

Controller Victor Laktushin acknowledged: "The 19th of February I witnessed a UFO. That evening I was working in the control tower and the incident took place right in front of my eyes. As I was watching, little bright dots were flying up to this group of four orange-red lights from the left. About four minutes later the lights seemed to fade away. One of the aircraft was out on the runway. I asked them if they could see a UFO and they confirmed that they could."[51]

That night there were at least three separate video recordings of the UFO spotted at different locations in St. Petersburg. These Russian videos, which were aired on TV, look identical to the photos I took of the light formations on January 23, 1997, over Phoenix. Could it have been the same unexplained phenomena? As Russian air traffic controller Victor Laktushin stated, "I can only say it was definitely an unidentified flying object."[52]

Contrary to Russia, Belgium, China, Japan, and other countries that openly investigate UFO sightings, the U.S. government's official stance is that they no longer investigate UFOs. Although 15 million Americans claim they've seen them, the government continues to dismiss them.

It is notable that during so many UFO sightings, including the select few I have shared here, the "unknowns" never seemed to intentionally hurt or threaten anyone. When you consider what could have happened to the nuclear bases in Montana or to the airborne craft in Argentina, the imagination conjures up grave consequences. Those behind the unexplained phenomena were revealing their existence, getting our attention, nothing more. That seems to be what occurred throughout Arizona on March 13.

Is that why on April 1, 1997, the Pentagon reiterated the same pronouncement they had made in 1969? It had been 30 years since their original assessment that there was no threat. If our military was professing this, perhaps during the past 30 years they had confirmed that whatever was visiting us wasn't malevolent. I hoped so. I also hoped that the congressional committee meeting on UFOs held in Washington, D.C., that same month would shed some light on the government's position.

In April 1997, leading UFO experts met with representatives of ten congressman in Washington, D.C., to discuss the situation. I wondered if anything would change. Excerpts from this meeting were later aired on the Sci-Fi Channel program *Sightings*.

One of the most prominent leaders in the cause for disclosure is Steven Greer, M.D., a North Carolina physician and founder of CSETI (Center for the

Study of Extraterrestrial Intelligence). He stated that in response to information provided at the meeting, the government leaders have been "interested, surprised, at times shocked. No one has been laughing."

Confirming the 1997 rash of sightings in the U.S., Major George Filer, a retired USAF aerospace engineer, said, "They're seeing them right now in Arizona. I had people call me the other day from New Hampshire that said they had seen one the size of an ocean liner."

Even Apollo astronaut and moon walker Dr. Edgar Mitchell attested, "I've taken the position that I would like to see government—all governments—release whatever classified information they have. People are entitled to know exactly what the story is about UFOs, extraterrestrials, and so forth."

But that's not so easily accomplished. Barry Blitzer, press secretary for then New Mexico Congressman Steven Schiff, stated, "He's been getting the same runaround as the constituents have. Something is not right when a U.S. congressman can't get access to what should be declassified government information. Notably, there are missing documents. A lot of documents have been destroyed."

Astronomer Jim Mullaney agreed that all was not kosher. He stated emphatically at the 1997 Washington hearings, "It's quite clear that over the past decades there have been [radio] signals received. What disturbs me deeply as an astronomer is that detection of radio signals from other civilizations is nice and clean and safe. That means they're out there. Yet even something like that has not, 'til this day, been officially released."

After enduring three years of official stonewalling, Dr. Greer created the Disclosure Project, a nonprofit research project working to fully disclose the facts about UFOs, ET intelligence, and classified advanced energy and propulsion systems. As the project's director, he took matters into his own hands. On Wednesday, May 9, 2001, 400 military, government, intelligence, corporate, and scientific witnesses came forward with their evidence at the National Press Club in Washington, D.C. The hope was that the weight of this firsthand testimony, along with supporting government documentation and other information, would establish without any doubt the reality of these phenomena. In addition, it would clearly substantiate the need for open congressional hearings, which were last held in the 1960s by the House Science and Astronautics Committee.[53]

But as dramatic and informative as the May 9, 2001, meeting turned out to be—again, nothing transpired after it ended.

Even John Podesta, former chief of staff for President Bill Clinton, made a plea to the Pentagon in December 2002 to release its classified UFO files. Podesta is part of an initiative by the Coalition for Freedom of Information formed in 2002. Among other pertinent data, they want the air force to hand over documents on Project Moon Dust and Operation Blue Fly, secret operations that supposedly existed decades ago to investigate UFOs and retrieve objects of unknown origins. Like many other serious researchers and experiencers, members of the coalition want to legitimize the scientific investigation of unexplained aerial phenomena.

Podesta told CNN, "It is time for the government to declassify records that are more than 25 years old and to provide scientists with data that will assist in determining the real nature of this phenomenon."[54] His call for disclosure was impressive, but to date the results, if any, have not been divulged to the public.

It makes one curious why our country is so closed-mouthed and cynical about the subject while other countries, including Belgium and the former Soviet Union, have been openly embracing UFO phenomena for years.

On July 16, 1999, the French published an important document called the COMETA Report, entitled "UFOs and Defense: What Must We Be Prepared For?"[55] This 90-page report is the result of an in-depth study of UFOs, covering many aspects of the subject, complete with photos and physical evidence. COMETA, the committee that authored the report, was made up of French military, scientists, pilots, researchers, and administrators. Their conclusion: UFOs are real and extraterrestrial origin cannot be ignored.

COMETA also surveyed the organization of UFO research in the U.S., Great Britain, and Russia. They reported that in the U.S., the media and the polls show a marked interest and concern by the public, but the official position, especially of the air force, is still one of denial, more precisely that there is no threat to national security. They also write that in actuality, declassified documents, released under FOIA, show another story—one of surveillance of nuclear installations by UFOs, and the continued study of UFOs by the military and intelligence agencies.

On the other hand, a January 2000 *New York Times* article expounds that China has an elite group of researchers who are studying the unexplained sightings openly.[56] Mexico is another example of a country where the witnesses, scientists, and Ufologists are now afforded access and respect. The Japanese government has even financially supported the building of a UFO museum. They are trying to educate people regarding UFOs, so, as they so eloquently avowed, "We can work towards universal peace." The saucer-shaped UFO Museum in Hakui, Japan, houses one of the most extensive collections of both data and artifacts in the world.

Perhaps the West should follow Japan's lead. The problem is getting our country to own up to the truth and, most of all, to reveal what it knows. Perhaps then we can begin to accept reality, and honestly work towards universal harmony. (See appendix A for more quotes from prominent people in the 1940s to the present concerning the reality of UFOs.)

11. Things Are Looking Up

I couldn't believe what I was finding now that I was seriously looking. What's more, I couldn't believe I was researching this topic. I was used to compiling and disseminating information on vital health issues. Never in my wildest dreams did I foresee delving into this tenuous realm of the unknown, and even more unlikely, sharing it with others.

Before the Phoenix Lights appeared, I was content to live my quiet, uncomplicated life in ignorance of what might lie beyond. I had been so busy doing my part as a devoted wife, mother, physician, and educator that I had no idea what was going on around me, or above my head. But now that I had discovered this new world, I couldn't stop finding out more. The more credible information I found, the more I searched; the more I searched, the more I found. My thirst for the truth was so unquenchable that I had pushed my professional life aside for close to three years in pursuit of it.

In 1999, I got word that *Unsolved Mysteries* was airing a special on the Phoenix Lights. It was reaffirming that the uncanny Arizona event was still alive and kicking. Like myself, the producers were more dazzled by the quality of the witness accounts than the Air National Guard's questionable explanation for the phenomena.

Unsolved Mysteries host Robert Stack began the program by stating that for

UFO buffs it's always the same story: an unprecedented event, followed by an official brush-off. He told the viewers that it happened again in Phoenix, Arizona, where a series of spectacular sightings had the entire state buzzing about UFOs and visitors from beyond. Stack reiterated that even though the military said the strange lights were just flares, the witnesses said otherwise. "There was one little problem with the military explanation. They said they only dropped flares between 9 and 10 P.M., but the most impressive sightings occurred earlier, between 8 and 9 P.M." The highly credible eyewitness accounts seemed to indicate that there was something other than flares in the Arizona skies, Stack said.

Among numerous testimonials, a commercial pilot proclaimed, "I've been flying for 29 years now and I have not been able to figure out what I was seeing." Stack explained that between 8 and 9 P.M. the Phoenix Lights traveled over three hundred miles and were seen by hundreds of witnesses. Then at 10 P.M. Michael Krzyston shot the videotape that would provide the basis for the official explanation.

As they showed footage of military flares drifting in a disorderly pattern, you could hear Stack's voice saying, "The military says that flares like these dropped at night would look like this. Judge for yourself." They displayed Mike Krzyston's video of a slightly curved, but perfectly spaced hovering array. You immediately noticed the difference. It was dramatic. The flares obviously could not stay in an equidistant line—but Mike's did.

The pilot asserted, "I'm certain that the lights that I saw were not aerial flares as used by the military. I've seen them from the ground. I've seen them from the air. And these weren't flares."

Stack assured the viewers, "For the military the case is closed. But for hundreds of eyewitnesses the question remains, 'Did the Phoenix Lights come from somewhere beyond the stars?'"

Then Mike Krzyston observed, "We've got to learn to accept certain things in life. We've been sending radio signals out to space for over 50 years now to locate intelligent life. So why would it be hard for us to think that at some point in time, somebody finally answered the call?"

After pressuring the Arizona National Guard for a reenactment for almost three years, the military must have felt the need to answer ours. One week before the third anniversary of the statewide event, the Air National Guard announced publicly that three Snowbird units—the New York, California, and Michigan ANGs—were going to be deploying a barrage of flares for the next two weeks. The headlines on the front page of the *Arizona Republic* on Tuesday, March 7, 2000, read: "Sky Lights to Be Flares, Not UFOs, Guard Says. It's . . . the Return of the Fabled 'Phoenix Lights'!"

Whether they were using this ploy as damage control or to confuse the issue didn't matter. What did matter was that by the second night, the military's attempt to persuade others that the Phoenix Lights events were their own flares backfired. When they tried to form a triangle with the flares, not only was it upside down, but it looked nothing like what we had witnessed or photographed previously.

In addition, the characteristics of their flares were significantly different from the true unknowns. They were not huge amber orbs, but much smaller. They looked white with multicolored sparks, flickered frantically, emanated visible smoke trails, moved extensively, and did not stay in formation. After three years of waiting for a reenactment of the unsolved mystery, we were now convinced that what we had seen and documented in the skies over Arizona was not military, but UFOs.

For the record, after the third day of deployment—and the onslaught of mockery by the press—the Guard units canceled the rest of their scheduled runs. We now had the irrefutable proof that we needed. The phenomena called the Phoenix Lights were not flares, and to this day, they remain unexplained.

After the local and national media flurry concerning the strong suspicion that the Phoenix Lights probably weren't military flares had died down a bit, I persuaded Jim Dilettoso to share his thoughts about the possibilities of unearthly explanations.

Jim had been studying and authenticating these phenomena for more than 20 years, and he had accumulated an impressive database of hundreds of pictures from many countries. I was thrilled when he finally sat down with me for an in-depth interview, even though I was aware he was imparting his speculations. I asked him why he got involved in the subject.

"My job is that I defend the people's right to say that they saw something. Because if I don't defend them, they can't. And then other people will call them nuts and loony and crazy. They have no recourse. So it's not only about testing pictures. That's just the medium that I use. My job is to protect people's rights to say that they have seen something very unusual and not be ridiculed."

"You have to respect that," I said. "But tell me, is whatever it is occurring more now, or are we just starting to recognize and acknowledge it?"

"It's been going on for many years, and now more people are paying attention. They also have the tools to capture what they see. A third [factor], and in a different category, is that there are more unusual sightings. I think it's happening more often, larger and bigger, around the world."

"Do you think these things might be extraterrestrial in origin?"

"I think that more and more ETs are now coming to see how Earth behaves in its final phase of spiritual growth. I think that's why they come here. I think that the legends of God, free will, and spiritual development are true and that we are a very advanced species. We have tremendous potential, more unique than any other species. The fact that many people have picked greed and violence instead of development has freaked out the ETs. They're coming here to say, 'Man, look at this. They have all these available resources and tools and look what they do.' I think they're going to let us proceed to our own destiny. That's why I think they contact people and then erase their memories, so that there is no interference with free will and destiny."

Jim's words were reminiscent of statements I had already catalogued from others, including Astronaut Al Worden and scholar Zacharia Sitchin.

"Are you saying that we're more advanced than they are?"

"I think we are. As bioforms with spirits and potentials, we may be the most genetically advanced and spiritually advanced in potential of any other species. You look at the descriptions of many other aliens and they look atrophied. I think that that's the way they developed, and they reached their maximum. We're probably derivatives of the humanoid type or they preceded us. I'm not really sure. I'm still trying to figure it out. I don't think humanoid ETs are more advanced in spiritual potential or spiritual achievement. Could we say that Albert Einstein, with his technical wisdom, was more advanced than a pigmy shaman priest? Which one is more advanced, really?"

I pondered Jim's comments. "I guess for most people it would take experiencing a true unexplained happening firsthand before they'd believe that it is feasible. Short of that, how do you even attempt to raise public awareness and global consciousness to begin to accept the possibilities?"

He cracked a smile. "We've got to do it with music—a rock and roll concert!"

"Seriously, Jim, what is your take on the Phoenix Lights? What do you think is going to happen?"

"I think within two or three years the spiritual growth of the people who have been affected by it will begin to demonstrate itself. We're going to have national, international leaders in the field who will come out of the trenches of Phoenix. I think the Phoenix Lights had nothing to do with global awareness of UFOs. I think the balls of light affected the consciousness of people here at a deep level and that those people, regardless of whether the Phoenix Lights are remembered or not, will take their position in their activities."

Our conversation reminded me of statements by witnesses whose consciousness had been deeply touched by the events. It seemed that there was an undeniable transformation, a spiritual awakening that took place in many of the witnesses. I wanted to delve more into this intriguing and perhaps integral aspect of the unexplained phenomena.

Two communications that I had received from witnesses to the giant floating triangle came to mind. The first is a detailed personal account that illustrates the point. It was sent on October 26, 1997, to Village Labs and Bill Hamilton by a Tucson medical doctor trained in chemistry and physics. His family was traveling up I-10 towards Phoenix for the state swimming championships at ASU when they experienced the March 13 sighting.

I have been a psychiatrist for 22 years, board certified since 1984, and got my private pilot's license in 1985. I moved to Tucson from New Jersey in September 1991. I have never observed anything in the sky that I could not explain until the night of March 13, 1997. We saw a row of approximately seven bright reddish-orange glowing orbs to the northwest at about 8:20–8:25 p.m., just east of South Mountain and just west of Camelback Mountain. Then they moved over the west edge of the Gila Indian Reservation moving slowly south along I-10. In an instant, the lights were directly overhead. While our car was traveling at about 65 mph they seemed to hold directly overhead for about five to ten minutes, still holding formation at about 1,500 feet. With the moon roof open, we could hear no aircraft engine noise whatsoever. It was a diamond within a diamond pattern something like this:

▲

southeast

▲

✶ - - - - - - - - - lead light

✶   ✶

✶

✶   ✶

●- - - - - - - - trailing light

I was impressed by the perfect symmetry of these lights. With a good deal of time to observe closely, these lights did not seem to be connected to anything. It was as though the light or glow itself was the object. I could see stars immediately around a light and within the formation itself. From lead to trailer, the formation was about 300 yards across. There was no evidence of a flame, ionization, or smoke trail. The light itself did not seem to be illuminating either an attached physical craft or object or the ground. The lights formed no beams as a searchlight might. Altitude did not seem to change at all, and the formation slowly moved to the southeast toward Casa Grande. There were no obvious aircraft nearby . . .

The doctor, who asked to remain anonymous, continued his account in writing by stating that after the lights passed out of sight, no one in the car spoke, nor did they mention it to anyone during the swim meet. The memory of the event just vanished, until several months later when he happened to be channel-surfing on TV and came across *Strange Universe* reporting on the Phoenix Lights. The doctor's written communication continued: "It actually took three months for our memories to come back. It really felt more like a sudden flood of recalled events, rather than the slow return of memory." His next description echoed numerous witness testimonies:

During the intervening three months and since, our lives changed in some very interesting ways, all for the positive! Clarity of thought, concentration, and productivity increased. Moods of all involved improved significantly. We have been aware of these changes only in retrospect. There has been a dramatic increase in a sense of love and connectedness between my wife, myself, and our daughter that remains difficult to explain.

I asked my wife about the lights months later and wondered why we had not stopped to watch. She stated very matter-of-factly, "We were told not to worry, that this was not for us to be concerned about, that we were to keep driving." She said that there was not a voice that said this, but that it was clearly communicated to her somehow. On separate occasions, I asked my daughter and then her friend the same question. They both gave the same answer without having talked about it with each other beforehand. I experienced the same communication. We no longer talk to each other about the experience. We do, however, continue to be awed by it and apparently continue to have benefited from it. I have been forever changed by it.

My next step was to contact the doctor. He was eager to share the details of how the sighting had affected him and his family.

"There was definitely a profound aftereffect. Since the mass sighting our whole family is calmer, optimistic, excited with what we know is coming, a huge change of some type," he said. "Even in my practice I look at things more spiritually now. It's not just diagnosing and giving medicine, it's more of 'what are you doing this for, where are you going?' What's the spiritual side for the patient? But there is humility enough to say, 'at your own pace.'"

The recollections of the second witness to the giant floating triangle, Shala, who shared the experience with her husband, Max, that night, were strikingly similar to my own. A former skeptic and a MENSA member, she felt certain that behind the lights there was a presence observing them, just as surely as she and her husband were scrutinizing the phenomenon.

Her words touched off the memory of my own intense feelings in 1995 of an intelligent presence when I stepped out onto the balcony to get a shot of the two orbs near our house. I sensed I was being watched for weeks after the oval objects had disappeared. I replied to Shala, "Fascinating. Has this affected you since?"

"Of course it has affected me. It kind of changes your whole outlook on everything. For example, politics. Because it seems less important when you realize that there are other *beings* out there visiting us, with I'm sure military hardware and all kinds of things. It's ridiculous to get into squabbles in Northern Ireland, Bangladesh, the Middle East. You know what I'm saying? When this was my life as a war correspondent, to cover all these areas, I felt it was important. It's taken on a whole different type of importance to me now."

What she shared next was in keeping with what most experiencers, including myself, of unexplained phenomena had realized. "Well, the March 13 sighting totally reinforces what I'm saying. We should be citizens of the world. We shouldn't have boundaries. We need to be here to protect the planet. Now that I saw what I saw it makes me feel much more like that. That we are the inheritors of this planet because we were given intelligent life."

I had to interject that it seemed that I too had been enlightened as to how much we have right here on Earth, that we must preserve our incredible resources, stop abusing and destroying, and appreciate the splendor of life and living. After the statewide sightings, I found myself more focused on the importance of conservation and global awareness. It seemed that many Phoenix Lights witnesses agreed that our sighting caused an "awakening" for all who truly experienced it and a powerful connectedness to the rest of the universe.

In fact, among other witnesses, Shala and the doctor also reminisced about their own past near-death experiences. They admitted openly that distant thoughts and feelings, long buried, were rising to the surface since the Phoenix Lights sighting.

In the midst of considering the spiritual "light beings" described in Native American folklore, postulations of numinous biblical close encounters, and the curious transformation taking place within the minds and behaviors of the witnesses, I wondered if there might be a possible connection between all unexplained phenomena. Was there a link between the UFO experience, near-death, out-of-body, and other mystical light experiences? The consistent and positive aftereffect attested to by the experiencers was too essential to disregard. I began calling each experience an *Unexplained Phenomenon*—or *UP*—as in "up" in the sky, or even more aptly as in "things are looking *UP*."

12. Consider the Source—The NDE/UFO Connection

While reflecting on the reawakening of past near-death experiences in the other Phoenix Lights witnesses, I began remembering, visualizing a powerful experience I had had as a child, an incident that changed my life. Could there be a connection to what happened to me then and what was occurring now?

Let us return to January 1997, weeks before the mass sighting, and months before I began my intricate inquiry into the source and meaning of the Phoenix Lights. Almost two years had passed since that fateful February evening when my husband and I had witnessed the amber orb pyramid just yards from our bedroom window. It could not be explained, nor could it be denied—I had the evidence.

On January 9,1997, I checked out a dozen books from the library to explore the possibilities. I knew little about the topics, but grabbed books at random on near-death experiences, holistic medicine, Edgar Cayce, and other intriguing subjects that I never had the desire, much less the time, to research. After a couple of weeks flew by, I finally picked up the first book, *Closer to the Light* by Melvin Morse, M.D. It is an acclaimed scientific study of children who have experienced near-death. I had no idea where this innocent choice would lead me.

As I began reading the true-life accounts, as told by children who had clinically died and were brought back to life, a chilling sensation ran through my body. When one child described coming to some sort of barrier after he drowned, I thought, *That happened to me.* Reading further about a child having a short "life review," another child hovering over his body, and yet others seeing *beings of light,* I had a realization. This had happened to me. It was as if a light bulb turned on in my brain, illuminating a cascade of memories. Recall of an experience that had been tucked away for so many years flooded my thoughts. Vivid images and feelings saturated me. I picked up book after book on near-death experience to validate it. As I did, I became assured that what had occurred over 40 years before was just that, a near-death experience (NDE). (See appendix C for a typical near-death experience as described by Raymond Moody, M.D., the father of NDE research.)

Due to advancements in life-saving technologies, millions of the near-dead around the world have been brought back to life and have been willing to share their psychic experiences, something that was unheard of a few decades ago and certainly not prevalent during my medical training in the early 1970s. Most people who have had an NDE will tell you that when they were clinically dead they suddenly separated from their earthly body, hovered above it, looking down at whatever was going on at the time, and then traveled through a tunnel towards a bright light. Frequently they will see loving spirits, even departed relatives, on the "other side" of this life. Many hadn't realized they had experienced near-death until recently, when they happened upon an explanation of it on TV or in literature. My case is a perfect example.

I consider myself spiritual, with a strong belief that love combined with high moral values and a positive attitude are imperative for optimal growth and maturation. I am proud of my heritage and its spiritual and moral foundations. Throughout my childhood, I was blessed with a strong, loving family, based on these values. But the fact is that organized religion didn't enter into our lives. Therefore, what I will describe next wasn't something that I had heard about, read, or would have ever dreamed up.

The year was 1956. I was eight years old. I needed major dental work and was instructed that I would be sedated. I don't recall the precise anesthetic used, but inhaled sedation could have been precarious, even deadly for a child, as we learned from a *60 Minutes* report that aired in January 1999. I remember that a mask was put over my face. Whether it was ether or some other anesthetic infiltrating my body I can't say for sure. But I do know one thing. The following experience affected the rest of my life.

While under anesthesia, I fell into a deep sleep. At least my body was asleep.

The Phoenix Lights

My mind was alive. I began to experience myself being slowly pushed through what seemed to be a revolving door. There was a strange harp sound, like a haunting musical tune repeating over and over again; I felt myself slowly turning around and around. I could move no farther. I hit a barrier, again and again. In horror, I realized that if I got past the barrier, I would be dead. I then began a life review.

The life review usually consists of a detailed reliving of one's life, every second of it. The intriguing part is that not only do you feel what you felt at the moment, you also feel how the other person in the situation felt as well. For example, if you insulted someone, you feel how the other individual felt—hurt, angry, saddened—as a repercussion of your actions. The person you offended might then go home and start an argument with their spouse or hit their child out of frustration—all because of your thoughtless or inappropriate behavior. You see and feel it all in your life review.

On the other hand, if you were gracious and caring to another person, you would be filled with the wonderful sensation of love and appreciation that they felt because of your kindness—even from small gestures of kindness. In other words, when you die, you get to relive every moment of your life and the consequences of your behavior—how your actions affected everyone around you. What goes around does come around, after all.

The deceased, in this case, ultimately returns to Earth, or sometimes has the choice of whether or not to do so. The next thing they know they are back in their body. It is an interesting phenomenon, particularly since statistics show that many people who have experienced near-death come back transformed. They have not only glimpsed the "other side," they also now know what is most important in life.

My own short life review was intense, focusing on my close relationship with my mom. My mom could have been and done anything she wanted, but she chose to direct her energies towards the good of the family. And now here I was, her only daughter, going to die and leave her. At that moment I realized that if I should die, my mother would be devastated. I was terrified. How could this be? I couldn't die—for her, I couldn't.

Next I was shooting up above the Earth and then hovering peacefully, floating among the billowy clouds. I noticed three giant robed *beings of light* over me. They seemed immense, but I wasn't frightened. I felt safe, even curious about my new situation. I tried to see their faces, but the large luminous white hoods that covered their massive heads hid their features. I recall this event so vividly. How could I ever have forgotten being drenched in the incredible shower of love that they shared with me? What's more, they seemed to know me.

138

They knew who I *was,* deep inside. I was in awe of these strange figures, white glowing forms without visible faces, and feeling the beautiful energy radiating from them. I wondered who were these brilliant beings? Why were they so huge? For what purpose were they looking down at me, and at our planet?

As I turned my head to gaze at Earth, I saw people going about their daily activities. It was as if my eyes were super-powered telescopes that could peer into the lives of everyone down there. I saw the milkman delivering milk, door to door, petting a dog, smiling at the neighborhood paperboy. Children were skipping and laughing on their way to school, hopping haphazardly over chalked hopscotch drawings on the pavement. The storekeeper was opening his shop, sweeping the stoop, putting out his sign to begin his workday.

A realization came over me. I could sense what everyone was going to do next. In fact, I *knew* what was going to happen next. Wait a minute—if I knew what was coming next, then these benevolent light beings must also know.

As I gazed down towards Earth, I realized that everything everyone was doing seemed planned, predestined. My astonished mind searched for logical answers. Would that mean that everything we do as humans is already designed for each one of us, already written? Does that mean that we have no control over what happens to us, the events that come before us, the people we meet, the adversity or good fortune that enters into our Earth existence, the twists and turns of daily living?

As this absurd revelation was sinking in, my mind was flooded by another thought. I realized that each individual might not have control over what lies ahead, but as humans we do have control over how we interpret these events, how we treat people and other living things we come into contact with, and how we deal with the circumstances that shape our lives.

If this were true, would it mean that our own actions and reactions, the results of the multitude of lessons we learn throughout our lifetime, will lead us to who we will become in our future? What we will become as the human race on Earth? Is that what *they* are watching?

I had led a sheltered life up to this point, so this was a profound concept for a naive child. I was baffled. Apparently these *beings* were observing what we do with certain situations: if we grow strength from within or buckle in a crisis; if we learn from our mistakes; if we take advantage of the opportunities presented to us, or let them pass us by; if we appreciate our every breath; if we are kind and loving to other living things or selfish and self-serving; if we are true to ourselves.

I was there, in this *other place.* Perhaps it was another dimension, another realm of reality. Somehow I had traveled to a time and space outside our own to realize these wondrous *beings* exist. They were with me looking down on Earth, looking down on us. Did that mean that our whole existence was being observed? I asked myself, *If these mysterious, loving beings are watching over us and noting our reactions to stimuli, is humankind but an experiment?*

As I contemplated this poignant question, a majestic male voice uttered, "It's not your time. You must go back. There's a reason you must go back."

Suddenly I was back in my body, coming out of the anesthetic, sensing that something had happened during the procedure, and it wasn't just the dental surgery. I remember hearing, "We're not going to let you go yet," as my eyes began to focus. I turned my head to view the oral surgeon and his nurse moving about with instruments. There was chaos in the small office area. The nurse whispered to the surgeon, "Thank God, she's okay! That was a close call."

As I started to come to they asked me over and over if I was all right, reassuring me that everything had turned out fine. They told me that I had to stay in the dental chair in the prone position for a long while. They never revealed that anything out of the ordinary had happened during the procedure. They never shared that something had gone wrong. But to this day, I know that it did.

For weeks after this curious journey, I didn't speak to anyone about it. Not even to my parents. What could I have said? How could I have explained to someone else what was so incongruous, yet so real to me? How could I verbalize any of it? For many days, alone in my thoughts, I pondered why I was allowed a glimpse of this truth. For months, even years, I wondered what it all meant and whether or not to share it. I didn't. I kept this wondrous experience private, safe within my own thoughts.

Where had I been? What had I seen? And why? For a long time afterwards, I searched the sky for my three giant friends above the clouds. But alas, they were nowhere to be found. With only my thoughts to trust, I relived the strange events. Eventually, the actual memory of my experience became buried in my subconscious, but the *feelings* remained.

I had gained knowledge beyond my tender years and took the insights seriously. I began to evaluate every event that came before me, trusting that it was there for a reason, trying to take advantage of each opportunity that came my way. I began to appreciate everything—cloud formations, sunsets, the uniqueness and beauty of every living creature on Earth, from the tiniest flower to the tallest tree, colors, sounds, tastes, touch—with a new consciousness and from a new perspective.

Even my voice became a tool for my newfound zest for living. I spent hour after hour singing, developing a beautiful gift that I felt had been given to me. It was up to me to cultivate and share it. I did so, passionately using my voice so that others could treasure the delight of song, believing (as I do to this day) that music is food for the soul.

After a time I no longer had the sinking feeling of futility, thinking that we have no control over what happens to us, but rather a feeling of joy. Through this near-death experience, I became aware that I did have control over my destiny. I started to look at my life in a more astute and positive way, realizing the potential in everything around me. Even if something unpleasant happened, I always believed that something good would come from it, that I would learn from it and grow stronger. It certainly made it easier to cope with adversities that came my way.

I also believed that everything happened for a reason, that there was no coincidence. Or perhaps a coincidence was an anonymous gift from God. With that, I searched for the good in each situation, in each person I met along the way, to see how I could reap the most from that situation. I worked hard and took advantage of things that others might not have dared to accomplish, that others might not have seen right before them. Inevitably, something positive did come from such things. And so, I came to trust in my new understanding and in my freedom of choice. Even if I didn't have control over what came before me, I did have control over what I did with it, over my awareness, attitude, and appreciation.

I knew as well that there must have been a reason for this insight. There must have been a reason I came back to my body, perhaps one that would take many years to realize. I began to look at my existence in a new light. I engulfed myself in its guidance, trusting it from childhood onward.

Then on January 22, 1997, the floodgates of my buried near-death memory opened wide. The mystical connection was revived. A childhood experience that had been hidden in my psyche for over forty years was reawakened, and now I was *assured* that it was real. Near-death experience had been substantiated by medical science.

Was it just a coincidence that on the day I realized the truth of what had happened to me so long ago, three huge amber lights appeared in the skies above Phoenix? As I watched the spinning orbs of gold, it was as if something was confirming my revelation. Might there be a link between the glowing giants in my near-death experience, the three hovering orbs outside our bedroom window on my birthday eve in 1995, and the three spheres of amber suspended in the distance? I wondered if these balls of energy were connected to my past. Were they connected to my future?

Among the many who have studied these phenomena, acclaimed author and UFO experiencer Whitley Strieber would say that they are intimately connected. As he put it, "Hundreds of witnesses report they see balls of light that seem to have a conscious direction. In many cultures, they are associated with the soul of the dead. Something about the close encounter experience is deeply involved with death and the dead."[1]

Were these glowing orbs awakening all who noticed them, who truly experienced them, to something important? As I delved further into this topic, I found an abundance of scientific studies relating to these anomalous experiences. Respected scholars including Dr. Kenneth Ring of the University of Connecticut, Dr. Bruce Greyson of the University of Virginia, Dr. Stuart Tremlow of the University of Kansas, Dr. Raymond A. Moody Jr. of the University of Nevada, Dr. Michael Grosso, Dr. Gary E. Schwartz of the University of Arizona, and Dr. John Mack of Harvard University had already substantiated that there was a strong correlation between all unexplained phenomena.

For the most part, an UP takes the experiencer to another world, which is attended by beings bathed in glorious light and ruled by a Supreme Presence, who guides the person through a profound learning process before sending them back to live longer on Earth. Upon return, the individual is never the same. Dr. Raymond Moody contends, "They are transformed. They embrace life to its fullest and express the belief that love and knowledge are the most important of all things, because they are the only things you can take with you."[2]

When the experiencers return they not only have a thirst for knowledge, they feel an urgency to change themselves and the world for the better. Moody asserts, "Sense of urgency is a phrase that comes up again and again . . . frequently, they are referring to the shortness and fragility of their own lives. But they are often expressing a sense of urgency about a world in which vast destructive powers are in the hands of mere humans."[3]

I knew firsthand what that "sense of urgency" felt like. I also felt the need to learn whether researchers had come to the same conclusions regarding UFO phenomena. One researcher had. According to author Raymond Fowler, Betty Andreasson Luca is one of the most credible UFO contact experiencers ever documented. What I found intriguing about her case was that the entities Betty met called themselves The Watchers, caretakers of Earth's life forms, therefore equating themselves with The Watchers of antiquity who claimed to fulfill this function.

In the 1970s, Betty talked about meeting tall beings who look like us and call themselves our Elders. Where do they come from? Most scientists believe it most unlikely that humanoid creatures like us could evolve elsewhere. But the human appearance of these entities indicates some genetic or other kind of relation to humankind. Interestingly, patients who experience past life regressions also talk of these Elders as teachers in between life cycles (see, for example, *Many Minds,*

Many Masters, by Brian Weiss, M.D.). Regarding his near-death experiences, Dannion Brinkley (in *Saved by the Light*) speaks of Elders relaying future events years before they actually occurred. Could these Elders be part of our genetic past, part of our spirit world? Could there be a connection between these supposedly different worlds of unearthly entities and ours?

In *The Watchers,* Fowler poses a number of questions: If these Elders were among the types of entities who influenced Sumer and initiated civilization on Earth, did they alter primate life forms to create Homo sapiens? If they, too, were a form of Homo sapiens, how could we explain their paraphysical nature?

Many people worldwide—from different cultures, religions, backgrounds, and beliefs—have experienced these phenomena. One thing is strikingly consistent: The experiencers have similar stories to tell, receive similar messages. How is that possible, unless the experiences are real and connected?

Dr. Jacques Vallee, astrophysicist and UFO researcher, postulates a convincing argument that humans have been interacting with nonhuman entities since the beginning of human history. Elves, fairies, pixies, trolls, and the like have been an integral component of folklore and folk history worldwide. Our human myths are overflowing with tales of peculiar, yet loving, creatures interacting with us.

Is it possible that UFO and near-death experiences are genuine? I knew I had experienced near-death. No one could convince me otherwise. But contact with alien creatures? That seemed too incongruous. I had always stayed away from anything relating to the UFO "communication" scenario—movies, films, books. Yet now I had to face this topic head on.

How could any study of the UFO experience be complete without a thorough look into the realm of extraterrestrial contact? We study other life forms, and if we want to examine an endangered wildcat, for instance, we sedate it from afar with an anesthetic, transport it to a sterile lab, study it, probe it, maybe even tag it, and then put it back in its natural environment. When it comes to, it will most likely remember little or nothing of what took place.

Is it possible that unearthly intelligent entities can extract us from a bed, car, or field with a beam of light, as so many experiencers have been reporting? Then study us and place us back exactly as they found us, leaving us with little or no memory of what occurred? I reminded myself that for the preservation of many nearly extinct species of wildlife we do just that on a large scale. I also assured myself that our intentions in so doing are honorable. If this is happening to us, the reason for it might be something we don't understand or want to deal with. If so, perhaps we should.

David Jacobs, Ph.D., UFO researcher and history professor at my Alma

Mater, Temple University, told me in a telephone conversation in 1999 that in polls at the time, one in 50 Americans exhibit at least four out of five common symptoms of UFO contacts! In other words, as many as 2 percent of our adult population might be experiencing something otherworldly. Dr. Jacobs pointed out that after examining the situation for the past 20 years, he believes that over eight million people have been contacted by UFO intelligences, many without their cognitive knowledge.

Certainly, skeptics balk at the claims of alien contacts, calling them dreams, hallucinations, a side effect of sleep paralysis, or fabrications of imaginations urged on by therapists during hypnotic regression. (You can find a comparison of alien contact and sleep paralysis data in appendix C.)

I discovered that Pulitzer Prize-winner and Harvard psychiatrist John Mack, M.D., was actually studying hundreds of alien contact cases at Harvard University's Peer Institute. Here was a renowned intellectual, a respected professor at one of the most prestigious institutions in the world, acknowledging the validity of these strange exchanges. He admits that when he began this work, the reports shattered all of his expectations and continue to challenge his sense of reality.[4] But he stresses that the experiencers are not at all motivated to believe in the "truth" of their experiences. In fact, they would like to find out that it was just a dream or psychological in nature.

In Mack's numerous studies there are apparently no recorded alien contact cases that proved to be caused by some other type of experience or trauma, even though investigators try to find other explanations for the encounters. There is substantial evidence that something extraordinary happened to the experiencers. Key factors supporting this conclusion include: missing time, physical findings, descriptions of UFOs by the experiencers (sometimes reported by others in the community as well), vivid descriptions of the beings themselves (even by small children), and psychospiritual aftereffects concerning Earth's ecology.

"I have never encountered anything similar to this in patients I have known to be traumatized by humans, or in psychotic patients suffering from delusions," Dr. Mack attests.[5] "It's a complicated, consistent narrative that operates clinically altogether like a real experience."[6]

Numerous other researchers are also convinced that such incidents are not imagined. The realization that the "alien" experience is genuine may deliver a shock to our consciousness, to our identity even as a species on this planet, as transforming as when humankind recognized that the Earth was not flat. This would also have profound implications for our scientific worldview.

There is nothing in our reality that can relate to it or prepare us for it. Society has conditioned our psyche as to what is acceptable. As much as we may try to deny the fact, we are still subject to a narrow set of reality rules. It gives us comfort to expect the sun to rise in the morning and to set every evening. But throughout human history, and particularly in the past 50 years, we have also been programmed not to acknowledge certain things outside the realm of scientific verification.

Theologians, philosophers, psychologists, scientists, and now even the media have created models of reality that are accepted by the masses as truth. We are convinced by science and those in power of what can be and what cannot be, based upon the rigid reality model of the times. Reports of UFOs, OBEs (out-of-body experiences), NDEs, ghosts, and a host of other "paranormal phenomena" do not fit these preconceived belief systems. So, for many years, reports of unexplained experiences have not been perceived or accepted as being part of our reality. They have been mocked or labeled as "crazy." If we can't measure it and reproduce it, it must not be so.

But according to many dedicated researchers, including Dr. Mack, we are closer to a new reality, a major epochal shift connecting us to something beyond ourselves.

As I continued my journey of discovery, I was thrilled to find that there was scientific substantiation for a correlation between unexplained phenomena and the type of people experiencing them. Dr. Kenneth Ring and Raymond Fowler came to the same conclusion. Through analytical and scientific studies, Dr. Ring was convinced that there are certain types of people who are more sensitive to experiences of this nature, more open to them to begin with, who would also remember and/or report these experiences more readily than others.

According to civilian and military statistics collected by Dr. Ring, only ten percent of people who sight an unusual object in the sky actually report it. Just think how many more people probably witnessed the Phoenix Lights who didn't acknowledge it. His studies also show that only one of three persons who survive a near-death incident will later describe having an NDE of some kind. It took me over 40 years to realize mine. With over 13 million adults in the U.S. verified by a Gallup Poll as having experienced an NDE, one can only imagine how many more have entered this other realm of time and space—and don't remember it.

As my worldview was changing, I felt it imperative to investigate the possibility of this change occurring in other experiencers. Would this inquiry lead me to a correlation between all unexplained phenomena? It did. One consistent link, which stood out in the research, was that a special "light" seemed to be present during most unexplained experiences, whether it was a near-death, out-of-body, or UFO experience. This *mystical light* seems always to have sparked a positive transformation, a spiritual rebirth or awakening. The experience was indeed an UP. (I compiled many examples of this light occurring during both NDEs and UFO contact; see appendix C.)

Researchers have confirmed that UFO contactees talk about the same type of entities as near-death experiencers do—human-shaped forms composed of light. I started collecting reams of information on all unexplained phenomena, particularly those referencing lights or light beings. What struck me was not only the persistent scenario of light in almost every UP, but the similarity of the experiences themselves—whether an OBE, NDE, or UFO encounter. It became clear that there was something connecting these phenomena.

Dr. Ring asks, "Could it be that the world of the NDE and that of the UFO experience, for all their differences, are not, after all, universes apart, but a part of the same universe?" Ring found that some experiencers in describing what purported to be an NDE began talking about UFOs and aliens in the same context. "Furthermore, there turns out to be a small but respectable number of persons in my sample who report having had (though, to be sure at different times) both an NDE and one or more UFO encounters."[7]

Fowler goes one step farther in stating, "These reports, coupled with Dr. Ring's findings of a UFO/NDE connection, seem to be telling us that whoever controls the UFO phenomenon is intimately connected with the afterlife of human beings."[8]

Thanatologist Dr. John B. Alexander, an expert on the study of death, echoes these findings in a paper he delivered during the UFO Abduction Study Conference held at the Massachusetts Institute of Technology in 1994. He maintained that there is indeed a striking commonality between NDEs and UFO encounters.[9]

Leading UFO researcher Jenny Randles acknowledges that British investigators have also noted this in some cases as early as 1982. She volunteered an example that, like my own, involved a near-death experience caused by a reaction to a drug administered by a dentist. The patient underwent the typical OBE and tunnel experience, but instead of entering a world of light, so typical in NDEs, he entered a UFO! Alien entities warned that the Earth was in trouble and that he had to return (another recurring theme of both NDEs and UFO experiences). He was then returned to the dentist's office, where he saw the dentist attempting to revive him.

Some UFO experiencers also report being contacted during an out-of-body experience. They refer to the incident as nonphysical, but genuine. They are certain that they were transported into another dimension that felt and looked real (see appendix C for the definition of OBE). Fowler and other UFO researchers make the case for UFO experiencers also approaching the light and even going through a tunnel to do so, oftentimes meeting a tall robed figure. Many NDErs experienced a similar situation. Some of their descriptions were similar to my NDE:

- We came to a place where there were many figures, some of them dressed in robes.[10]

- He was about seven feet tall and wore a long white gown.[11]

- It was all bright then . . . He was tall . . . He had a white robe on.[12]

- The light came closer at a high rate of speed. It then took on the shape of a man in a white robe.[13]

A number of NDErs interpret these beings as God, angels, or other religious figures. Even more prevalent are the thousands of reported NDErs who encountered entities who were deceased family or friends, also wearing white robes.

Is this possible? Are our deceased ancestors and loved ones actually in another dimension, another time and space, waiting for our arrival? Are we to believe that we could meet up with dead relatives and other kindly beings during these experiences and then again after we die? There are a multitude of examples from the writings of Drs. Morse, Ring, Sabom, and other NDE authorities that substantiate that we do.

- I see this guy with a long robe . . . I do not know him, but have the feeling he is one of my grandfathers. They have both died before I was born.[14]

- Instantly from the other side appeared my Uncle Carl, who had died many years earlier.[15]

- I remember seeing the *light* . . . Suddenly hands were reaching to me, and I saw my grandparents. The hands and my grandparents weren't just part of the *light,* they were the *light.* My grandparents had been dead for several years.[16]

- There were all my relatives, my grandmother, my grandfather, my father, my uncle . . . They all came towards me and greeted me. My grandparents were dressed all in white and they had a hood over their heads.[17]

After it sank in that this phenomenon could be real, the thought was consoling, particularly for those of us who have experienced the death of a loved one. To realize that we might see this person again after we die is uplifting and reassuring. It helped make my own parents' deaths—from terminal cancer and a sudden massive heart attack—more endurable. It is encouraging that many researchers and experiencers alike are substantiating this wondrous possibility.

"I recognized my grandfather and a girl I had known when I was in school, and many other relatives and friends," one person said in *Life After Life,* by Dr. Moody. "I felt that they had come to protect or guide me. It was almost as if I were coming home, and they were there to greet or to welcome me. I had the feeling of everything light and beautiful."[18]

I began wondering, where is home? Are we looking at another dimension outside our realm of reality that we can also call home? This "other dimension" theme was a constant, mentioned in many of the reported cases of unexplained phenomena. Even though this "place" was nonphysical as we know it, somehow the experiencer had been transported into a dimension that seemed real. In many cases, this other dimension was a realm similar to Earth.

As I reviewed memories of my near-death experience, and then the February 1995 sighting when it felt as if the faded orbs were still there even though we didn't see them anymore, this "other dimension" idea made more sense.

After 30 years of dedicated research in the field, Raymond Fowler shared how his own perceptions, as well as those of Dr. J. Allen Hynek, had changed concerning the UFO mystery. It seemed that they started out feeling that the unexplained objects were nuts-and-bolts spacecraft coming from another solar system, from another star system. But as time went by there were very bizarre things that UFOs did that seemed to indicate that their original assumption was wrong. I could relate to Fowler's line of reasoning: "Some of us began to think that maybe we're dealing with something that is able to penetrate our dimension from another dimension. They can take on material aspects here, but actually disappear and go somewhere else enabling them to perhaps bypass what we call the 'Law of Physics.'"[19]

Dr. Jacques Vallee postulates that the entities in an UP are themselves inter-dimensional. His theory asserts that they possess the uncanny ability to somehow shift between our reality and theirs at will. The more I investigated this intriguing premise, the more Dr. Vallee's contention was substantiated. And so it seems physicists today are just catching up with what most metaphysical traditions, notably Theosophy, Anthroposophy, and Qabala, have been saying for a long time. Many research scientists and astrophysicists are now hypothesizing that there may be as many as ten different levels of dimensional reality in our universe. Unfathomable folded dimensions of reality may be present along with ours, eluding detection by man-made technology, no matter how sophisticated.

When I discussed this with UFO researcher Linda Moulton Howe, she agreed: "Out of these experiences, it appears that a new cosmology is emerging that suggests there are more dimensions than this one. The Earth exists in one particular dimension that has an atomic frequency and matter/energy relationship that *beings* from other dimensions and other time lines can penetrate and overlap. There are many other universes that can be radically different from ours in both visual appearance and physical makeup. And intelligences other than human are forcing glimpses of these realities upon us."

A common characteristic of these other dimensional realities seems to be timelessness. This is a significant feature in NDEs, OBEs, and UFO encounters.

Investigator Phyllis Atwater writes, "Almost every single person returns knowing time does not exist. They come back knowing time is a matter of consciousness: past and future are really qualities of perception."[20]

Melvin Morse, M.D., confirms this finding in *Closer to the Light*. One of his NDE patients said, "I think the difference in me was caused by the way I now saw time. I realized that time as we see it on the clock isn't how time really is."[21]

Physicist Stephen Hawking states, "You can think of ordinary, real time as a horizontal line. Early times are on the left and late times are on the right. But you can also consider another direction of time, up and down the page. This is so-called imaginary direction of time, at right angles to real time. The idea of imaginary time is an intellectual leap of the same order as believing that the world is round. I think that imaginary time will come to seem as natural as a round earth does now. There are not many Flat Earthers left in the educated world."[22]

Does that mean that each of us possesses the innate ability to "imagine" ourselves into other *unearthly* realms? Perhaps through the millennia we have lost the knowledge of how to get there and the belief that we can.

When recalling my NDE, I could relate to the idea of somehow traveling to this timeless realm of existence, meeting tall robed light beings, communicating through telepathy, as described by other NDErs:

• I heard a voice . . . but like a hearing beyond the physical senses.[23]

• Without talking with our voices it just registered in my brain.[24]

Is telepathy also present in UFO experiences? It seems that the anonymous Tucson physician and his family (cited earlier) clearly received telepathic messages during their Phoenix Lights sighting.

Researchers, including Raymond Fowler, make a strong argument that UFO subjects communicate with nonearthly entities in a nonverbal manner:

- 1944: They're calling my name. It sounded as if someone jumped into my head.[25]

- 1949: I'm hearing it in my head . . . He is talking to me, but I don't see any mouth moving.[26]

- 1967: I'm talking with them, but they're not talking through their mouths. I think it was a transformation of thought.[27]

Telepathy seems to be a highlight for the experiencer during all UPs. Everything is out in the open. Perhaps we on Earth also have this intuitive ability of silent communication, which has been lost to us through the ages. My husband and I, as well as many other "connected" people, have it on occasion. Perhaps telepathy is something we all possess.

The experiencers who share their stories have obviously come back to Earth, to our time and space, to tell us about their experiences. Those who do return tell us of *beings of light,* a relative, stranger, or a loving entity who telepathically imparts the same fundamental communication: *You have to go back* (or) *you have the choice to do so.* Many state that they would have liked to remain, but for assorted reasons returned. (For testimonials of this aspect of the NDE experience, see appendix C.)

Those who do come back feel that they have unfinished business to address before returning to the *world of light.* It is also noteworthy that people who have tried to take their life know it was wrong, and when they return to Earth assert that they will never attempt suicide again.

Fowler makes an intriguing observation: "All of the scenarios imply that the greeters at death's door are fully aware of the identity, given task, and death date of the NDEr."[28] He assures us that the primary difference is that NDErs are brought to this point because of temporary physical death, whereas alien contactees are brought to this point because they are chosen to be shown the world that lies beyond so-called physical death. This again illustrates a connection between life after death and unexplained phenomena. (The striking similarities between UFO encounters and NDEs, according to Fowler, are summarized in appendix C.)

Could *they,* the greeters, possibly be us? Is physical death just another step in human evolution? If our ancestors have gone on ahead of us to continue their existence and growth in a world beyond our own physical awareness, are humans in this plane of existence an embryonic form for *their* civilization? Could it be that an advanced society, existing in another dimension, is supervising NDEs and UFO phenomena? And could this "other place," this physical-like civilization complete with clothes, buildings, and even spacecraft as reported by some experiencers, be occupied in part by humans who have entered that dimension through the death process? Do we return again and again to repeat the balanced exchange between energy and matter?

What about telepathy? What are the *beings* from beyond imparting? Most often the UP experiencer comes back awakened. They experience an enhanced awareness that transforms them for the better.

In *Saved by the Light,* Dannion Brinkley shared the revelations from his NDE: "It's wild when you start to realize that there's a type of interwoven fabric between us and everyone else. 'Love thy neighbor as thyself' and 'Do unto others as you would have them do unto you.' That it's not only practical, that it's the law. I was waiting to be judged—but I never was judged; I judged me. I had to look at me as though I were a powerful, spiritual being after I left the earth. That's how everyone's going to review their life."[29]

Perhaps that is what *they* want us to do before we leave this earthly plane. Because there is more. Through telepathy, the *being* imparted a warning to Brinkley. Scenes from a horrible world war accompanied the message, but the being assured him, "It can be changed and you can help change it. This is not carved in stone, but we (who live here on earth) have the opportunity to change this." Then this being told Brinkley that he had to go back to prepare a way to renew others and their spirits in a world that was no longer secure.

This last statement seems to be a recurring one that impacts many who experience an UP. After receiving nearly a quarter of a million letters from people claiming contact, with more than 30 thousand detailed descriptions of the encounter, Whitley Strieber acknowledges: "Whether it comes from deep within us or from out among the stars, we are most certainly dealing with a communication from another world. Again and again, the letters I've received present one consistency; the witness is challenged, often with devastating power, to look at self and life in a new way."[30]

And that was exactly what was happening to me. Because of the Phoenix Lights and my subsequent search for answers, I was slowly but surely looking at the world and myself differently. Topics I had considered gibberish, "out there," New Age, were making more sense to me. My spirituality was blossoming big time. In addition, I was taking the gnawing urge to share my concerns for the survival of humanity and our planet seriously. But why?

Are these entities aware of what may lie ahead for us, trying to warn us to change our violent, destructive ways before it is too late? Are they affecting our collective consciousness by waking us up to this reality, one person at a time? From my own UP experiences and certainly from all the volumes of verification I was gathering from experts and other experiencers, I was coming to believe that there is a connection to something out there just waiting to be grasped by each one of us.

In turn, everyone has the choice of whether or not to perceive it. As humans we have free will, opportunities for growth, throughout our lives. Taking advantage of these opportunities, or not, is a personal decision. As I learned in my NDE, life is a series of causes and effects. Everything we choose to do will have an inevitable positive or negative effect on us and those around us. Liken it to the ripple effect of a pebble tossed into a pond. The rings of energy spreading outwards from that pebble can be far-reaching indeed.

Our reality, our choices, and ultimately our destiny begin with our thoughts and beliefs. These are the seeds of an action. These seeds are stronger than we have ever imagined. It is our free will to cultivate these thoughts, these seeds, to fruition. Obstacles are opportunities for growth. We are limited only by what we believe. A thought, a decision based on that thought, and then the action from that decision will ultimately represent who you are. Thoughts, decisions, actions are all based on your own free will.

The potent energy in thoughts that are used to create fear or hurt can also be used to end it. Through life's experience, we learn that our flaws and blunders can be traced back to our own fears. What makes free will so powerful is that through positive thought and conduct we can change that fault or failure into a strength.

If you want to change your life, change your thoughts. If you want a pleasant existence, fill your mind with pleasant thoughts, fill your life with pleasant deeds. Each one of us has this precious gift of free will. Use it judiciously and with love, and you will reap the benefits—we will all reap the benefits.

Which brings us to the most significant realization that UP experiencers bring back. Unconditional love is the prime directive for humankind. My research showed that this knowledge alone has changed the lives of those who have experienced an unexplained phenomenon. NDE researcher Phyllis Atwater confirms, "Over and over again, I hear survivors tell of the love they experienced and how they want now to emulate that love, to develop and expand that love, so it will become a daily reality in their lives. They want to keep it alive and growing."[31]

Graphic descriptions come from patients who have survived death:[32]

• Love is the main reason for our existence as human beings in our physical bodies. We must understand love in a holistic sense, altruistic love.

• We cannot fully experience love unless we also know compassion, the ability to know pain and loss—not just our own pain and loss, but the ability to feel pain and loss of others.

Dr. Raymond Moody corroborates this encouraging aftereffect. "Upon their return, almost all of them say that love is the most important thing in life. Many say it is why we are here. Most find it the hallmark of happiness and fulfillment, with other values paling beside it."

To add to the mystery, many UFO subjects come back from their separate experiences with the same understanding. Here are additional messages of love from patients, friends, and me as gleaned from our UP experiences:

- Learning love is what life on Earth is all about.

- Love is God. God is Love.

- Love transcends all religions and cultures. It is what unites us all.

- Love creates positive energy. Love is healing.

- Do what you love to do and you will do it well.

- Every action of love has a reaction of love.

- Each soul shines with the *light of love* in various degrees. If you are filled with love, your soul shines brightly and strong. If you possess little love, your soul is weak and dim.

- The more love you have to give, the greater you are.

- Love is Truth.

- FEAR = False Evidence Accepted as Real.

- Fear and love cannot exist simultaneously.

- When we put our trust in love, there is no room in our soul for fear.

- To live in the *light* is to let love be your guide.

- Law enforcement is most often accomplished by fear and guilt. We have the power within us to enforce ourselves on a "higher level" by embracing love and respect for life.

- We can create paradise on Earth if we learn to love each other as ourselves.

- Teach our children love, with love—and we will spread love throughout the world.

- Love and knowledge are the only things you take with you at death.

- If you travel through life with *light* and *love* in your heart, you will bridge the gap between the seen and unseen energies that can reconnect you to the *Source*.

What's more, the love and devotion that are felt by the experiencer during and after an UP are not limited to people. They also include a love and earnest regard for our planet. It has been reported by researchers and experiencers that in many instances the *beings,* whether spirit or ET entities, are very worried about Earth's ecology. As Fowler substantiates, "This concern was a primary component of the alien's message to humankind."[33]

Dr. Kenneth Ring's studies also reveal that UFO contactees and NDErs return from their encounters with a great concern for the environmental state of Earth, and, like Dannion Brinkley, some even experience a terrifying vision of global cataclysm to clarify the point.

Dr. Ring incorporated the subject into his Omega Project and scientifically studied the data. He notes that 85 percent of UFO experiencers and almost 80 percent of NDErs report an increase in concern over the welfare of our planet following their UP, while 50 to 60 percent state that it had strongly increased. "The heightened sensitivity to ecological matters and to the condition of our Earth generally seems, statistically at least, to be among the most important value changes that follow extraordinary experiences."[34]

Most of us probably never think about this issue, at least not seriously. If we examine our legacy as a species, the multitude of wondrous things we have accomplished as a civilization, particularly in the past century, many of us have looked the other way when neglect and abuse have been inflicted upon our own planet. We might "talk a good game," but do we do anything about it? With our busy schedules and minute-to-minute concerns, it is easy to embrace our short-term needs and brush aside the long-term consequences. After all, like most other species, our existence is predicated on surviving, thriving, and multiplying. We are wired for the short term, a fact compounded by the high-tech revolution, which overfeeds our cravings for a quick fix. Along the way, many have ignored the results of our negligent behavior. Perhaps somewhere in the back of our minds we hope that someone is going to bail us out. But could that "someone" be us? And could the time be now? It certainly seems as if these intermediary intelligences are alerting us to that.

When we step back and look—really see our careless actions—do we recognize in ourselves the mind-set of children who use this planet as a playground, mauling it, spray-painting it, draining and destroying its precious resources with little thought for the future?

Do you think about what is going to happen once the rain forests are depleted? Do you consider the horrors to humankind and other forms of life when latent pathogenic organisms, such as the dreaded Eboli virus, are released by this vandalism? Do you wonder why the hydrogen fuel cell, which emits water as a by-product and replenishes life-sustaining oxygen in our environment, isn't being used *now* instead of dangerous nuclear and fossil fuels? During your hectic day do you ponder what will happen if our air becomes too polluted to breathe, our water too polluted to drink, our seas too polluted to sustain life?

Experiencers do. As an outgrowth of the insight imparted by the *beings,* many return with prophecies and warnings that they take to heart. UFO experiencer Whitley Strieber is a prime example, claiming that he was told in 1986 about the dangers of the ozone hole over the Antarctic, long before scientists even understood the implications. He also predicted that the ultraviolet light would cause extreme crop damage and affect animal and human immune systems.

The message from these "ambassadors of the light" is consistent: Our Earth is a finely tuned and balanced organism. If there is a disruption of this exquisite ecosystem, it can have a cumulative effect.

Case in point: pollution of our oceans, which can cause a decline of the microscopic marine life—the foundation of the food chain in the sea. This can significantly change the temperature of the oceans and in turn change climate, affecting habitats, particularly in the sea coastal regions, and even turn grazing lands into deserts. The greenhouse effect caused by the buildup of carbon dioxide in the atmosphere and the ozone hole depletion in the upper atmospheres creates global warming, changing our weather conditions and inevitably our food and natural resources. As we now know, this dangerous set of circumstances has already been set in motion. Scientists are postulating that the same fate may have befallen the now desolate planet of Mars.

Steve Neill, an artist and ET experiencer, expresses his personal concern about our planet. "I think that it's really evident that we've separated ourselves from nature. We have a sense that nature is over there and we're over here. That this world was made for us to do whatever we want, to trash it in the name of personal gain and profit. And I think we're in danger of becoming extinct."[35]

Psychotherapist Yvonne Smith heads one of the more than 250 support groups for UP experiencers in the U.S. She verifies these pressing communications of the future from more than 100 cases. "People have been told that there is going to be devastation. That there's going to be tremendous Earth changes. They're shown these images of tremendous earthquakes, hurricanes. It's something that's put into their mind."[36]

Like me, those who have received this important message feel a responsibility and passion to share it, in hopes that these adversities can be prevented. The good news is that most experts and experiencers agree that the future is not written in stone. With awareness and action, our mistakes can be undone by the self-corrective and rebalancing forces inherent in the universe. But again, it is our responsibility to make that happen.

On March 9, 2000, the Associated Press released the findings of the National Museum of Natural History in Washington, D.C. The story ran in the *Arizona Republic:* "Many scientists fear the increasing loss of plant and animal life. It's not just 'stop the extinction' and things bounce back immediately. It takes a long time—10 million years before anything resembling it reappears."

As if confirming that, in a telepathic communication, an ET informed a witness, "As time goes by, mankind will become sterile. They will not be able to reproduce because of the pollution of the land and the waters and the air and the bacteria and the terrible things that are on Earth."[37]

Realizations about Earth's environment are such an important part of the aftermath of an UP, might "unearthly" entities be trying to wake us up to these infractions? By implanting visions and prophecies in the minds of experiencers are they urging us to take responsibility for our actions? Are they letting us know that Earth has a significant place in the cosmos and that as a species we cannot be permitted to destroy it? The communications from these *beings* concerning the failure of our species to take proper care of the Earth aren't just meant for Americans alone. It is a worldwide proclamation.

In his book *The Alien Intent,* British researcher Raymond A. Robinson notes, "The subject is given a message to spread to the rest of humankind about the error of our ways, and the dire warning that if we do not change, the human race will suffer extinction. The message of extinction is nearly always the same, ranging from nuclear wars that will wipe us all out to huge disasters (similar to Nostradamus's predictions), and always on a megalithic scale of 'One.' It is never of a minor nature."[38]

The cards are laid on the table. It is now up to us to decide how we want to play our hand. This urgent concern was duly expressed by His Holiness the Dalai Lama in 1992, "These *beings,* these creatures, they are very upset. We are destroying their physical and spiritual homes. They have no choice, but to become physical and come back and try to stop us."[39]

Raymond Robinson agrees. "They appear to be able to give the victim precognitive skills and a heightened perception of the Universe, together with a degree of clairvoyance where none existed before the encounter. It could mean that there is a genuine exchange between us and them, in order to fulfill an agenda of gradual human enlightenment not only as to their presence, but also as to our place in the Universe as a whole."[40]

An experiencer concurs. "The message is—wake up, grow up, the sandbox that you are littering is not your own, you are not alone, you do not have to feel the sense of isolation and separation that you have felt, you are part of a bigger community."[41]

As I read the case studies, it became evident that Unexplained Phenomena had positively transformed people's lives as a consistent aftereffect. The experience puts the events of one's life in perspective. The experiencer comes back thinking about what good they have done and how they can help to improve the lives of those around them. Some claim that it is the exposure to a higher being that has guided them to a certain clarity; others say it is the peace and comfort that comes from knowing that there will be life after life.

Whether it's a UFO experience or NDE, the positive effect is inevitably revealed. The revelations that follow each experience are consistent, an experience of oneness, a connection to others and to our planet, a sense of knowing, an understanding of a new reality. Moreover, researchers are finding a strong connection between the unexplained experiences of the twentieth and twenty-first centuries and the works of great philosophers from Plato to Christ, as well as a connection with such documents as the Tibetan Book of the Dead and St. Paul's experience in the Bible.

Dr. Moody elaborates. "The great Hindu sages themselves said that just by being in the presence of a highly evolved *being,* the less evolved gets a shock of the spirit, kind of like a laying on of hands. By being in close contact with these entities we are actually reaping an influx of energy."[42]

UP experiencers also come away with a feeling of being connected to the universe, that we are all interconnected, with interwoven dependencies of male/female and plant/animal, that all life must be equal in importance, for it shares a universal consciousness. There is no real distinction between one life form and another; we are all dependent and interlinked with each other. We are *One.*

This may sound like a Buddhist or Native American philosophy. Could their long-held beliefs be close to the truth? After all, their fundamental principles of balance and respect have endured the test of time. One only needs to recognize that the tiniest of insects is dependent on the smallest flower, which in turn is dependent on the insect, so that each short life may flourish. The mighty mountains are dependent on the flow of the streams and the strength of the winds to shape their futures. We are all part of a complex, interwoven system of connections and interdependencies. And when people realize that, they begin to live their lives in a way that makes the world a better place.

Apparently, we are also connected to a divine *Source* or creative center of being in the cosmos. "Experiencers of unexplained phenomena come to appreciate that the universe is filled with intelligences and is itself intelligent,"[43] as Dr. Mack put it. There is a sense that everything in the universe is connected.

After experiencing an NDE during a cardiac arrest, a 62-year-old, no-nonsense businessman stated: "The first thing I saw when I awoke in the hospital was a flower, and I cried. Believe it or not, I had never really seen a flower until I came back from death. One big thing I learned when I died was that we are all part of one big, living universe. If we think we can hurt another person or another living thing without hurting ourselves, we are sadly mistaken. I look at a forest or a flower or a bird now, and say, 'That is me, part of me.'"[44]

As happened with this patient, people can be suddenly introduced to the greater reality surrounding us, the first step of a long-term spiritual awakening, through a variety of ways, including: UFO encounters, NDEs, OBEs, epiphanies, guru contacts, powerful and/or lucid dreams, mystery quests. To a large extent, the psychological impact is the same for any of these "knocks": common changes in belief and attitude such as increased love, environmental awareness, and a connectedness to the universe. Ultimately, any knock will do as long as it starts to wake you up to the world, yourself, and the consequences of how you live.

The final result is that all UPs help the experiencers to develop a new appreciation for their place in the universe. Respect and wonder grow for the mysterious and sacred spirit of the natural world.

UPs are a kind of spiritual outreach program from the cosmos. We and the higher or alien beings evidently come from a common *Source*. Perhaps these entities, whatever their origin or agenda, are trying to help us reconnect to that *Source* and awaken us to our potential and destiny. They are also giving us the choice of how we want our future to play out. And love is at its core. It is up to us to find it within, cultivate it, and share it if we are to survive as a species.

Think of your mind as a parachute. It won't work unless it is open. To be closed-minded is to shut off the most precious source of energy that this universe and its beings possess.

The strength of our own wills, our own positive spirits, can lead to a strong collective consciousness—a powerful and brilliant energy source that will help us recover that which we have lost. We can heal ourselves and our planet with our own free will—with our own willpower.

As we begin to develop our potentials as multisensorial beings, we may face a quantum leap of knowledge relating to the nature of humanity and our intimate connection to the rest of the universe. There is a realm that truly exists outside our own. *They* will know when we embrace the reality of its existence.

13. The Journey Was Part of the Gift

As the days, months, years rolled on in my own process of discovery, the long-term impact of the Phoenix Lights experience continued. I was now looking at my life and everything in it with a new perspective and appreciation. Witnessing the lights was a gift. The journey to find the source and meaning was a bonus. I would have never chosen this path. But now that I had stumbled upon it, I was realizing more and more how awesome, exciting, scary, and cool it was—all at the same time. I was also beginning to grasp the impact of the new experiences, new knowledge, and new insight I had accumulated. I'm not alone.

How far we've expanded our knowledge as a civilization in just the past few years—it seems we have learned more about the Earth and the cosmos in the last two decades than in all recorded history. Are we as a species embarking on a monumental expansion of our intellect, reaching out into the universe of space and into our minds? Is humankind at large on the verge of understanding what experiencers of unexplained phenomena have known for millennia? Are we now moving towards our next evolutionary level, the positive maturation and spiritual advancement of consciousness itself?

I had to ask myself if our current knowledge of physics, astronomy, and the paraphysical sciences is just in its infancy. Perhaps, in the scheme of things, we are just beginning to learn. Philosopher and psychologist William James once stated, "Our science is but a drop, our ignorance a sea." Western scientists are only recently even admitting to the possibility of unexplained phenomena and that they may actually have been with us since the beginning of human life on this planet.

More impressive still, the Hubble space telescope is altering the face of science at record speed. It can view much farther out into space from Earth than we have ever been able to before. It is giving us a peek at the future and at our past. Many scientists now agree that by looking back 14 billion years, the telescope has shown us evidence of vast changes in the universe that we never suspected before. Marty Caidin, science writer, aviation historian, and pilot who covered the space program for 30 years, recently stated with conviction, "Ninety-five percent of everything we believed is now in the trash can!"

Joining astronomers and astrophysicists, Caidin is investigating clues supplied by the Hubble, findings that challenge our concepts of space, gravity, and time. These have been part of the framework that defines our existence and reality. It seems that our foundation is now being bulldozed to clear the way for a new reality, and, it is to be hoped, for a better reality for humankind.

Even though Einstein's theory of relativity has been around since 1915, scientists are increasingly convinced that space, gravity, and time are linked together in the way that an orchestra is. Think of the universe as a symphony of different notes, different levels, different sounds, but playing the same melody. In other words, an UP may not be "out there" at all. Maybe these unexplained phenomena have always been right here with us. We just don't get to see them or feel them unless we're open to them or invited.

Scientists are also realizing that life is not as fragile as we have presumed, but tenacious and ever present. Going one step farther, perhaps there are even life forms that do not have a physical form at all.

SETI (Search for Extraterrestrial Intelligence) Institute radio-astronomer Seth Shostak reminds us that we are the "new kids" on the galactic block. The galaxy has been around for 10 to 12 billion years, but the Earth for only four and a half billion years, he says. He believes that there might be civilizations out there that are way ahead of us, and not just by a hundred or a thousand years. "They could be a billion years more advanced than we are."[1]

Graham Hancock, author of *Fingerprints of the Gods,* agreed with Shostak: "We live on a planet revolving around a star in the middle of an unknown infinity of space. Isn't it arrogant and stupid to imagine that we're the only life in this enormous universe? If you take our ancient texts seriously, they all tell us that the universe was created as a home for life, that the universe is full of life. I think it's obvious that there are many other intelligent life forms in the universe and I don't dismiss for a moment that they have visited Earth, perhaps in the past . . . perhaps even now."[2]

Or could these mysterious "unearthly" visitors possibly be us—time travelers—visiting the present from our own distant future? Whatever the case, if advanced *beings* have discovered our existence, maybe we should ask what we would do in their place? What if one day NASA discovered a thriving civilization on another planet or from another time and realized that these intelligent beings were several steps below our own evolutionary development? We know enough about sociology, psychology, and theology to recognize that the worst thing we could do is just barge in. It would cause either panic or worship. But an advanced and caring society would slowly infiltrate, cautiously affect the mass mind, and get the inhabitants conditioned to the idea that they might be visited someday. Gradually the mass mind, the collective consciousness, would begin to accept the idea that this isn't so "Earth shaking."

Renowned astronomer and the scientific consultant of our government's only public study of UFOs, Dr. J. Allen Hynek so aptly observed that in science things are very frequently in steps. The first step is often complete disbelief. Then there comes a state where people say, "Well, it might be so." And the third stage or final stage is, "Gee, I knew that all the time."

It seems that we are getting closer to this final stage with each passing day. Are we just around the corner from discovering a galactic neighborhood waiting with open arms for our arrival? Are we soon to realize that whoever has been communicating for all these years, perhaps for millennia, has also been watching us advance technologically and spiritually so as to comprehend the possibilities? Are they waiting for us to realize that we are spiritual beings with potential to affect this world through our positive energies?

We all need contact with this positive energy, with our soul, the spirit within us, the essence of who we are. As we have learned, this strong, loving, fulfilling force seems to be connected to a greater *Source*, an exquisitely powerful but peaceful energy. Some call it intuition, a guardian angel, or inner voice, which through us imparts a soft, gentle thought or feeling. If we trust it and embrace it, this precious offering has the potential to produce incredible outcomes.

There is something about being touched by the *light* that helps us to understand this truth. The realization of a new reality seems most potent when it comes to us through UP events because:

• It is unexpected.

• It connects us directly with the primary *Source* of spiritual energy.

• The experience helps to awaken us to our true potential as spiritual beings.

• It is transforming, enriching our awareness and appreciation of the spiritual blessings that are possible.

But you do not have to have an extraordinary experience to tap into the glorious possibilities. Scientific studies have shown that you need only be open to and educate yourself about them in order to experience the positive effects. And these results are long term. The enlightened are far more aware of our Earth, the delicate balance of life upon it, the paramount importance of the dissemination of knowledge and love, and the duty of each individual to help in the effort to save our planet and ourselves from destruction.

Every one of us has the capacity—and the choice—to connect with this strong affirmative force, as well as to recognize our innate telepathy, messages in dreams, precognition, and other healing spiritual gifts.

If people examined their lives closely, most would probably realize that they too have been touched by this compassionate guidance. Through faith, meditation, and prayer, we all have the potential to tap into this spiritual connection, a direct pipeline that weaves its wondrous thread through every one of us, through the living and the dead, to connect us all to each other and to the cosmos.

The most comforting thing of all is that we are not alone. Millions of us have been touched by an UP and know that what we saw, what we experienced was real. Without fear of ridicule or reprisal, we can hold our heads up high in the knowledge that these phenomena can finally be brought out into the open. We can finally acknowledge them, address them, and analyze them.

Our realities and beliefs have changed throughout our evolution. It is time we accept that other realities exist, realities that we cannot see or measure with our sometimes limiting human and technological faculties, at least not yet. But they are real nonetheless.

Before the advent of the microscope, we had no idea that trillions of minuscule organisms were thriving in abundance all around us, even within our own bodies. This truth eluded our senses and our scientific prowess for centuries. Just a few short years ago, we discovered that every living cell possesses electromagnetic energies. This revolutionary finding helped us develop the MRI (magnetic resonance imaging), which detects disease noninvasively. Even though we cannot see these potent, healing energies or microbial living entities with our human eyes, they do permeate our lives.

We have yet to decipher a way to scientifically detect and verify unexplained phenomena. Have we been searching on the AM dial for an FM frequency? Could it be that the time is fast approaching when scientists, scholars, even inquisitive children who embrace the wonder of an UP will be able to unveil that which has so curiously escaped our intellectual and scientific grasp?

The unexplained phenomena that thousands witnessed on March 13, 1997, throughout Arizona and the mysteries experienced across the globe teach us that *they* are part of us. *They* may be appearing from another time and space, from a different vibrational frequency, from a higher *Source*—but *they* have communicated their ethereal messages to us for thousands of years and will continue to communicate through the skies of planet Earth, the spiritual encounters that are unexpected blessings, and in the minds of those who are open to them.

My quest for the truth has led me to confirm my own connection. After exploring the unexplained phenomena that have touched my life, searching for answers, I now believe that the encounter I experienced as a child was a precursor or groundwork for what happened to me later.

The three magnificent *light beings*, my own loving spiritual friends who gently guided me and comforted me all these years, returned to my reality in 1995 to reawaken me to theirs.

Just three weeks after the Arizona mass sighting, I ventured onto our balcony to seek their advice, asking the heavens for a sign that this was real. My prayers were answered.

When I stepped inside and slipped back into bed, I fell into a deep sleep. Suddenly I was sitting in the passenger seat of a car with a man who I felt cared deeply for me. I didn't think it was my husband, but I wasn't sure who it was.

As we approached a stoplight, we saw to our horror a two-story tractor trailer truck, the biggest one I've ever seen, enormous and black, barreling around the corner at excessive speed. There was no way this monstrous vehicle was going to stop, so my driver swerved to try to avoid a collision. Our car was dragged backwards. I felt the impact of the crash, no pain but the pressure of being pushed at a tremendous speed. I then felt as though I were being pulled out of my body by a powerful suction and immediately engulfed in a kaleidoscope of white light beams. An incredible rush of euphoria filled me. I was becoming the *light.* Love penetrated me as I floated peacefully in the center of this radiant energy. I tried to look down at my body. I couldn't see it. It wasn't there.

Then the thought occurred to me that there was no way we could have avoided a collision. There was no way we could have survived a crash with the gigantic vehicle. We would surely have been crushed. That would mean that I must be dead, but I was still alive. Something of me was still alive. I was still thinking.

All I knew for certain was that it felt so wonderful, so safe, so loving. I was floating, and thinking at the same time, *What I'm experiencing must be the essence of who I really am—my spirit, my soul. We must not die when our body does—we do go on—in another form. Then it is true—the essence of who we are does live on after we die.*

With that thought, I felt myself sucked back into my body with a jolt. My eyes opened and I turned my head to see my husband asleep next to me. The euphoria I had been feeling lingered, as did the sensation of love.

What happened? It felt so real . . . I was still feeling it. How could it just have been a dream? I dream most nights and can usually remember my dreams. This was no ordinary dream. It was an experience. An experience so fantastic that I didn't dare share it with Frank at the time. I knew I wasn't prepared for it, so I kept it to myself.

A week later, exactly one month after the Phoenix Lights statewide event and just hours after the couple from Rainbow Valley videotaped daylight amber orbs hovering on the horizon, Frank shuddered in his sleep, as if he were having a bad dream. I woke with a start and asked him if he was all right. He gasped, "We're okay, we're okay. We were almost in a car accident, but I swerved to the right to avoid a collision and saved us. We're okay. I saved us."

Shocked by his reply, I responded without hesitation, "Wait a minute, Frank, what almost hit us?"

"Shush, go back to sleep," he muttered, as he turned on his side and fell asleep.

I lay there in disbelief. How could he have had the same dream I had? Thoughts and vivid images started racing through my mind. Thoughts so foreign to me, so engaging, that I felt compelled to write them down.

As if in a hypnotic state, I slipped out of bed and walked slowly downstairs to the study. I picked up a pen and began writing. My eyes remained closed as illuminating knowledge flowed effortlessly through me.

It was not until morning that I realized what had transpired. As I read for the first time what I had written, I wondered what possessed me to write it. Somehow I knew. It was this anonymous gift, this treasure from beyond that prompted me to embark on my seven-year journey of discovery.

It is an honor to share this gift with you . . .

I don't know about other living creatures in the vast universe, but questions keep permeating my mind about the ones who are trying to get our attention now.

What if these beings are as advanced spiritually as they are technologically?

What if they want to share this beautiful and wondrous future with us?

And what if they have already met our spirit world and know firsthand that the essence of who we are is pure? They may only be trying to help us recognize the positive spirit deep within and teach us to know ourselves for who we really are . . . before we destroy our world.

Each and every one of us is a powerful being with the strength and wisdom to deeply appreciate our Earth and every living creature on it.

It is time we view ourselves in a New Light.

This can begin by searching within ourselves to find goodness and love so that the consciousness of humankind can elevate spiritually above petty differences, envy, greed, lies, hatred, abuse, violence, and fear.

That is our destiny . . .

But only if each one of us chooses to look within our own soul for the answers . . .

They are there. It isn't too late.

Humankind can begin this very moment to learn and grow so that our future will benefit from our newfound knowledge, not be pulled down by our self-serving primal ignorance.

It is so very important to look within yourself . . . and to believe.

Judge yourself each and every day.

There will come a time when you will indeed judge every moment of your own life . . . the good things, the bad, the kindness, and the wrath that you and you alone have brought to other human beings, to other living things, to our Earth. You will feel what it felt like to be on the receiving end.

Near-death experiencers have told us time and time again that when we die we go through a life review. God does not judge us . . . we judge ourselves.

So maybe we should judge ourselves now.

Think clearly about how we treat others, the energy and dedication we put into our relationships, especially our family . . . as well as our relationship to other living things we touch, in this short but precious existence.

So when our time does come, we won't have to endure pain and sadness, but rather . . . we will be drenched in the ecstasy of our own love—in the magnificent light of love.

And if each of us truly looks deep within, the positive energies emanating from the goodness each one of us possesses will be shared around the world.

Then . . . our beautiful journey to a new reality will have begun.

Afterword

I hope that my journey for answers has touched your mind and spirit. If so, then I have succeeded as an educator and as a messenger. But I am only one cog in the wheel on that road of discovery. There is much exploring yet to be done if we, as a civilization, are to reveal the source and meaning of unexplained phenomena.

There is little doubt that something extraordinary *is* going on for which we have no definitive explanation. Even with all the advanced technology and empirical data we have acquired, are we any closer to proving, conclusively, that these elusive events, which seem to be occurring at a faster pace worldwide, truly exist?

Not yet. But we do have the next best thing. We have ourselves, multisensorial sentient beings, who can experience and document these awesome happenings firsthand. Though our present scientific prowess cannot provide an answer to all the mysteries that abound, many of us have felt something, seen something, even photographed something that is indeed *real* to us. We sometimes capture images in our mind's eye or through the camera lens that cannot be denied, replicated, or explained. Ultimately, it will be our own choice—our awareness, attitude, and appreciation of these findings—that will reveal the stunning truth.

The Phoenix Lights

In the meantime, I felt it imperative to share my story on the chance that by coming forward it might help make it easier for you to share yours. If we continue to keep these "knocks" behind closed doors, we will be silencing the very keys that could unlock the gateway to this glorious new reality. My final reflections may help illustrate what I mean.

At 10 P.M. on October 10, 2001, one month after the most horrific incident in modern U.S. history, I lay in bed pondering the terrifying events and their potential consequences for humankind.

My pensive state was interrupted by the unsettling words relayed on the evening news. Every TV station was reporting on the most recent terror— anthrax. As I switched to another news program, they were elaborating on the equally frightening possibilities of nuclear mass destruction. My heart was pounding and my head spinning with visions of human heartache, devastation, and extinction.

I began to meditate . . . *Are you watching out there? Do you know what's happening down here on Earth? Why haven't you shown yourselves? Can you help us?*

In an instant, three huge amber lights were hovering in a massive triangle array over the Phoenix city landscape, again in the same location. I rushed onto the balcony and took several shots before the lights disappeared from view.

The sight was a reassuring affirmation . . . *They* do know, *they* do care, *they* do hear our prayers, and *they* can communicate with us. The real question is . . . are we listening?

As an extra for the reader, I offer ten suggestions to help you build your own connection to the lifelines of the living energy universe.

1. Become aware of what is going on in your life, your choices and their potential outcomes, how your actions will affect both you and those around you. If you just go through the motions of daily living and repeat the same mistakes over and over again, you will likely continue going around in circles. Only you can break the cycle.

2. Surround yourself with people who make you smile, who appreciate and respect you for who you are. There is nothing more damaging to your mental and physical health than being around others who berate you, take advantage of you, or abuse you in any way. Take note, and if you are in that type of situation, do something about it. There is help out there. Confiding in someone you trust (a counselor, clergy, teacher, or relative) is the first important step.

3. Develop a positive attitude. The positive energies this produces and radiates will benefit you and those around you. Refuse to feed into negative thoughts or deeds. Taking yourself too seriously can also be harmful to your health. Laughing relieves as much tension as crying. Studies confirm that a good belly laugh does wonders for your whole body—chemically, physically, and psychologically.

4. Appreciate whatever it is that is put before you. As they say, *I cried because I had no shoes until I saw a man who had no feet.* Appreciating every moment to the fullest will fill your life with new perspectives and can help you reconnect to the guiding energies available out in the living energy universe.

5. Take care of your body, your earthly container. It is yours to cherish, nourish, and maintain. Deep breathing and aerobic exercises, such as walking, biking, or swimming for ten to 30 minutes each day, circulate life-giving oxygen throughout your body, replenishing organs, muscles, your brain. Studies show that a high oxygen intake helps your body cells burn more of the food you consume in addition to stored fat. Daily exercise can reduce the incidence of depression, keep your immune system and bones vital and strong, and promote optimal cardiovascular health.

   Stick to a low-fat (including dairy products rich in calcium and protein), well-balanced eating plan rich in fruits and vegetables (complex carbohydrates), fiber (especially whole grain), and soy products. Start looking at product labels, steering clear of saturated and hydrogenated fats, as well as products that contain them. Instead, increase your omega 3 fatty acids by eating fish (especially salmon) and flax seed. To help decrease triglycerides, blood sugar, and blood pressure, stay away from the "white stuff": sugar, salt (NaCl), white bread, flour, potatoes, rice, and pasta. Starches with color are better, such as whole grain breads, sweet potatoes and yams, brown rice, whole wheat or spinach pastas. But keep these carbohydrates to a minimum. Load up on tomatoes; they contain the antioxidant lycopene and heart healthy P3 tomato factor, especially when heated as in stewed tomatoes or tomato sauce. And try a few almonds a day for a snack. They not only decrease LDL, the "bad" cholesterol, but almonds contain vegetable protein, plant sterols, and are rich in fiber and vitamin E. By cutting down portion size and spreading your intake across five or six small meals throughout your day, instead of two or three large ones, this plan will help you control your food cravings, keep those pounds off, and give added energy. We're not talking about a diet here, but healthful eating that will become a healthy lifestyle.

Save one meal over the weekend to eat what you want. It will be that special perk to keep you going for the following week. It's worked for me for 20 years. It is also important to hydrate your body by drinking about eight glasses of pure water per day. Another alternative is brewed teas, particularly green or black teas, which are packed with antioxidants.

Most important, become mindful of your body's messages to you. You'll know when you should seek medical attention.

6. Prayer, meditation, or yoga can stimulate your right temporal lobe and help connect you directly with the unseen positive forces of the universe, which in turn can help heal your body, mind, and spirit.

7. Find a peaceful place inside or outside your home that gives you joy. This will be your special retreat. It can be a small quiet area set with photos of loved ones, small trinkets that make you smile, books or other written materials that are close to your heart, aromatic candles, plants, and music that will fill your senses with a glorious calm.

Take five to ten minutes a day to sit silently in this area, savoring the tranquility of your special space. This quiet time will slow your heart rate and reduce your blood pressure, which in turn decreases stress on your body and mind and increases your sense of control.

Either lie down on a comfortable surface or sit in a cozy chair with feet flat, spine straight, arms relaxed, and your hands resting, palms open, on your lap. With eyes closed, concentrate on a comforting or beautiful thought. For example, visualize a sunset or waves lapping a pristine beach or a lush garden filled with brilliantly colored flowers swaying in the breeze. Start breathing in slowly through your nose for a count of five and then slowly out through your mouth for a count of five. This five-second regimen corresponds to the natural ten-second heart cycle—not only calming you, but also improving your cardiovascular status. As little as two minutes of deep breathing a day can help lower your stress level.

If you have more time, with eyes closed, first picture a deep well. Think of a problem in your life as if it were a rock. Throw that rock into the well and feel it falling farther away, farther down the shaft until it hits bottom. The problem is gone for now. The heaviness each problem produced on your being dissipates as each problem is tossed into the well. After you complete the process of releasing your problems, close the cover of the well. Again concentrate on that comforting thought and deep breathing technique. These simple methods will not only relax your body, they will also help elevate your mind to a higher level of consciousness. You will become aware of the openness that is needed to receive wondrous energies from the universe.

8. Envision a goal. It is always best to set an end objective in your mind and then plan how to get there, instead of just having scattered and haphazard thoughts and hoping things will turn out the way you want them to. Start by figuring out what you want to achieve. For example, paying your bills or how you would like a meeting this afternoon to go. Concentrate on different ways of "getting there," asking for guidance along the way. Inevitably, you will hit upon a plan that you feel will work for you. Then pursue it.

You will be surprised by how easy it becomes to receive "ideas" with practice. If you are open to it, you will become aware that the answers to queries and concerns come to you for the asking. Ultimately, you will begin to trust your inner voice and intuition, as well as the guidance from beyond. You have tapped into a comforting and positive realm that is here to help us grow and learn.

9. Self-doubt is the result of the fear of failure. We all fail. It's learning from the failures and continuing to improve that will lead you to success. Live with love, not fear, and spread this living energy to everyone around you, especially your family. Build on that love. If you look for the good in others, you

will find it. Cultivate it within yourself and plant the seed in others. This positive energy will come back to you manyfold.

10. Take a few minutes each day to reach out to another living being, be it a person or animal. Give your loved one a hug, make that phone call to someone you haven't spoken to in a while, take time to caress a pet, help a neighbor, visit someone who is ill, spend precious moments reading to a child. Caring, loving actions touch others to the core.

Connecting to these lifelines of the living energy universe will promote your own personal health, healing, mental well-being, and peace of body and spirit. May the *Source* be with you.

Appendix A
What Others Believe—
Impressive Quotes

Concerning the article by Thomas Ropp, "Real-World Ufology Usually Lost in Space in Hollywood," in the *Arizona Republic*, July 13, 1997

Ropp wrote about Dr. Steven Greer, a specialist in the medical emergency field from North Carolina who travels with his research group to sites where UFO activity is common, then attempts to communicate with unidentified craft through light patterns and tones recorded from other encounters with UFOs. Ropp tells us that in February 1992, a scientific team led by Greer went to a volcanic region outside Mexico City. When they encountered a mile-wide triangular-shaped craft, similar to the one reported by thousands of witnesses across Arizona in March, light sequences were exchanged when the craft came within a couple hundred yards of them. All data was documented and recorded. Interestingly, Dr. Steven Greer and his CSETI group were also in Arizona on March 13, 1997, allegedly doing the same thing!

E-mail to author from Phoenix Light investigator and witness Bill Hamilton, November 14, 1997

1. We did an analysis of the mystery lights on video and compared them to the lights on illumination flares and they differ in waveform. The mystery lights reveal a coherent waveform with a superposition of the RGB (red/green/blue) components of the light, whereas the flares show ragged waveforms with no coherence.

2. The Maryland ANG stated they dropped LUU2 magnesium flares, which burn bright white. This flare drop was accomplished and the planes landed at 8:30 P.M., according to the Tucson paper and a source at Davis-Monthan AFB, PIO Lieutenant Keith Shepherd. The lights we [Tom King and Bill] videotaped appeared to be amber colored and were taped at 9:50 P.M.

3. A superimposition of the Krzyston light footage onto daylight footage shows an array of lights to be lower than the crest line of the Estrella Mountains and in front of the Estrellas, between the Estrella Mountains in the south and North Mountain and Shaw Butte in the north. These lights were in front of the Estrella Mountains at about half the elevation of the highest peak, or 4,515 feet. We not only videotaped these lights, which did not alter their relative positions, nor descend or drop, but two of us viewed these lights through a 24X Celestron spotting scope and we could see rapidly pulsing orbs of yellow-orange light. We could not and did not see any aircraft in the vicinity of these lights, no suspension apparatus for the lights such as a balloon or parachute, no smoke or sparks, just dazzling lights that did not illuminate the surrounding terrain, such as flares commonly do for military training exercises. These lights turned on in sequence and went off in sequence. I have received similar reports from Ohio, Nevada, Pennsylvania, New York, California, and Canada of these lights lining up in formation or dancing around or moving vertically upward.

4. Arizona director of MUFON, Tom Taylor, sighted these orbs a few days later in a group of three, mentioning that one ascended. Very strange activity for a flare.

5. We have a segment of daylight footage taken near the Buckeye Hills (Rainbow Valley). This shows two of these so-called flares glowing in the hills with a blue sky and no parachutes visible. One of these orbs fades out as we see them do at night, then suddenly reappears at a higher altitude, and then jumps to a higher altitude—behavior uncharacteristic of flares.

6. The first appearance of this formation of 8 + 1 lights was seen around 7:30 P.M. hovering over the Superstition Mountains in the east and the last seen over the Buckeye Hills the next morning at 2 A.M. Hence, these were not flares. The largest object seen on March 13 was a structured black triangle seen passing over I-10 headed toward Tucson around 8:30 P.M. The witnesses estimated the width of this triangle in excess of two miles.

E-mail update from Bill Hamilton, May 17, 2003

In an attempt to ascertain the timing and details of the flare ejection by Maryland Air National Guard A10 Warthog airplanes, I filed an FOIA request to the National Guard Bureau. Today I received a response. Needless to say, there are no direct answers to my questions, but there is data provided that clarifies some of what happened on March 13, 1997.

The 175th Fighter Wing of the Maryland Air National Guard engaged in a training exercise operating out of Davis-Monthan AFB in Tucson, flying several sorties to the bombing and gunnery range of the Barry Goldwater Test Range. An earlier statement indicates the night exercise was conducted on the North Tac Range.

The Barry Goldwater Gunnery Range, which extends from the Cabeza Prieta National Wildlife Refuge in the south to Interstate 8 near Gila Bend in the north, and from the Tohono O'odham Reservation to Yuma on the west, contains three tactical subranges—North Tac, South Tac, and East Tac—which are used for live fire and simulated artillery and bombing activities in air force pilot training.

Among other aircraft deployed, 8 A10 aircraft were dispensing flares during the exercise on the bombing range. The flare tubes number four with two flares per tube for a total of eight flares per airplane or 64 flares total. Two night operations were conducted, one on March 13. A total of 117 Luu-1 flares and 130 Luu-2 flares were dispensed during the operation. The Luu-1 flares burn for 30 minutes on the ground. The Luu-2 flares are dropped from about 1,000 ft and hang by parachutes, burning for about five minutes to illuminate the operations on the ground. They burn bright white. These are used less these days because of interference with night-vision goggles.

The commander of Operation Snowbird is Lieutenant Colonel Louis Pawlik. He was the one to provide the limited information in answer to my request.

I now have a map showing where the North Tac, South Tac, and East Tac ranges are located.

A recreation of this event on March 8, 2000, during the time when Operation Snowbird was conducting training exercises, was made from the direction of Gila Bend near the North Tac range. Those who taped the flare display and viewed it that night (who also viewed the amber lights on March 13) easily identified the recreation as flares and could see the sparks and smoke trails. This was also seen and recorded by Jim Dilettoso. These witnesses all contend that the lights seen on March 13 and the following January 14 did not appear to look like flares. All events were viewed by some witnesses using binoculars or telescopes. The amber lights have a clear round shape and do not morph in shape as do flares. Airplane lights were also visible during the recreation event, but no airplane lights were seen over the anomalous amber lights.

Sincerely,

Bill Hamilton

Executive Director

Skywatch International, Inc.

http://www.skywatch-research.org

UFO Quotes from Prominent People

J. Edgar Hoover, in response to a government request to study UFOs, wrote in 1947: "I would do it, but before agreeing to do it, we must insist upon full access to discs recovered. For instance, in the L.A. (or La.) case, the Army grabbed it and would not let us have it for cursory examination."[1]

General Walter Bedell Smith, director of the CIA from 1950 to 1953, divulged in a memo to the National Security Council:

The Central Intelligence Agency has reviewed the current situation concerning unidentified flying objects which have created extensive speculation in the press and have been the subject of concern to Government organizations . . .

Since 1947, approximately 2,000 official reports of sightings have been received and of these, about 20 percent are as yet unexplained. It is my view that this situation has possible implications for our national security which transcend the interests of a single service. A broader, coordinated effort should be initiated to develop a firm scientific understanding of the several phenomena which apparently are involved in these reports . . .[2]

General Douglas MacArthur, stated in a *New York Times* article (October 8, 1955), in true military fashion: "Because of the development of science, all the countries on earth will have to unite to survive and to make a common front against attack by people from other planets. The politics of the future will be cosmic, or interplanetary."[3]

He made this assertion again on May 12, 1962, in an address to the U.S. Military Academy at West Point.

Lieutenant Colonel Lawrence J. Coyne, U.S. Army Reserve helicopter pilot with 3,000 hours of flying time, was one of four airmen who had a close encounter with a UFO on the night of October 18, 1973, while flying in a U.S. Army Huey utility helicopter in the vicinity of Mansfield, Ohio. Lieutenant Colonel Coyne described his experience at a UN UFO hearing in 1978:

With the aircraft under my control, I observed the red-lighted object closing upon the helicopter at the same altitude at a high rate of speed. It became apparent a midair collision was about to happen unless evasive action was taken. I looked out ahead of the helicopter and observed an aircraft I have never seen before. This craft positioned itself directly in front of the moving helicopter. This craft was 50 to 60 feet long with a gray metallic structure. On the front of this craft was a large steady bright red light. The design of this craft was symmetrical in shape with a prominent aft indentation on the undercarriage. From this portion of the undercarriage, a green light, pyramid-shaped, emerged with the light initially in the trail position. This green light then swung 90 degrees, coming directly into the front windshield and lighting up the entire cockpit of the aircraft. All colors inside the cabin of the helicopter were absorbed by the green light. That includes the instrument panel lights on the aircraft.[4]

In a statement to the Special Political Committee of the United Nations, November 27, 1978, Lieutenant Colonel Coynes concluded: "As a result of my experience, I am convinced this object was real and that these types of incidents require a thorough investigation. It is my own personal opinion that worldwide procedures need to be established to effectively study this phenomena through an international cooperative effort . . ."[5]

Victor Marchetti, a former CIA official, wrote an article for *Second Look,* published in 1979 and entitled "How the CIA Views the UFO Phenomena," in which he stated:

> We have, indeed, been contacted—perhaps even visited—by extra-terrestrial beings, and the U.S. government, in collusion with the other national powers of the earth, is determined to keep this information from the general public. The purpose of the international conspiracy is to maintain a workable stability among the nations of the world and for them, in turn, to retain institutional control over their respective populations. Thus, for these governments to admit that there are beings from outer space . . . with mentalities and technological capabilities obviously far superior to ours, could, once fully perceived by the average person, erode the foundations of the earth's traditional power structure. Political and legal systems, religions, economic and social institutions could all soon become meaningless in the mind of the public. The national oligarchical establishments, even civilization as we know it, could collapse into anarchy. Such extreme conclusions . . . accurately reflect the fears of the "ruling classes" of the major nations, whose leaders (particularly those in the intelligence business) have always advocated excessive governmental secrecy as being necessary to preserve "national security."[6]

Lieutenant Colonel Philip J. Corso, member of President Eisenhower's National Security Council and former head of the foreign technology desk at the U.S. Army Research and Development Department, led a double life while in the military, supposedly researching and developing weapons for the army while, clandestinely inside the Pentagon, he was responsible for the army's most deeply held secret, Roswell. Shortly before his death in 1998, he asserted that the military seeded U.S. industry with technology from that wreckage:

> Artifacts harvested from the spacecraft led to today's integrated circuit chips, fiber optics, lasers, and stealth technology . . . The message from my book that I'd like to see is that the younger generation look at this and see what we did and see that these beings exist. Give permission. The young people of this world and this country want to hear it, they want it.

Give it to them, rather than tell lies and make stories. They're not stupid. It's their information. It doesn't belong to the army or Dept. of Defense. It's theirs. If it's classified—take the classification off and give it to them.[7]

Harry S. Truman, during his presidency, commented at a White House Conference on April 4, 1950: "I can assure you that flying saucers, given that they exist, are not constructed by any power on Earth."[8]

President Gerald Ford, when he was a congressman, sent a letter, dated March 28, 1966, to L. Mendel Rivers, Chairman of the Armed Services Committee, in which he said:

In the firm belief that the American public deserves a better explanation than that thus far given by the Air Force, I strongly recommend that there be a committee investigation of the UFO phenomena. I think we owe it to the people to establish credibility regarding UFOs and to produce the greatest possible enlightenment on this subject.[9]

President Jimmy Carter pledged during his election campaign in May 1976: "If I become President, I'll make every piece of information this country has about UFO sightings available to the public, and the scientists. I am convinced that UFOs exist because I've seen one . . ."[10] (Statement confirmed by White House special assistant media liaison, Jim Purks, in an April 20, 1979, letter.)

President Ronald Reagan was often quoted referring to the possibility of an alien threat. In describing discussions held privately with General Secretary Gorbachev, he said:

. . . When you stop to think that we're all God's children, wherever we may live in the world, I couldn't help but say to him, just think how easy his task and mine might be in these meetings that we held if suddenly there was a threat to this world from some other species from another planet outside in the universe. We'd forget all the little local differences that we have between our countries and we would find out once and for all that we really are all human beings here on this Earth together.[11]

Representative Jerry L. Pettis (R-California) stated in 1968 during the House Committee on Science and Astronautics hearing on UFOs:

Having spent a great deal of my life in the air, as a pilot . . . I know that many pilots . . . have seen phenomena that they could not explain. These men, most of whom have talked to me, have been very reticent to talk about this publicly, because of the ridicule that they were afraid would be heaped upon them . . . However, there is a phenomenon here that isn't explained.[12]

Dr. Carl Sagan, professor of astronomy and space sciences at Cornell University, wrote in the 1963 *Encyclopedia Americana* section on "Unidentified Flying Objects":

It now seems quite clear that Earth is not the only inhabited planet. There is evidence that the bulk of the stars in the sky have planetary systems. Recent research concerning the origins of life on Earth suggests that the physical and chemical processes leading to the origins of life occur rapidly in the early history of the majority of planets. The selective value of intelligence and technical civilization is obvious, and it seems likely that a large number of planets within our Milky Way galaxy—perhaps as many as a million—are inhabited by technical civilizations in advance of our own. Interstellar space flight is far beyond our present technical capabilities, but there seem to be no fundamental physical objections to preclude, from our own vantage point, the possibility of its development by other civilizations.[13]

Dr. Margaret Mead, world-renowned anthropologist, was also a UFO believer. In a 1974 interview in *Redbook* magazine, she acknowledged it:

There are unidentified flying objects. That is, there are a hard core of cases—perhaps 20 to 30 percent in different studies—for which there is no explanation. . . . We can only imagine what purposes lie behind the activities of these quiet, harmlessly cruising objects that time and again approach the earth. The most likely explanation, it seems to me, is that they are simply watching what we are up to.[14]

Dr. Stanton T. Friedman, nuclear physicist and well-known UFO researcher, was responsible for the original investigation of the Roswell, New Mexico, incident. He worked on nuclear-fusion propulsion systems in the 1960s and has since become one of the strongest voices among scientists in the Ufology field. He always begins his lectures in the same way: "I say the evidence is overwhelming that planet Earth is being visited by intelligently controlled extraterrestrial space-craft and that we're dealing with a cosmic Watergate, the biggest story of the millennium. Then I back it up with five large-scale scientific studies."

Interestingly, he and Carl Sagan were classmates at the University of Chicago from 1953 to 1956. Dr. Friedman has been quite candid and critical about Sagan's lack of real research into the UFO phenomenon, declaring that Sagan did his UFO research by proclamation, not investigation. In a prepared statement submitted to the House Science and Astronautic Committee UFO Hearings in 1968, Friedman posed and answered a series of key questions about the UFO phenomenon:

> To what conclusions have you come with regard to UFOs? I have concluded that the earth is being visited by intelligently controlled vehicles whose origin is extraterrestrial. This doesn't mean I know where they come from, why they are here, or how they operate. What basis do you have for these conclusions? Eyewitness and photographic and radar reports from all over the earth by competent witnesses of definite objects whose characteristics such as high speed maneuverability and hovering, along with definite shape, texture, and surface features, rule out terrestrial explanations.[15]

Dr. J. Allen Hynek, chairman of the department of astronomy at Northwestern University and scientific consultant for air force investigations of UFOs from 1948 until 1969 (Projects Sign, Grudge, and Blue Book), made numerous comments about the scientific implications of the UFO phenomenon after his stint in the government facades, including:

> There exists a phenomenon . . . that is worthy of systematic rigorous study . . . The body of data points to an aspect or domain of the natural world not yet explored by science . . . When the long awaited solution to the UFO problem comes, I believe that it will prove to be not merely the next small step in the march of science but a mighty and totally unexpected quantum jump.[16]

American Institute of Aeronautics and Astronautics (AIAA) UFO Subcommittee, established in 1967 to look into the UFO question, issued several reports and statements, including in-depth studies of two UFO incidents. The UFO Subcommittee stated that its "most important conclusion" was that government agencies consider funding UFO research. They also criticized the conclusion of the Condon Report as the personal views of Dr. Condon.[17]

Dr. Richard Haines, a research psychologist, specialized in pilot and astronaut "human factors" research as chief of the Space Human Factors Office for the Ames NASA Research Center in California, from which he retired in 1988. He states, "We're not dealing with mental projections or hallucinations on the part of the witness but with a real physical phenomenon."[18] A principal focus of his UFO research concerns aircraft cases and the electromagnetic effects that UFOs have repeatedly had on aircraft, as with the "Foo Fighter" phenomena. In a paper he presented at the MUFON International UFO Symposium in 1992, he stated:

> Reports of anomalous aerial objects (AAO) appearing in the atmosphere continue to be made by pilots of almost every airline and air force of the world in addition to private and experimental test pilots. This paper presents a review of 56 reports of AAO in which electromagnetic effects (E-M) took place onboard the aircraft when the phenomenon was located nearby but not before it appeared or after it had departed. Reported E-M effects included radio interference or total failure, radar contact with and without simultaneous visual contact, magnetic and/or gyrocompass deviations, automatic direction finder failure or interference, engine stopping or interruption, dimming cabin lights, transponder failure, and military aircraft weapon system failure.[19]

Dr. Jacques Vallee, astrophysicist, computer scientist, and world-renowned researcher and author on UFOs and paranormal phenomena, worked closely with Dr. J. Allen Hynek. Commenting on the need for science "to search beyond the superficial appearances of reality," Vallee contended in his 1990 book *Confrontations:*

> Skeptics, who flatly deny the existence of any unexplained phenomenon in the name of "rationalism," are among the primary contributors to the rejection of science by the public. People are not stupid and they know very well when they have seen something out of the ordinary. When a so-called expert tells them the object must have been the moon or a mirage, he is really teaching the public that science is impotent or unwilling to pursue the study of the unknown.[20]

In his book, *Forbidden Science,* published in 1992, Vallee chronicles how the government has deliberately misled the scientific world, the media, and the public regarding its information on UFOs and paranormal research:

. . . Phenomena were deliberately denied or distorted by those in authority within the government and the military. Science never had fair and complete access to the most important files . . . All over the world people had begun to observe what they described as controlled devices in the sky. They were shaped like saucers or spheres. They seemed to violate every known principle in our physics . . . Governments took notice, organizing task forces, encouraging secret briefings and study groups, funding classified research, and all the time denying before the public that any of the phenomena might be real . . . The major revelation of these Diaries may be the demonstration of how the scientific community was misled by the government, how the best data were kept hidden, and how the public record was shamelessly manipulated.[21]

Dr. Bruce Maccabee, Navy Optical Specialist, said:

After over 30 years of study I have found that there are sightings which involve multiple witnesses, some of which involve photographs, some of which involve coincident radar detections, and some of which involve effects on the environment (electromagnetic effects, "landing traces") which remain unexplained after investigation and analysis. In some of these cases the descriptions or photos of the objects or phenomena are sufficiently explicit to make it obvious that the objects were not natural phenomena or flying craft made by man, but rather flying craft made by some other intelligent beings. What I have found in my own investigations is consistent with what the air force told the FBI in 1952: "sightings for which there is additional corroboration, such as recording by radar or sighting from the ground . . . have never been satisfactorily explained . . . it is not entirely impossible that the objects sighted may possibly be ships from another planet . . ."[22]

Gordon Cooper, astronaut (*Mercury-Atlas 9,* May 15, 1963; *Gemini 5,* August 21, 1965) and Colonel USAF (Ret.), wrote in a letter, dated November 9, 1978, to Granada's Ambassador Griffith at the United Nations:

. . . I believe that these extraterrestrial vehicles and their crews are visiting this planet from other planets, which obviously are a little more technically advanced than we are here on earth. I feel that we need to have a top level, coordinated program to scientifically collect and analyze data from all over the earth concerning any type of encounter, and to determine how best to interface with these visitors in a friendly fashion. We may first have to show them that we have learned to resolve our problems by peaceful means, rather than warfare, before we are accepted as fully qualified universal team members. This acceptance would have tremendous possibilities of advancing our world in all areas. Certainly then it would seem that the UN has a vested interest in handling this subject properly and expeditiously.[23]

On several occasions, Cooper described his own sightings over Germany in 1951: "Several days in a row we sighted groups of metallic, saucer-shaped vehicles at great altitudes over the base, and we tried to get close to them, but they were able to change direction faster than our fighters. I do believe UFOs exist . . ."[24]

Dr. Edgar Mitchell, astronaut on the Apollo and other missions and a pioneer in the UFO movement, has for the past 25 years been one of the heroes of the movement, integrating science and spirituality. He believes that the mind is interactive with the body. From his unique perspective, Dr. Mitchell concludes: "The universe we're in is a self organizing, trial and error, learning, intelligent, interactive universe . . ." He believes that there needs to be a global mind change so that each one of us realizes our interconnectedness, that we are a part of something much bigger, and that we have a purposeful existence and meaning. Dr. Mitchell isn't afraid to speculate and even to discuss Earth's place in the galactic community. He passionately stated:

We are stewards of this planet. We need to be responsible for it. Perhaps our visitors . . . are looking at us and saying, "Well, which way are these guys going to go? Are they going to be so dumb headed and unconscious that their behavior destroys the planet? Or are they going to wake up, become conscious, become planetary citizens, become cosmic citizens?" Make this a cosmic civilization and join the rest of the community.[25]

In an article in the *Arizona Republic* on October 12, 1997, entitled "Ex-Astronaut Believes in Alien Arrival," journalist Richard Ruelas writes of Dr. Mitchell:

The 67-year-old said that when he went to the moon 26 years ago, it was conventional wisdom, religiously and philosophically, that we were still the biological center of the universe, but few, if any, thinking, knowledgeable people accept that theory anymore. The most likely scenario is that life has organized everywhere environmental conditions permitted.

Mitchell discussed his theory that alien craft have been captured and dissected, with that technology being used on military and other planes. Mitchell believes that reverse engineering has been going on for decades under a parallel government administration, separate from the president and the highest-ranking members of the Pentagon, and that it has been kept confidential. He had recently met with high-ranking military officials from several countries who admitted involvement with alien technology and hardware. He verified that what got his attention was talking with people of stature, of military and government credentials and position and hearing their renditions and their desire to openly share their stories with the public. He urges that we can't deny the firsthand experiences of these credible witnesses that are in advanced years and are anxious to tell their side. Mitchell assures us that the evidence points to a very large disinformation and misinformation effort around this whole area. "One must wonder, how better to hide something out in the open than to say 'it just isn't there.' You're deceiving yourself if you think this is true." He elaborates that it is a disinformation effort that is concerning here, not the fact that they have kept the secret, because they haven't kept it secret. "It's been getting out to the public for 50 years or more."[26]

In the briefing document, *UFOs: The Best Available Evidence,* by Don Berliner (December 1995), there are dozens and dozens of similar quotations from key military and government personnel, and scientists from countries around the world, including Argentina, Belgium, Brazil, Canada, China, France, Germany, Greece, Hungary, Indonesia, Japan, Spain, Switzerland, USSR/Russia, and Zimbawe, just to name a few. Two particular quotes touched me deeply, nudging me onto a whole new road of inquiry.

Major-General Pavel Popovich, pioneer cosmonaut, was called the "Hero of the Soviet Union." He also held the position of president of the All-Union Ufology Association of the Commonwealth of Independent States. Popovich told a MUFON International UFO Symposium in 1992:

The UFO sightings have become the constant component of human activity and require serious global study. In order to realize the position of man on Earth and in the universe, Ufology, the scientific dealing with man and the world . . . the influence the UFO has on people, as well as the effects it produces, should become the items of special research. The UFO's interaction with the environment, the behavior that it motivates, and its genesis, also presenting interesting areas for concentrated study. Today, many specialists have come to the opinion that [UFO] phenomenon research should be taken up along with understanding and comprehension of other unexplained phenomena . . . The results of these studies should aid in the survival of the people on Earth . . ."[27]

Al Worden, Apollo 15 astronaut who later became a poet, discussed his views in a lengthy interview for a documentary for the twentieth anniversary of the landing on the moon. He began by commenting on the "UFO interpretation" of the vision of the prophet Ezekiel in the Bible, that a literal translation describes very clearly a spacecraft with the ability to land vertically and take off vertically. He asserts that it was an object that looked very much like the lunar module that the U.S. used on the moon, and if it was going to land vertically and take off vertically, it had to come from someplace and go back some place. Worden stated in the documentary:

In my mind the universe has to be cyclic, so that in one galaxy if there is a planet maybe that has arrived at the point of becoming unlivable, you will find in another part of a different galaxy a planet that has just formed which is perfect for habitation. I see some kind of intelligent being, like us, skipping around the universe from planet to planet as, let's say, the South Pacific Indians do on the islands, where they skip from island to island. When the first island blows up due to a volcano, they will have their progeny on all these other islands and they will be able to continue the species. I think that's what the [alien] space program is all about.

Astronaut Worden also believes that Earth was probably visited in the past by extraterrestrial explorers. In his own words:

I think we may be a combination of creatures that were living here on Earth some time in the past, and having a visitation, if you will, by creatures from somewhere else in the universe, and those two species getting together and having progeny. I am not at all convinced that we are not the result of that particular union some many thousands of years ago. If that is the case in fact, a very small group of explorers could land on a planet and create successors to themselves that would eventually take up the pursuit of, let's say, inhabiting the rest of the universe.

186

Appendix B
Continuing My Journey for Answers

After discovering the poignant and revealing quotes cited in appendix A, I continued my quest for answers by searching out reference books and scientific data on the most reliable information about UFOs. I wanted objective and subjective views from experts in the field. I was trying to stick to credible authorities, but even so, my sense of reality was shaken as I entered a world so foreign that I began wondering why I was even exploring it.

On the surface, this "questionable" subject matter was clouded by derision and strange pronouncements. But as I delved further, I was amazed to discover that journalists, anthropologists, scientists, professors, even medical doctors were dedicating their life's work to this exploration. Many had been lauded and awarded for their works; others were chastised or discredited. Their valiant efforts touched me to the core.

I remembered seeing a thought-provoking TV documentary in the 1970s that had addressed much of what I was researching. It was called "In Search of Ancient Astronauts." Learned professionals subsequently lambasted it as outrageous and unsubstantiated. I recalled that Erich von Daniken, the author of *Chariots of the Gods: Unsolved Mysteries of the Past,* on which the documentary was based, not only suggested captivating theories about our own origins on Earth, but also highlighted archeological finds that have yet to be explained, including the pyramids, ancient aircraft models, a 37-mile-long "landing strip" carved into the barren Peruvian spurs, and the like.

Von Daniken asked some good questions. Did astronauts visit the Earth 40,000 years ago? Is there evidence of a prehistoric airfield in the Andes? Did extraterrestrial beings help set up the giant stone faces that brood over Easter Island? Where did thousand-year-old electric batteries come from? What were the "fiery chariots" that brought "gods" to Earth as depicted throughout the Bible? How could an ancient Sanskrit text contain an account that sounds exactly like a journey in a spaceship, complete with a graphic description of the force of gravity? Von Daniken wonders why all over the world there are fantastic ruins and improbable objects that cannot be explained by reference to conventional theories of archeology, history, or religion. Von Daniken's book was published in 1970, and yet we are no closer to answering many of his questions.[1]

He postulates that we may have been visited—and possibly even seeded here on Earth—by other life forms many thousands of years ago. At the time of his suppositions, he was laughed at and censured. His theories have been ostracized for many years. I'm not defending his hypothesis, only questioning how we can continue to close our minds to the possibilities he introduced three decades ago. Today, scientists are mining the surface of Mars, finding new evidence confirmed by the Hubble telescope, and discovering the very essence of life, the amino acid glycine, existing in deep space. For the first time, we have proof that there is life beyond Earth and perhaps, as the NASA scientists postulated to Jim Dilettoso, potential doorways into other galaxies.

Our own galaxy is said to be about ten billion years old. Our sun is only four and half billion years old. Earth is therefore a young planet. We now have telescopic and satellite verification that in our galaxy there are billions of stars, there are billions of possibilities. Taking into account that there are a hundred billion other galaxies, each with a half trillion stars, there are probably more stars out there than there are grains of sand on all of Earth's beaches. In other words, the cosmos may be teeming with life.

Let's imagine for a moment that we continue to advance our space exploration and send a scientific team to Mars or another planet and they find intelligent life forms. How would intelligent beings, even just a hundred years less advanced than we are, react to us—our spaceships, space gear, lasers, computers, wireless communicators, submersibles, helicopters, all-terrain vehicles, holograms, virtual technology, and so on? Might they think we are "the gods" ascending from the heavens?

Von Daniken postulated a similar premise 30 years ago. He goes a step farther, however, to sketch an outline of the subsequent development of that planet. He postulates that the site of the spacecraft landing would be proclaimed as holy ground and praised as a place of pilgrimage to celebrate the fantastic gods. To sanctify the area, the peoples would erect temples and pyramids, dictated by strict astronomical laws. After a time, these regions might be destroyed by natural causes or wars only to be rediscovered over and over again by generation after generation and interpreted according to the beliefs of the time. Von Daniken suggests, "This is the stage we have reached."[2]

Even though these conjectures about ancient astronauts are purely speculative, what of the many still unexplained artifacts that may have been left behind? There is a cave drawing in the mountainous Asian region of Kohistan, representing the exact position of the stars as they actually were 10,000 years ago. Lines in the depiction join Earth and Venus. What do we make of thousand-year-old space flight navigation charts, computer astronomy from Incan and Egyptian ruins, a map of the land beneath the ice cap of Antarctica, electric elements with copper electrodes and an unknown electrolyte, and electric dry batteries, which work on the galvanic principle, displayed in the Baghdad Museum?

The meaning of other puzzling archeological finds such as the 50-ton statues on Easter Island and the Sumerian cuneiform tablets showing stars and planets are still being debated. But one interesting fact cannot be debated. It seems that very similar stories were being told during these ancient times on different continents and belonging to different cultures and religions. How did these stories and traditions of flying gods, strange heavenly vehicles, and miracles travel worldwide and end up being recorded in the Bible, the Mahabharata, the Epic of Gilgamesh, and the texts of the Eskimos, American Indians, Scandinavians, and Tibetans? It has been suggested that these uniform texts stem from direct observations of events that were witnessed by civilizations across the globe.

References to mysterious flying machines from the heavens also seem to be a recurring theme throughout history. Every culture in every era has written about strange objects and lights in the sky, called chariots, flying shields, or wheels of fire.

Some researchers, including archeologist David Hatcher Childress, attest that if we try to extract the core of the multitude of myths and legends, flying in ancient times was the rule, not the exception. Take a look at his book, *Ancient Indian Aircraft Technology.*[3] His data are compelling.

Gene M. Philips, founder and president of the Ancient Astronaut Society, believes that some museums are hiding thousands of artifacts that do not conform to their narrow doctrines of anthropology. According to Philips, an exact replica of a flying object, called a stylized insect, used to be on display in the Smithsonian Museum. The Smithsonian even sold replicas in their shop. But after the Ancient Astronaut Society interpreted the object as a prehistoric space shuttle, the Smithsonian removed the original from display.

And what about present-day manifestations? A new breed of scientist, theologian, astronomer, and mathematician is taking enigmatic phenomena, known as *crop circles,* seriously.

These wondrous formations of intricate patterns, which appear primarily in grain fields, but also on snowy mountainsides, beaches, and elsewhere, seem to be undeniable evidence of an intelligent design. Where do they come from and what are their intentions? Crop circles occur worldwide, are apparently meant for everyone, and are so large that they can only be viewed from above: they appear fully formed overnight without damaging the grain. Most curious to me are the reported discs or amber orbs flying above or hovering low over the fields before the crop circles appear.

In a TV documentary on crop circles aired on the Learning Channel in 2003, crop circle expert Colin Andrews, author of *Circular Evidence,* said that almost from the start reports of aerial phenomena have been associated with the appearance of crop circles. People have even reported beams of light before the crop circles were discovered. In many cases, sightings of little balls of orange light were witnessed dancing over and in the fields, followed by the discovery of crop circles. "What is so strange is that these lights appear to be moving purposefully. That for me is what sets it apart from natural phenomena to one that may be controlled by an intelligence of some sort or in itself may be intelligent," Andrew asserts.[4]

In the documentary, Steve and Gillian Trench, UFO/crop circle witnesses, shared their unexplained experience of August 1994. Their description and video evidence were strikingly similar to ours: "It was like a clear sphere, orange inside. The whole thing was spinning."[5] A crop circle subsequently appeared in the field.

Another witness, Tom Blower, extrapolates on his own sighting, "They look like orange balls of light. You can see that they were revolving and emitting orange light from the bottom."[6]

Is it a coincidence that in close proximity to a June 1991 sighting of golden balls in the skies of England are numerous hills that still carry the names that they were given hundreds of years ago, one of which is Golden Ball Hill?

Authorities and skeptics have conjectured many "earthly" explanations for the causes of crop circles, including the wind, satellite-based weapons systems, scanners, even porcupines rolling around in the fields, and hoaxers. And the

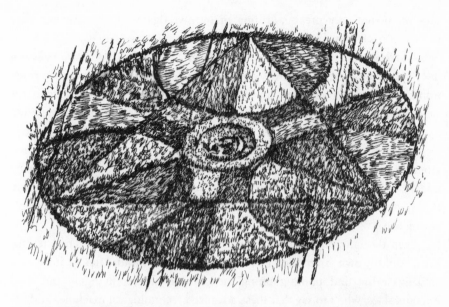

Representation of a Crop Circle: The Wiltshire Formation, Winterbourne Bassett, Wiltshire, England

This particular crop circle caught my attention. Alvin Swimmer, Ph.D., associate professor of mathematics at Arizona State University, showed me the original photograph. It is almost identical to the pyramid formation of amber orbs that Frank and I witnessed outside our bedroom window in 1995.

This 150-foot complex checkerboard pattern appeared on June 1, 1997, in a barley field in Winterbourne Basset. The diameter of the three part-circles is exactly the same as a circle that would fit precisely inside the triangle. Dr. Swimmer explained to me that this formation illustrates that a circle contained by an equilateral triangle is half the size of the circle containing the triangle—a Euclidean design.

orbs of light have been said to be a natural, yet erratic phenomena called ball lightning.

But if these spheres were just super-heated energy, then how could they create the complex, mathematical patterns so characteristic of crop circles, or for that matter, the similar hovering and traveling orb arrays reported in Arizona and throughout the world?

According to most researchers, the true crop circles couldn't possibly be made by anyone or anything here on Earth because they are interwoven and intricately laid, not at all the way they would be if crushed by human means. In addition, the energy pattern in the lattice structure under the microscope inside the crop circle is different from anything seen before. Studies show that they are very mathematically precise, leading many investigators to believe that they could not have been produced naturally.

Add to this the growing reports and photographic evidence of amber balls and discs appearing close to the areas prior to their formation. Wherever they come from, it seems as though their appearance in our skies and the intricate patterns subsequently etched on our lands are touching us in benevolent and creative ways.

In addition to UFO sightings, biblical inferences, and multiplying crop circles popping up around the world, there seem to be other remnants of *their* attempts at communication with us as well. Unexplained artifacts are being unearthed globally at unprecedented rates. Reports of ancient airplanes, bizarre skulls, prehistoric batteries, and anomalous hieroglyphics add fuel to the smoldering fire.

Even though some of these discoveries seemed a bit far-fetched to me, because of my own experience, I tried to keep an open mind. After all, if we were actually seeing and photographing inexplicable objects flying in our own Phoenix skies, who's to say that these advanced technological machines and the intelligent entities controlling them haven't been visiting us for millennia? It surely seemed as though people throughout human history had been reporting them. I kept wondering why these detailed accounts by reputable people were never included in our volumes of history books.

My research became so exhaustive that I thought you might appreciate a summary of the more interesting findings.

- On a Peruvian plateau, ornaments were discovered made of smelted platinum, which begins to melt at 1800 degrees C.

- In Lebanon, there are glasslike bits of rock, called tektites, in which radioactive aluminum isotopes have been found.

- In Egypt and Iraq, there is a piece of cloth, a fabric so intricate that today it could be woven only in a special factory with great technical expertise.

- At Delphi in Greece, there is an ancient pillar made of iron that is still not ravaged by phosphorus, sulfur, or the effects of weather.

- In Yugien, China, parts of a belt made of aluminum, a metal that has to be extracted from bauxite under tremendous chemico-technical circumstances, were retrieved from a grave.

Gene M. Philips and the Ancient Astronaut Society have studied more than 150 ancient sites in 30 countries, and unearthed in Eastern Europe 5000-year-old masks resembling the "grey" aliens.

Ancient electric devices and batteries have also been retrieved. In 1961, Wally Lane, Mike Mikesell, and Virginia Maxey, co-owners of the LM&V Rockhounds Gem and Gift Shop in Olancha, California, went into the Coso mountains to look for unusual rocks. They found a fossil-encrusted geode on February 13, 1961, on a mountain peak 4,300 feet high, about 340 feet above the dry Owens Lake, six miles northeast of Olancha. Geologists estimate that about 10,000 years ago Owens Lake was as high as the top of the peak. Later, the X-ray of the object revealed a shape resembling a spark plug, according to Paul Willis, the editor of *INFO Journal* (International Fortean Organization).[7] Based on an approximate stratification and the composition of the outer crust, the object was dated from 250,000 to 500,000 B.C.E.

The ancient battery in the Baghdad Museum, as well as others which were discovered in Iraq, all date from the Parathion occupation between 247 B.C. and 228 A.D.

It also seems that similar batteries may have been used in ancient Egypt, where several objects with traces of electroplated precious metals have been found at different locations. There are numerous anomalous finds from other regions, which suggests use of electricity on a grander scale.

Ancient glyphs have come under fire by researchers and skeptics alike. Are they evidence of ancient visits from the heavens? This next example is one of the most intriguing hieroglyphs—and it is authentic.

Some people have suggested that the engravings in the Abydos Temple are in the shape of a helicopter or Cessna type of aircraft, a boat or submarine, a UFO or disc-shaped craft, a bigfoot or Roswell type of alien with four fingers, and a glyph that seems to end with a jet airplane.

Again, apparently Sumerian, Indian, Greek, New Guinean, Australian, European, and American native literatures describe many devices that resemble flying machines and submersibles. There is even awareness of these things in Greek mythology and much earlier in Hittite literature.

Where did the ancient and indigenous peoples get the ideas for such drawings and myths?

Another interesting account, which I discovered during my extensive research, concerned a finding in 1938 by a team of archeologists led by Professor Chi Pu Tei of Beijing University. They found a series of interlinked caves at Balan Kara-Ula, a district on the border of China and Tibet, which contained skeletons of small *beings* with delicate frames, but rather large skulls. At first, an assistant thought that the caves had been the habitat of an unknown species of ape. But as Professor Chi Pu Tei pointed out, "Who ever heard of apes burying each other?"[8]

On the walls of the caves were rock drawings that portrayed *beings* with round helmets. Engraved in the rock were a sun, moon, earth, and stars connected by groups of pea-sized dots. They also stumbled on 716 large round stone disks, each about two centimeters thick (0.8 inches), which looked like Stone Age gramophone records. Each had a tiny notch on the side, a hole in the center, and a fine groove spiraling out from the center to the rim, which contained a continuously inscribed double-line of closely packed characters. But no one could decipher the message they contained. They were stored in Beijing for 20 years before Professor Tsum Um Nui broke the code. The speaking grooves relayed a shocking tale that was officially suppressed by the prehistory department of the Beijing Academy.

The discs were, however, sent to Russian scientists in Moscow for examination. Their findings corroborated those of the Chinese scientists. When the discs were placed on a special turntable, they hummed and vibrated at a very high frequency. The scientists suggested that they had been exposed to very high voltage and were part of an electrical circuit.

Dr. Tsum Um Nui decided to publish the findings in spite of the position of the academy. In 1963, his paper, entitled "The Grooved Script Concerning Space-Ships which, as Recorded on the Discs, Landed on Earth 12,000 Years Ago," was released. But again the West did not take it seriously until 1967, when Russian philologist Dr. Viatcheslav Zaitsev published the extracts of the story in *Sputnik* magazine. The whole tale is said to be preserved in the Beijing Academy, as well as in historical archives in Taipei, Republic of China.

The spiral records told of a space probe by the inhabitants of another planet who crashed in the Bayan-Kara-Ula mountain range, how their peaceful intentions were misunderstood, and how many of them were hunted down and killed by the neighboring cave dwellers, the Kham tribe.

According to Professor Tsum Um Nui, one of the lines of the hieroglyphs read: "The Dropas came down from the clouds in their aircraft. Our men, women, and children hid in the caves ten times before sunrise. When at last they [the Kham] understood the sign language of the Dropas, they realized that the newcomers had peaceful intentions."[9] The local Kham tribe regretted that the aliens had crash-landed in such a remote and inaccessible mountain range and that there was no possibility of building a new spacecraft so the Dropas could return to their own planet.

After the discovery of the skeletons and discs, archeologists and anthropologists learned more about the isolated Bayan-Kara-Ula area, much of the information verifying the account recorded on the discs. Legend speaks of small, yellow-faced *beings* who came from the clouds in the distant past. They had huge bulging heads with spindly bodies and were so ugly and repulsive that they were hounded down by local tribesmen. It is noteworthy to mention that these stories not only validate the skeletons, discs, and cave drawings originally discovered in the caves by Dr. Chi Pu Tei, dating 10,000 B.C.E., but also that, at the time, the cave area was still inhabited by two odd-looking tribes known as the Dropas and Khams. These people were frail, averaged only about five feet in height, and were neither typically Chinese nor Tibetan.

Amazingly, more than three years after I discovered this startling historical data, a FOX TV special, broadcast in April 2000, confirmed it.[10] They showed the same round discs with a hole in the center and a wedge cut on one side. Only these identical objects weren't found in a cave. NASA's own cameras had photographed them as they hovered around a broken tether out in space!

David Soretta, a former defense department subcontractor, had been studying NASA's possible interest in UFOs for more than 15 years. He believes this incident, which has become legendary on the Internet as the Tether Incident, may substantiate the reality of UFOs.[11]

On February 25, 1996, 100 miles above Africa, a 12-mile-long electricity-conducting tether attached to an experimental satellite system suddenly broke and within seconds the satellite drifted almost 100 miles away. Nitrogen gas gathered around the tether, subsequently turning it into a gigantic fluorescent light floating in space. As the televised program shows the documented footage, the tether seems to attract something strange.

David Soretta elaborates, "You see a swarm of what may be UFOs flying around it. And when the cameras zoom in on these objects, we see giant discs passing behind this tether." He measured the UFO as approximately two to three miles in diameter against the 12-mile length of the tether. If it was farther behind the tether than he thought, it might have been much larger. Soretta points out that to him, this provides proof that in quantum physics these UFOs are utilizing very advanced forms of gravity energy and zero point energy.

As the film footage shows the object turning at high speed, he assures us that the G-forces on a turn like this would flatten any astronaut into a pancake, thus showing some other intelligence.

Sorretta then corroborates the tie to our ancient past: "In 1938, high in the mountains of China, archeologists discovered these round stones with a black dot in the middle and a little notch out of the side. The discs also had a carved spiraling wave that radiated from the center to the outside periphery. It is a perfect match. I believe that these Dropa stones were made as artifacts to record what the ancient peoples of China saw in the skies—the same thing we are seeing on this tape."

When I found this next report on the Internet, by a presumed hieroglyph authority, I had enough time to transfer part of it into my journal before my computer alerted me that I had entered a prohibited site. My computer then crashed. Try as did, I was not able to bring it up again to procure the author or verifiable references, which, by the way, were extensive.

> When I first saw the hieroglyphs on the I-beams, I immediately recognized a similarity with the Greek and Phoenician alphabets. Indeed, both of them have a common origin and belong to the same "family" as the many different Semitic alphabets—Aramaic, Sabaeic, Samaritan, Hebrew, Protocanaanitic, Nabataeic, and Arabic—which all originate from the hieroglyphic alphabet, one of the four main groups of Egyptian hieroglyphs (the others being two- and three-syllable signs and ideograms).
>
> In this context I was able to decipher both I-beams and translate their inscriptions using languages from the same context and language families as the alphabets. They say: DIREQH ELE/ECE and OSNI. DIREQH is related to the Hebrew *Derekh,* meaning "way, path, journey." ELE could be a plural of *El,* meaning "God," like the Hebrew *Elohim,* and ECE is related to the Egyptian *ase,* meaning "to introduce" or "to approach." So, depending on whether we read the second sign as a "lambda/lamed" or a "gamma/gimel," we can translate it alternatively (since we don't know the grammar) as "the journey of the gods," a prayer, like "Go with God," or "a journey to approach/introduce." I translate OSNI as the Egyptian *asni,* meaning "to make to open," either philosophically, as in "to open for a contact" or "to open the consciousness," or, in a practical sense, as in "Open here."

The author asks:

> But why would extraterrestrials speak and write like Phoenician, Hebrew, or Egyptian? Maybe because it's the language of the gods, who introduced it on Earth. In fact, the ancient Egyptians believed their hieroglyphic system had been brought to them by Thoth or Tehuti, the God of Wisdom, one of the Neteru "Watchers" who traveled in the celestial barks on the celestial Nile—the Milky Way. Is it a coincidence that the mathematical system of both ancient Sumer and Egypt was based on 12, when here we meet beings with 12 fingers? We find 12-toed footprints on Anasazi petroglyphs in the

Canyonlands of Utah, USA, and a 12-fingered Sky Kachina in the tradition of the Laguna, Hopi, and other Pueblo Indians. The Brazilian Ugha Mongulala believe their Ancient Fathers, who came from the stars, had six fingers and six toes as signs of their divine origin.

As I was pondering these curious data, I happened to catch part of a radio interview that confirmed some of the claims of extraterrestrial visitation that I was accumulating—claims that we have been visited in the past, that there was in fact a UFO crash at Roswell in 1947, that alien bodies were retrieved, and that the ETs had a distinct similarity to what had been described in the ancient writings.

Respected UFO researcher and journalist Linda Moulton Howe was interviewing a retired first lieutenant who was with the U.S. Army Signal Corps and served as a CIA administrator at an army base in the southeastern USA from 1957 to 1960. According to his bio, he also helped analyze top-secret cases gathered for the Air Force's Project Blue Book investigation of UFOs.

The following is a brief excerpt from the first broadcast on the North American syndicated radio program *Dreamland,* on May 31, 1998,[12] and rebroadcast on *Coast to Coast AM* hosted by Art Bell on all-night radio, June 1–2, 1998.[13]

Linda Moulton Howe: "Now, how was the autopsy/dissection of the six-fingered humanoid film presented to you? What was the explanation of how this had occurred?"

Lieutenant: "They just said that this was done at Roswell, the same day or day after the same. I think the craft was picked up at night, that some time during the next day this autopsy was performed there at the military base, and also an autopsy was performed in town in the little clinic or hospital they have there . . ."

Howe: "You said that they sort of resembled us in a humanoid-shape way?"

Lieutenant: "Yes, they did resemble us. That particular alien, the six-fingered alien, you might say it didn't resemble us completely. It looked like a miniature man with a smaller head, but it wasn't the great big narrow face with the big eyes. It didn't have ears like we have; it had a little circle around a hole inside of its skull. The ears didn't look like ours. The nose looked basically like ours and the mouth was smaller."

I called Linda Moulton Howe for verification of the lieutenant's credibility. She assured me that according to her research the testimony of her guest on the subject of the Roswell aliens was reliable. She also told me that after the broadcast the retired lieutenant received death threats and was at that point in hiding.

To return to the discussion of possible alien visits described in the Bible, acclaimed UFO investigator and author Raymond Fowler, who has degrees in biblical studies and New Testament Greek as well as graduate training in the study of Hebrew, refers to numerous biblical references of UFOs and what he calls The Watchers.

The origin of The Watchers stretches all the way back to the dawn of civilization in Babylonia at Sumer. In fact, the very word for Sumer (Shumer) means literally "Land of the Watchers."

In recent years, Dr. Zecharia Sitchin has published a number of books on the possible connection between extraterrestrial contact and Sumerian and other ancient writings.

Dr. Sitchin postulates that ancient myths are not myths but true historical and scientific texts, and that the Bible itself should be read as an historic/scientific document. He notes that texts that predate Genesis state that early Sumerian writings describe a planet orbiting the sun on an oblique to the others and of such a long orbit that it only makes one complete circle every 3,600 of our years. He puts forth that if this theory is correct, it suggests how an inhabited planet, called Planet X by astronomers, could have once been close enough to Earth (between Mars and Jupiter) for them to reach us with some type of short-range vehicles.[14]

Dr. Sitchin assures us that his study of history shows several time periods during which knowledge and progress have suddenly leaped forward and that they do seem to be 3,600 years apart. He observes, "To me this is highly suggestive that these intelligent beings have taken advantage of their proximity to Earth on several occasions and have helped us to advance and progress every time."[15]

Similar to astronaut Al Worden's take, Dr. Sitchin is convinced that the evidence shows that we may well be mixed breed descendants of humans and extraterrestrials. "In fact," he says, "according to ancient records the females who these *beings* married were offspring of Adam himself, created by an earlier genetic manipulation. We have only recently discovered the key to our genetic structure, the twisting coils of DNA, which are depicted on a Sumerian artifact from 5,000 years ago!" The esteemed scholar urges, "Don't call them aliens, because we look like them and they look like us."[16]

Excerpts from the #1 news radio station in Arizona—KTAR Radio—on the Fourth Anniversary of the Phoenix Lights Mass Sighting, aired March 13, 2001[17]

Host Preston Westmoreland: "The Phoenix Lights, a statewide phenomenon that has never been adequately explained. Of all the people who have looked into it, one of the greatest experts is Peter Davenport, the director of the National UFO Reporting Center in Seattle, Washington."

Peter Davenport: "This case is not closed by any means. I think the definitive work is yet to be written."

Host: "How would you rate the mystery of the Phoenix Lights sighting with other sightings that you are in contact with on a daily basis?"

Peter: "In my judgment, the events that took place over Arizona four years ago tonight remain the most dramatic UFO sighting report that I'm aware of."

Host: "That's amazing, because you are privy to just about everything that's going on."

Peter: "It's just astonishing to me that people are still awakening to the events that took place four years ago. What flabbergasts me about the political leadership in your state and in this country generally is that they are pretending that these events did not take place. They're sweeping them under the carpet. I wish there were more brave souls championing this type of event to try to get to the bottom of it."

Host: "Mr. Dilettoso, as the chief investigator here in Arizona, is there any new information?"

Jim: "Regardless of what happened in Phoenix and what people believe it to be—flares, military, or extraterrestrial—the same situation has been happening in other places around the world; same kinds of lights, same formation. And in the analysis, they test out to be the same. Other people have analyzed the lights by using a repeatable spectral analysis procedure. We can't get a match on flares. We can't get a match on Hale-Bopp. The only thing we can get a match with are lights photographed on film on November 13, 1917, in Fatima, Portugal! Now I find that very curious because it was a huge event in the Catholic Church, our Lady of Fatima appearing to tens of thousands of people. And here we have what has been viewed as a cross between a military exercise and visitation of ETs happening in Phoenix—almost a hundred years later. And the film that was shot by the woman we know as Dr. X, a prominent M.D. here in town . . ."

Host: "We had her on our program last year. She has a lot of photographs . . ."

Jim: "Yes, that's right. And her film—not the video—the film, when you analyze it and blow up the lights, it's like looking at ripples when throwing a rock into a pond. Analyzing all the ripples, you can then view it like a fingerprint. And I find it very interesting that the 1917 Fatima event is the *only* match we have been able to get."

Host: "What do you think it is?"

Jim: "As you know, what I try to find out is what it isn't first, eliminating things like airplane lights, flares, and Hale-Bopp. Which leaves the conclusion of what it might be. I do not think that it was a military exercise. If the military did come into play, it is because they viewed it as an event of phenomenal proportions. Which leaves it as something similar to either a mystical angelic event, as the Catholic Church views it in Fatima, or *light beings* that came here via bursts of gamma radiation. I'm viewing it as a complete mystery of ultimate proportions."

These next two articles appeared as lead stories on Netscape on February 15, 2003:

BEIJING, China—A team of Chinese scientists is to head out to the far west of the country to investigate a mystery pyramid that local legend says is a launch tower left by aliens from space. Nine scientists will travel this month to probe the origins of the 50–60 meter (165–198 feet) tall structure—dubbed "the ET relics"—in the western province of Qinghai, China's state-run Xinhua agency said on Wednesday. The mystery pyramid sits on Mount Baigong, has three caves with triangular openings on its facade and is filled with red-hued pipes leading into the mountain and a nearby salt water lake, Xinhua said. Rusty iron scraps, pipes and unusually shaped stones are scattered around the inhospitable and largely uninhabited area, it said.

A research fellow at a nearby observatory of the Chinese Academy of Social Sciences, Yang Ji, told Xinhua that the theory the pyramid was created by extraterrestrials was "understandable and worth looking into." "But scientific means must be employed to prove whether or not it is true," Yang said. Xinhua has not given any details on the age of the structure, or any other possible explanations for it. But a study carried out by a local smeltery suggests the pipes are very old, Liu Shaolin, the engineer who carried out the analysis, told Xinhua. These findings have made the site more mysterious, says Qin Jianwen, a spokesman for the Delingha government. "Nature is harsh here. There are no residents let alone modern industry in the area, only a few migrant herdsmen to the north of the mountain," Qin said. This will be the first time scientists are heading out to study the mysterious site near Delingha City in the depths of the Qaidam Basin, according to sources with the Haixi Mongolian and Tibetan Autonomous Prefecture.[18]

WASHINGTON (AP)—Proof that life exists outside the boundaries of Earth continues to elude scientists, but President Bush's budget suggests that "space aliens" may be out there. And it could just be a matter of time before they are discovered. In a brief passage titled "Where Are the Real Space Aliens?" Bush's budget document released Monday says several important scientific discoveries in the past decade indicate that "habitable worlds" in outer space may be much more prevalent than once thought. The finds include evidence of currently or previously existing large bodies of water—a key ingredient of life as we know it—on Mars and on Jupiter's moons. Astronomers also are finding planets outside the solar system, including about 90 stars with at least one planet orbiting them. "Perhaps the notion that 'there's something out there' is closer to reality than we have imagined," the passage concludes. The president calls for $279 million next year and $3 billion over five years for Project Prometheus, which includes building the Jupiter Icy Moons Orbiter.

"This mission will conduct extensive, in-depth studies of the moons of Jupiter that may harbor subsurface oceans and thus have important implications in the search for life beyond Earth," the budget reads. The budget is the second time in recent months that the Bush administration has addressed questions about life in space. On December 24, the White House issued a September determination by Mr. Bush in which he followed his predecessors' lead by issuing a determination exempting the Air Force facility near Groom Lake, Nevada, from environmental laws allowing the release of classified information about the area. Groom Lake is the place that UFO buffs call Area 51. "I find that it is in the paramount interest of the United States to exempt the United States Air Force's operating location near Groom Lake . . . from any applicable requirement for the disclosure to unauthorized persons of classified information concerning that operating location," the president wrote.[19]

Appendix C:
Exploring UPs—
Unexplained Phenomena

Typical near-death experience described by Raymond Moody, M.D., the father of NDE research[1]

- A buzzing or ringing noise, while having a sense of being dead.

- Peace and painlessness. While people are dying, they may be in intense pain, but as soon as they leave the body the pain vanishes and they experience peace.

- Out-of-body experience. The dying often have the sensation of rising up and floating above their own body while surrounded by a medical team and watching what's going on down below, feeling comfortable. They experience the feeling of being in a spiritual body that looks like a sort of living energy field.

- The tunnel experience. The next experience is that of being drawn into darkness through a tunnel, at an extremely high speed, until reaching a realm of radiant golden-white light.

- Rising rapidly into the heavens. Instead of a tunnel, some people report rising suddenly into the heavens and seeing the earth and the celestial sphere as they would be seen by astronauts in space.

- People of *light*. On the other side of the tunnel, or after they have risen into the heavens, the dying meet people who glow with an inner *light*. Often they find that friends and relatives who have already died are there to greet them.

- The *being of light*. After meeting the *people of light*, the dying often meet a powerful spiritual *being* whom some have called God, Jesus, or an angel. Also, although they sometimes report feeling scared, they do not sense that they are on the way to hell or that they have fallen into it.

- The life review. The *being of light* presents the dying with a panoramic review of everything they have done. In particular, they relive every act they have ever done to other people and come away feeling that love is the most important thing in life.

- Reluctance to return. The *being of light* sometimes tells the dying that they must return to life. Other times, they are given a choice of staying or returning. In either case, they are reluctant to return. The people who choose to return do so only because of loved ones they do not wish to leave.

In a near-death experience documentary called "Life After Death," which aired on the Learning Channel in November 2000, scientists trying to simulate an NDE in the laboratory claimed that they could cause a loss of consciousness, precipitating the visual cortex to respond by perceiving a long tunnel and bright lights. In addition, researchers, including Dr. Michael Persinger of Ontario, Canada, have also been able to electrically stimulate the temporal lobe, creating similar feelings of movement, out-of-body floating, and a sense of "presence."[2]

But quite clearly, these induced OBEs do not replicate all of the characteristics of a true NDE. The significant presence of deceased loved ones, the life-altering life review, and the message that most times transforms the experiencer are blatantly absent from these laboratory test results.

A comparison of sleep paralysis and the experience of alien contact

The top five features of sleep paralysis are:

- waking up paralyzed

- sensing a presence

- feeling of terror

- buzzing noises

- strange lights

There are at least seven features common in descriptions of a so-called alien contact:

• waking up paralyzed

• sensing a presence

• feeling of flying

• strange lights

• the person is sometimes missing

• the contactee experiences missing time

• UFOs are frequently reported by others as seen around the time of the experience

Researcher Dr. Thomas E. Bullard agreed with Dr. John Mack's evaluation of the validity of the "alien experience" in a 1987 article by stating, "Reality best explains where this unified picture of purposes and motivations originates."[3]

Examples of *light* and *light beings* occurring during both NDEs and UFO contact

Investigator Raymond Fowler confirms, "When NDErs and abduction subjects enter the *light,* they are confronted by a presence (seen or just sensed) that radiates and engulfs them with pure unconditional love that is indescribable."[4]

Dr. Raymond A. Moody, Jr., the "father of near-death experience" concurred, "The most incredible common element in the accounts I have studied is the encounter with a very bright *light.* Not one person has expressed any doubt that it was a *being of light.* The love and warmth, which emanate from this *being,* is utterly beyond words."[5]

NDErs elaborate:

• I floated . . . into this pure crystal *light* . . . I didn't actually see a person in this *light,* and yet it has a "special identity." It is a *light* of perfect understanding and pure love . . .[6]

• The *light*'s what was talking to me. The love which came from it is just unimaginable, indescribable.[7]

• I noticed a bright *light* ahead . . . I was absorbed by it as if engulfed by a force field. I cannot describe how it felt, except to say it was divine . . . I was inside bliss.[8]

What really amazed me was the identical scenario occurring during, of all things, alien contact. While being hypnotically regressed, a UFO contactee shares:

• I'm where there is *light* . . . Words cannot explain it . . . It's a greater love.[9]

• Oh, the *light* is all over. It is wonderful. I cannot explain the wonder and beauty and love and peace. It is so joyous![10]

Not only was there a spiritual *light* consistently described in both circumstances, but in many cases of both NDEs and UFO experiences there were also energy *light beings* observed. A UFO experiencer under hypnosis describes:

• And there are other forms that look like people, but they're *light* . . . They're just like human forms, but they're *light*! There's no features.[11]

• Oh-h-h. The Great Door has been opened. It's so bright! So bright in here. Oh and . . . I see something coming. There's . . . such a bright *light,* and there's *beings* coming, and they're all *light*—they're *light beings.* Those *light beings* are coming over . . .[12]

It didn't take long to find many examples in NDE research as well, particularly in the writings of author Melvin Morse, M.D., who shares almost identical descriptions of *light beings* as related by his pediatric patients who had experienced near-death:

• *Beings of light* on either side of me . . . *Beings of light* told me that I could return to my body.[13]

• There was someone else there, a Guardian Angel or something . . . made of *light.*[14]

In the renowned scientific study called the Omega Project, headed by Dr. Kenneth Ring at the University of Connecticut, an NDEr stated, "Suddenly I was suspended in total *light* . . . I was dressed in a flowing, glowing *light* and floating right beside me was somebody else."[15]

In *Life After Life,* Dr. Raymond Moody elaborates on yet another strange but wondrous phenomenon during a near-death experience. Not only does his subject transform into *light,* he changes colors, "I left my body . . . I took on the same form as the *light* . . . The form I took had colors . . . orange, yellow, and a color that was indistinct to me. I took it to be indigo, a bluish color."[16]

This last quote reminded me of similar statements made by an alien contact patient during hypnotic regression:

• I don't see where Bob [her husband] is . . . the area is bluish color . . . starting to get a lavender color . . . [my] whole body looks like it's becoming *light*.[17]

• Oh! [breathless] I can see the . . . Elder is changing to a white *light being* and . . . the grey is changing into a light blue one as we're running closer to the *light* and . . . I'm starting to change into a golden-colored *light!* This is beautiful . . . I'm just engulfed in *light* and blending into that *light*.[18]

Definition of an out-of-body experience (OBE)

It is a situation where someone finds his essence (soul or spirit) moving out of his body into a nonphysical realm. At this point the person's body may be visible to observers, but his essence is no longer in the physical realm. Even though the OBEr is able to see his own physical body and the physical realm surrounding it, he cannot interact with it. His body just passes right through physical objects as if they weren't there at all. Near-death experiences usually begin with this out-of-body experience.

Testimonials concerning returning to life after clinical death

• My particular company lost 42 dead. All 42 of those guys were there . . . They didn't want to go back. That was the basic tone of our communication. They were all happy right where they were.[19]

• My older brother, who had been dead since I was a young fellow . . . patting me on the shoulder, saying, "It's entirely up to you . . . If you want to stay and you don't want to be back in your body, and you see how bad shape it's in, you can stay, and I'll be right by your side and everything is going to be fine."[20]

• We're here to show you the way . . . If you do not wish to go, don't be concerned. We'll be back for you.[21]

• They said I had solved most of my problems and could now go either way. That meant I could either stay with them in the *light* or go back to my body. It was up to me . . .[22]

Like me, others come back with varied explanations as to why it was not their time:

• Go back. Your work on Earth has not been completed . . .[23]

• It is not time yet . . . You have work to do.[24]

• I hear a voice say, "Go back!" . . . and whoever spoke said my work on Earth wasn't over yet, that I had to go back to complete it . . . All I heard was his voice; it was loud, thundering, just like a clap of thunder coming out of nowhere.[25]

Many do not want to return:

• I started to move toward something I knew was white *light* . . . I knew I had a choice to go forever into the *light* or stay. An enormous sadness filled me, like nothing before or since.[26]

• There it was—a tunnel of *light* with a very bright *light* at the end . . . I was talking to this *light* . . . I didn't want to go back. That was the last thing I wanted to do . . . "Why can't I stay?" I yelled.[27]

Raymond Fowler's summary of the striking similarities between UFO encounters and NDEs[28]

• Being in an OBE state

• Traveling toward a bright *light*

• Being greeted by a loving *being*

• Experiencing oneness

• Seeing *beings of light*

• Being transformed into *light*

• Communicating by telepathy

• Being brought "home"

• Having a feeling of "timelessness"

• Exhibiting extreme reluctance to leave the place of *light*

• Returning with a sense that love is fundamental

• Showing extreme concern for Earth's ecological state

Endnotes

Chapter 3
1. Susie Steckner, "Object Seen Over State a Puzzle—Was It UFO?" *Arizona Republic,* March 18, 1997.
2. Ibid.
3. William F. Hamilton, "Phoenix Sighting—Summary Report—Mass Sighting in Arizona," Internet, March 1997.

Chapter 5
1. Susie Steckner and Chris Fiscus, "X-File Is Opened into Phoenix 'UFO,'" *Arizona Republic,* May 10, 1997.

Chapter 6
1. Chris Fiscus, "City Probe of UFOs Is Grounded," *Arizona Republic,* May 20, 1997.

Chapter 7
1. Richard Price, "Arizonans Say the Truth About UFOs Is Out There," *USA Today,* June 18, 1997.
2. Ibid.

Chapter 10
1. The Learning Channel, "UFOs: 50 Years of Denial," aired March 1999.
2. Jacques Vallee, *Dimensions: A Casebook of Alien Contact.*
3. The Learning Channel, "UFOs and Alien Encounters," aired March 1999.
4. The Learning Channel, "UFOs Above and Beyond," aired March 2000.

5. Richard Haines, *Advanced Aerial Devices Developed During the Korean War.*

6. Sci-Fi Channel, *Sightings,* aired 1997.

7. Ibid.

8. Ibid.

9. The Learning Channel, "UFOs Uncovered: Dark Secrets," aired June 1999.

10. The Learning Channel, "UFOs: 50 Years of Denial."

11. The History Channel, "UFOs Then and Now."

12. The Learning Channel, "UFOs Uncovered: Dark Secrets"; NBC, "Confirmation: The Hard Evidence of Aliens Among Us," aired 1999.

13. The Learning Channel, "UFOs: 50 Years of Denial."

14. Ibid.

15. The Learning Channel, "UFOs Uncovered: Dark Secrets."

16. Ibid.

17. The Learning Channel, "UFOs Above and Beyond."

18. Ibid.

19. Ibid.

20. Ibid.

21. Sci-Fi Channel, *Sightings.*

22. The Learning Channel, "UFOs: 50 Years of Denial."

23. Ibid.; Don Berliner, et al., *UFO Briefing Document: The Best Available Evidence.*

24. Peter A. Sturrock, "An Analysis of the Condon Report on the Colorado UFO Project," *Journal of Scientific Exploration,* 1987; www.scientificexploration.org.

25. www.ufoevidence.org

26. Sci-Fi Channel, *Sightings.*

27. The Learning Channel, "UFOs: 50 Years of Denial."

28. The Learning Channel, "UFOs Uncovered: Dark Secrets."

29. Ibid.

30. Ibid.

31. Sci-Fi Channel, *Sightings.*

32. Ibid.

33. Ibid.

34. The Discovery Channel, "Into the Unknown," aired 2000.

35. Ibid.

36. Ibid.

37. Ibid.

38. Ibid.

39. Berliner, et al., *UFO Briefing Document.*

40. Wilfred De Brouwer, "Postface" in *SOBEPS Vague d'OVNI sur la Belgique—un Dossier Exceptional,* 1991.

41. Timothy Good, *Beyond Top Secret.*

42. Berliner, et al., *UFO Briefing Document.*

43. Sci-Fi Channel, *Sightings.*

44. Ibid.

45. Ibid.

46. Ibid.

47. The Learning Channel, "UFOs Uncovered: Dark Secrets."

48. Felix Y. Zigel, "Unidentified Flying Objects," cited in Berliner, et al., *UFO Briefing Document.*

49. The Learning Channel, "UFOs Uncovered: Dark Secrets."

50. Ibid.

51. Ibid.

52. Ibid.

53. 90th Congress, 2nd Session, "Symposium on Unidentified Flying Objects," July 29, 1968.

54. www.freedomofinfo.org/news/podesta.

55. Gildas Bourdais, "The French Report on UFOs and Defense: A Summary," www.cufos.org/cometa.

56. Elizabeth Rosenthal, "A UFO Boom Doesn't Worry China's Rulers," *New York Times,* January 2000.

Chapter 12

1. Whitley Strieber, *Confirmation*, p. 99.

2. Raymond A. Moody, *The Light Beyond*, p. 2.

3. Ibid., p. 38.

4. John E. Mack, M.D., *Abduction: Human Encounters with Aliens* (1994), appendix A, "A Brief Review of Issues Relating to Reality of the Abduction Phenomenon."

5. Ibid.

6. Sci-Fi Channel, *Sightings*, 1998, 1999; www.scifi.com/sightings.

7. Kenneth Ring, *The Omega Project: Near Death Experiences, UFO Encounters, and Mind at Large.*

8. Raymond E. Fowler, et al., *Watchers II, Exploring UFOs and Near Death Experience.*

9. John Alexander, *Comparative Phenomenology: Near Death Experiences and UFO Abductions*, pp. 342–347.

10. Melvin Morse, M.D., *Transformed by the Light*, p. 40.

11. Melvin Morse, M.D., with Paul Perry, *Closer to the Light*, p. 29.

12. Michael B. Sabom, M.D., *Recollections of Death: A Medical Investigation*, pp. 47, 76.

13. Ring, *The Omega Project*, p. 102.

14. Ibid., p. 101.

15. Raymond A. Moody, *Life After Life: The Investigation of a Phenomenon—Survival of Bodily Death*, pp. 55–56, 76.

16. Morse, *Transformed by the Light*, p. 4.

17. Sabom, *Recollections of Death*, p. 76.

18. Moody, *Life After Life.*

19. The Learning Channel, "Searching for UFOs," aired March 2, 1999.

20. P. M. H. Atwater, *Coming Back to Life: The After-Effects of the Near Death Experience.*

21. Morse, *Transformed by the Light*, p. 75.

22. Marilyn Vos Savant, quoting Stephen Hawking, *Parade* (June 13, 1999), p. 16.

23. Moody, *Life After Life*, p. 57.

24. Sabom, *Recollections of Death*, p. 47.

25. Raymond E. Fowler, *The Andreasson Affair, Phase Two: The Continuing Investigation of a Woman's Abduction by Alien Beings.*

26. Ibid.

27. Raymond E. Fowler, *The Andreasson Affair: The Documented Investigation of a Woman's Abduction Aboard a UFO.*

28. Fowler, et al., *Watchers II*, p. 290.

29. Dannion Brinkley, with Paul Perry, *Saved by the Light.*

30. Whitley Strieber, *Confirmation,* p. 86.

31. Atwater, *Coming Back to Life,* pp. 65–66.

32. Ring, *The Omega Project,* p. 178.

33. Raymond E. Fowler, *The Watchers, The Secret Design Behind UFO Abduction.*

34. Ring, *The Omega Project,* p. 181.

35. Sci-Fi Channel, *Sightings.*

36. Ibid.

37. Ibid.

38. Raymond A. Robinson, *The Alien Intent,* p. 52.

39. Mack, *Abduction,* p. 418.

40. Robinson, *The Alien Intent,* p. 52.

41. Sci-Fi Channel, *Sightings.*

42. Moody, *The Light Beyond,* pp. 34, 36.

43. Mack, *Abduction,* p. 407.

44. Moody, *The Light Beyond,* pp. 34, 36.

Chapter 13

1. The Learning Channel, "Cosmic Safari."

2. The History Channel, *History's Mysteries,* "Ancient Aliens," aired December 2, 1999.

Appendix A

1. J. Edgar Hoover, handwritten note to Clyde Tolson, July 15, 1947, in Berliner, et al., *UFO Briefing Document.*

2. General Walter Bedell Smith, 1952 memorandum to the National Security Council in Berliner, et al., *UFO Briefing Document.*

3. General Douglas MacArthur, *New York Times* (October 8, 1955).

4. Lieutenant Colonel Lawrence J. Coyne, Special Political Committee of the United Nations, November 27, 1978, in Berliner, et al., *UFO Briefing Document.*

5. Ibid.

6. Victor Marchetti, "How the CIA Views the UFO Phenomena," *Second Look* 1:7 (May 1979).

7. Lieutenant Colonel Philip J. Corso in "The Day after Roswell," www.obits.com/roswell.

8. President Harry S. Truman, White House Conference, April 4, 1959, in Berliner, et al., *UFO Briefing Document.*

9. Congressman Gerald Ford, Committee on Armed Services of the House of Representatives, 89th Congress, 2nd session, Hearing on Unidentified Flying Objects, April 4, 1966.

10. President Jimmy Carter, "The Night I Saw a UFO," *National Enquirer* (June 8, 1976).

11. President Ronald Reagan, White House transcript of "Remarks of the President to Fallston H. S. Students and Faculty," December 4, 1985.

12. Representative Jerry L. Pettis, House Committee on Science and Astronautics Hearing on UFOs, U.S. House of Representative, 19th Congress, 2nd Session, July 29, 1968.

13. Dr. Carl Sagan, "Unidentified Flying Objects," in *Encyclopedia Americana,* 1963.

14. Dr. Margaret Mead, *Redbook* (1974).

15. Dr. Stanton T. Friedman, Congressional Hearings, 1968, in Berliner, et al., *UFO Briefing Document*.

16. J. Allen Hynek, *The UFO Experience: A Scientific Inquiry*.

17. Ronald D. Story, *The Encyclopedia of UFOs*.

18. Dr. Richard Haines, *Observing UFOs, an Investigative Handbook*.

19. Richard F. Haines, "Fifty-six Aircraft Pilot Sightings Involving Electromagnetic Effects," MUFON 1992 International UFO Symposium Proceedings.

20. Jacques Vallee, *Confrontations: A Scientist's Search for Alien Contact*.

21. Jacques Vallee, *Forbidden Science*.

22. Bruce S. Maccabee, *UFO/FBI Connection*, pp. 230–232.

23. Astronaut Gordon Cooper, letter to Granada's Ambassador Griffith, United Nations, November 9, 1978, in Berliner, et al., *UFO Briefing Document*; www.cyber-north.com/ufo/united.

24. Article in *OMNI*, vol. 2, #6, March 1980.

25. Astronaut Dr. Edgar Mitchell in *Sightings*, Sci-Fi Channel, 1999.

26. Astronaut Dr. Edgar Mitchell in Richard Ruelas, "Ex-Astronaut Believes in Alien Arrival," *Arizona Republic* (October 12, 1997).

27. Major-General Pavel Popovich, MUFON International UFO Symposium, 1992, in Berliner, et al., *UFO Briefing Document*.

Appendix B

1. Erich von Daniken, *Chariots of the Gods: Unsolved Mysteries of the Past*.

2. Ibid.

3. David Hatcher Childress, *Ancient Indian Aircraft Technology*.

4. Colin Andrews, *Circular Evidence*.

5. The Learning Channel, "Crop Circles: In Search of a Sign," aired August 7, 2003.

6. Ibid.

7. forteansociety.tripod.com.

8. "UFOs and the Dropa Stones," www.unsolvedmysteries.com

9. Ibid.

10. FOX TV special, "UFOs: The Best Evidence Ever (Caught on Tape) 2," April 2000.

11. "Galaxy Clock; New Theory in Quantum Physics," www.UFONASA.com; www.astronomy.net; also, using any search engine, search for Tether Incident.

12. Art Bell's *Dreamland* syndicated radio program, May 31, 1998.

13. Art Bell's *Coast to Coast* all-night radio, June 1–2, 1998.

14. Zecharia Sitchin, *The Lost Realms, The 12th Planet, Genesis Revisited: Is Modern Science Catching up with Ancient Knowledge?, The Stairway to Heaven, The Cosmic Code*.

15. Sci-Fi Channel, *Sightings*.

16. Ibid.

17. KTAR Radio, *Preston Westmoreland Show*, March 13, 2001.

18. "China Baffled by 'Alien' Pyramid," Netscape, February 15, 2003.

19. "Bush Budget: Aliens May Be Out There," Netscape, February 15, 2003.

Appendix C

1. Moody, *Life After Life*.

2. Ring, *Omega Project*, p. 201; The History Channel, "UFOs Then and Now."

3. Dr. Thomas E. Bullard, "UFO Abductions—The Measure of a Mystery," *International UFO Reporter* 12 (November 4, 1987).

4. Fowler, *Watchers II*, p. 282.

5. Moody, *Life After Life*.

6. Ibid., p. 68.

7. Ibid., p. 64.

8. Atwater, *Coming Back to Life*, p. 43.

9. Fowler, *The Andreasson Affair, Phase Two*.

10. Fowler, *The Watchers*.

11. Fowler, *Andreasson Affair*.

12. Fowler, *Watchers II*.

13. Morse, *Closer to the Light*, p. 113.

14. Ibid., pp. 142, 152.

15. Ring, *The Omega Project*, p. 96.

16. Moody, *Life After Life*, p. 102.

17. Fowler, *The Andreasson Affair, Phase Two*.

18. Fowler, *Watchers II*.

19. Sabom, *Recollections of Death*.

20. Ibid.

21. Ibid.

22. Morse, *Transformed by the Light*, p. 4.

23. Moody, *Life After Life*, p. 76.

24. Ring, *The Omega Project*, p. 101.

25. Sabom, *Recollections of Death*, p. 54.

26. Ring, *The Omega Project*, p. 95.

27. Morse, *Closer to the Light*, p. 53.

28. Fowler, *The Watchers* and *Watchers II*.

Bibliography

Alexander, John B. *Comparative Phenomenology: Near Death Experiences and UFO Abductions.* [n.p.], 1994.

Andrews, Colin. *Crop Circles: Signs of Contact.* Franklin Lakes, New Jersey: New Page Books, 2003.

Atwater, P. M. H. *Coming Back to Life: The After-Effects of the Near-Death Experience.* New York: Dodd, Mead, 1988.

Barron, J. "Mysterious Fireballs Across the Sky Leave a Trail of Questions." *New York Times,* March 1991.

Basterfield, K. "Abductions and Paranormal Phenomena." In Proceedings of the 1992 Abduction Study Conference at MIT, 1992.

Berliner, Don, et al. *UFO Briefing Document: The Best Available Evidence.* New York: Dell, 2000.

Brinkley, Dannion, with Paul Perry. *Saved By the Light.* New York: Harper, 1995.

Bullard, Dr. Thomas E. "UFO Abductions—The Measure of a Mystery." *International UFO Reporter* 12, November 1987.

Carlsen, E., et al. "Sperm Counts Are Way Down." *British Medical Journal* 305, September 1992.

Childress, David Hatcher. *Vimana Aircraft of Ancient India and Atlantis.* Kempton, Illinois: Adventures Unlimited Press, 1992.

———. *Extraterrestrial Archeology.* Kempton, Illinois: Adventures Unlimited Press, 2000.

———. *Technology of the Gods: The Incredible Sciences of the Ancients.* Kempton, Illinois: Adventures Unlimited Press, 2000.

Chopra, Deepak, and Gary E. Schwartz, Ph.D. *Science & Soul: The Survival of Consciousness After Death.* Carlsbad, California: Hay House, 2001.

De Brouwer, Wilfred. "Postface" in *SOBEPS Vague d'OVNI sur la Belgique—un Dossier Exceptional.* Brussels: Belgian Society for the Study of Space Phenomena (SOBEPS), 1991.

Delgado, Pat, and Colin Andrews. *Circular Evidence.* London: Bloomsbury Publishing, 1989.

Devereux, Paul, and Michael Persinger. *Earth Lights Revelation,* London: Blandford, 1989.

Fowler, Raymond E., with introduction by J. Allen Hyneck. *The Andreasson Affair: The Documented Investigation of a Woman's Abduction Aboard a UFO.* Englewood Cliffs, New Jersey: Prentice Hall, 1979.

Fowler, Raymond E. *The Watchers, The Secret Design Behind UFO Abduction.* New York: Bantam, 1991.

———.*The Andreasson Affair, Phase Two: The Continuing Investigation of a Woman's Abduction by Alien Beings.* Albuquerque, New Mexico: Wildflower Press, 1994.

Fowler, Raymond E., Ray Fowler, and Betty A. Luca (illustrator). *Watchers II, Exploring UFOs and Near Death Experience.* Albuquerque, New Mexico: Wild Flower Press, 1996.

Good, Timothy. *Above Top Secret: The Worldwide UFO Cover-Up.* New York: Morrow, 1989.

———. *Beyond Top Secret.* London: Pan Macmillan, 1996.

Greyson, Bruce, M.D. "Near-Death Encounters with and without Near-Death Experiences: Comparative NDE Scale Profiles." *Journal of Near-Death Studies* 8, 1990.

Grosso, Michael. *The Final Choice: Playing the Survival Game.* Walpole, New Hampshire: Stillpoint Publishing, May 1986.

———. *Soulmaking.* Charlottesville, Virginia: Hampton Roads, 1997.

Haines, Richard F., Ph.D., ed. *UFO Phenomena and the Behavioral Scientist.* Metuchen, New Jersey: Scarecrow Press, 1979.

———. *Observing UFOs: An Investigative Handbook.* Chicago: Nelson-Hall, 1980.

———. *Advanced Aerial Devices Reported During the Korean War.* LDA Press, 1990.

———. "Fifty-six Aircraft Pilot Sightings Involving Electromagnetic Effects." MUFON 1992, www.nicap.dabsol.co.uk/bio-haines.htm.

———. *CE-5: Close Encounters of the Fifth Kind: 242 Case Files Exposing Alien Contact.* Naperville, Illinois: Sourcebooks, 1999.

Hancock, Graham. *Fingerprints of the Gods.* New York: Crown, 1995.

Henahan, Sean. "Sperm Decline/Environmental Estrogen Link?" *Access Excellence,* 1997.

Hill, Paul R. *Unconventional Flying Objects: A Scientific Analysis.* Charlottesville, Virginia: Hampton Roads, 1995.

Hopkins, Budd. *Missing Time: A Documented Study of UFO Abductions.* New York: Richard Marek Publishers, 1981.

Howe, Linda Moulton. *Mysterious Lights and Crop Circles.* New Orleans, Louisiana: Paper Chase Press, 2001.

Hynek, J. Allen. *The UFO Experience: A Scientific Inquiry.* New York: Marlow, 1998.

———. *Night Siege: The Hudson Valley UFO Sightings,* 2nd edition. St. Paul, Minnesota: Llewellyn, 1998.

Jacobs, David M. *Secret Life: Firsthand Accounts of UFO Abductions.* New York: Simon & Schuster, 1992.

Jung, Carl G. *Flying Saucers.* Princeton, New Jersey: Princeton University Press, 1978.

Maccabee, Bruce S. *UFO/FBI Connection.* St. Paul, Minnesota: Llewellyn, 2000.

Mack, John E., M.D. *Abduction: Human Encounters with Aliens*. New York: Ballantine, 1997.

———. *Passport to the Cosmos: Human Transformation and Alien Encounters*. New York: Crown Publishers, 1999.

Moody, Raymond A. *Life After Life: The Investigation of a Phenomena—Survival of Bodily Death*. Mechanicsburg, Pennsylvania: Stackpole Books, 1976.

———. *Reflections on Life After Life*. New York: Bantam, 1978.

———. *The Light Beyond*. New York: Bantam, 1989.

Morse, Melvin, M.D., with Paul Perry. *Closer to the Light*. New York: Ivy Books, 1991.

———. *Transformed by the Light*. New York: Villard Books, 1992.

Pringle, Lucy. *Crop Circles: Mystery of Modern Times*. Wellingborough, Northamptonshire, UK: Thorsons, 2000.

Randles, Jenny, and Peter Hough. *The Afterlife*. New York: Berkley Publishing Group, 1994.

Ring, Kenneth. *The Omega Project: Near Death Experiences, UFO Encounters, and Mind at Large*. New York: William Morrow, 1992.

Robinson, Raymond A. *The Alien Intent: A Dire Warning: The Truth Behind the Cover-Up?* London: Blandford, 1998.

Sabom, Michael B., M.D. *Recollections of Death: A Medical Investigation*. New York: Harper & Row, 1982.

Sagan, Carl, and Thornton Page, eds. *UFOs: A Scientific Debate*. New York: W.W. Norton, 1974.

Sitchin, Zecharia. *The Lost Realms*. Santa Fe, New Mexico: Bear & Co., 1990.

———. *The 12th Planet*. Santa Fe, New Mexico: Bear & Co., 1991.

———. *Genesis Revisited: Is Modern Science Catching up with Ancient Knowledge?* Santa Fe, New Mexico: Bear & Co., 1991.

———. *The Stairway to Heaven*. Santa Fe, New Mexico: Bear & Co., 1992.

———. *The Cosmic Code*. Rochester, Vermont: Bear & Co., 2002.

Story, Ronald D., ed. *The Encyclopedia of UFOs*. New York: Doubleday, 1980.

Strieber, Whitley. *Communion: A True Story*. New York: Beech Tree Books, 1987.

———. *Confirmation: The Hard Evidence of Aliens Among Us*. New York: St. Martin's Press, 1998.

Sturrock, Peter A. "An Analysis of the Condon Report on the Colorado UFO Project." *Journal of Scientific Exploration* 1, 1987.

———. *The UFO Enigma: A New Review of the Physical Evidence*. New York: Warner, 1999.

Vallee, Jacques. *Dimensions: A Casebook of Alien Contact*. Chicago: Contemporary Books, 1988.

———. *Confrontations: A Scientist's Search for Alien Contact*. New York: Ballantine, 1990.

———. *Revelations: Alien Contact and Human Deception*. New York: Ballantine, 1991.

———. *Forbidden Science*. Berkeley, California: North Atlantic Books, 1992.

———. *Passport to Magonia: On UFOs, Folklore, and Parallel Worlds*. Chicago: Contemporary Books, 1993.

von Daniken, Erich. *Chariots of the Gods: Unsolved Mysteries of the Past*. New York: Berkley Publishing Group, 1999.

Weiss, Brian L., M.D. *Many Lives, Many Masters*, New York: Simon & Schuster, 1988.

Zigel, Felix. Y. "Unidentified Flying Objects." *Soviet Life* 2(137), February 1968.

Television and Radio

Since many UFO programs were broadcast numerous times over the past seven years, I have listed pertinent radio, TV News, and documentaries for your edification.

ABC *Good Morning America*
ABC News
ABC News affiliate—KNXV 15, Phoenix
Art Bell Radio Show, *Coast to Coast*
Art Bell Radio Show, *Dreamland*
CBS News
CBS *This Morning*
CBS TV News affiliate—KPHO 5, Phoenix
CNN
CNN affiliate—(Ind.) KTVK NewsChannel 3, Phoenix
The Discovery Channel
    "Black Holes"
    "Into the Unknown"
    "UFOs Over Phoenix: An Anatomy of a Sighting"
Entertainment Tonight
Extra
FOX TV Network
    "UFOs: The Best Evidence Ever (Caught on Tape)"
    "UFOs: The Best Evidence Ever (Caught on Tape) 2"
FOX TV News affiliate—KSAZ TV 10, Phoenix
Hard Copy
The History Channel
    History's Mysteries, "Ancient Aliens"
    "UFOs Then and Now"
KTAR News Radio
The Learning Channel
    "Cosmic Safari"
    "Life After Death"
    "Searching for UFOs"
    "UFO-Alien Invasion Week: The Most Credible UFOs Caught on Tape"
    "UFOs: 50 Years of Denial"
    "UFOs Above and Beyond"
    "UFOs and Alien Encounters"
    "UFOs Uncovered: Dark Secrets"
MSNBC
    "Special Report on the Phoenix Lights"
NBC News
PAX-TV
    "Mysteries of the Unexplained—Crop Circles"
    "Unexplained Mysteries—Phoenix Lights"
SCI-FI Channel
    "100 Years of UFO Cover-Ups"
    Sightings
Strange Universe

Unsolved Mysteries
UPN
  "The Phoenix Lights"

Internet Sites

The Art Bell Website—www.artbell.com
Bill Hamilton's Website—www.skywatch-research.org
Disclosure Project/D.C. UFO Press Conference May 2001—www.disclosureproject.org
Journal and Society of Scientific Exploration—www.scientificexploration.org
National Institute for Discovery Science—www.nidsci.org
National UFO Reporting Center—www.UFOcenter.com
Scientific Frontiers—www.knowledge.co.uk/frontiers
UFO Evidence (in depth scientific research on UFO phenomena)—www.ufoevidence.org

About the Author

The internationally acclaimed physician and health educator Lynne D. Kitei, M.D., is leading the cutting-edge era of early disease detection and prevention as chief clinical consultant at the Arizona Heart Institute's Imaging/ Prevention/Wellness Center in Phoenix, Arizona. She is also a key witness to the still unexplained UFO mass sighting that took place throughout Arizona on March 13, 1997, called the Phoenix Lights.

Dr. Lynne received her bachelor of science degree in secondary science education, with minors in communication and voice from Temple University in Philadelphia, Pennsylvania. She received her medical degree from the Temple University School of Medicine and completed her post-graduate work at the Medical College of Pennsylvania.

Before her medical training, Dr. Lynne appeared in more than 40 featured and starring roles in professional musical comedies including: *Alice in Wonderland,* with Sherman Hemsley; *Oklahoma,* starring Gordon MacRae; *Guys & Dolls,* starring Betty Grable; and she understudied for Barbara Eden in *The Sound of Music.* She also played the role of Florence Arizona in the hit

Twentieth Century Fox/Coen brothers movie *Raising Arizona,* starring Nicolas Cage, Holly Hunter, Frances MacDormand, and John Goodman.

Dr. Lynne combined her artistic and academic talents during her residency to reach out to the community. She was called the "woman pioneer" of medical communications in *TV Guide* after creating and producing innovative TV news health reports for NBC in Philadelphia in 1976. Since that time, she has dedicated more than 25 years to promoting global public awareness, wellness, and health education.

Dr. Lynne has appeared as the resident health reporter for the NBC TV affiliates in Philadelphia, Pennsylvania, and Phoenix, Arizona, as medical consultant for KPHO TV news in Phoenix, Arizona, and has been featured on USA Cable, FOX TV News, and MSNBC. Dr. Lynne also wrote and appeared in more than one hundred 60- to 90-second health segments produced by Alcare Productions.

In addition to her duties as a medical communications specialist, Dr. Lynne is owner and president of Health Education Learning Programs. She has been lauded internationally as an award-winning producer, writer, and director of the "You Make It!" prevention/education video and workbook curriculum series.

Her AIDS, substance abuse, and teen pregnancy programs won the Telly Bronze Award in 1995, the National Education Film & Video Festival Silver Apple Award in 1994, the New York International Film Festival Finalist Award in 1992 and 1993, the Chicago International Film Festival Silver Hugo and Finalist Awards in 1993, the Columbus International Film & Video Festival Honorable Mention Award in 1991, and the Arizona Hemmy Award in 1993 and 1994.

Dr. Lynne has also been recognized in the *Who's Who of American Women,* was chosen Pennsylvania's Woman of the Year, and has been featured for her innovative work in publications such as the *Philadelphia Inquirer, TV Guide* magazine, *Runner* magazine, *Phoenix Magazine,* and *Physician's Management* magazine.

For more information, please see Dr. Lynne's website:
www.thephoenixlights.net